D1526875

ORIGINS AND ASPECTS

OF

OLYMPISM

By

John T. Powell, PhD, FACSM
Collaborator and Silver Medallist
of the International Olympic Academy

Published by
STIPES PUBLISHING COMPANY
10–12 Chester Street
Champaign, Illinois 61820
USA

ISBN 0-87563-502-4

-: Dedication :-

To
The Four Presidents
of the
International Olympic Academy
under whom I have been privileged to serve

Epaminonidas Petralias   **Athanassios Tzartzanos**

Professor Nicolaos Nissiotis   **Nikos Filaretos**

Permission has been granted by
Marie Hélène Roukhadzé, Head of Publications
Department, International Olympic Committee
to reproduce certain aspects of my
articles published in *Olympic Review*
and to Nikos Filaretos for extracts
reproduced from my speeches published in
the *International Olympic Academy's Annual Reports*

TABLE OF CONTENTS

Chapter   **Page**

Preface   iii

PART I

   I Ancient Greek Athletic Festivals   3
  II Opinions of Some Philosophers and Poets   27
 III Attitudes to Competition in the Ancient Games   45
 IV Some Thoughts About Ancient Olympia   57

PART II

   V The Contribution of the International Olympic
      Academy to the Understanding of Olympism   67
  VI The Olympic University   79
 VII University Education and Olympism   97
VIII Olympism and its Ethics 105
  IX Olympism and Science 117
   X A Personal Philosophy Derived from Olympism 127
  XI Creating an Olympic World 139
 XII Olympism, Sport and World Society 151

PART III

 XIII The Development of Olympic Athletes
      Are Laboratory Methods Enough? 169
 XIV Sport, Aggression and Violence 179
  XV The Limits of Ergogenic Aids in Sport 191
 XVI Sport-Teaching—Art or Science? 203
XVII Holism and Health 215
XVIII Aesthetics, Art and Movement 227

PREFACE

This book is primarily for those who study and take courses concerning the Olympic Movement and who are interested in the Olympic ideals and concepts.

It is also a tribute to the International Olympic Academy in Ancient Olympia - Greece, for the consistency with which it has presented the concepts of ethical behaviour, fair play and an abiding by the fundamental principles of Olympism, as expressed in the Olympic Charter.

The various chapters raise and pose questions which need answering and being acted upon, for the security and continuance of the Olympic Movement.

The vigour, integrity, idealism, ingenuity and effort of young people will all be needed in this worthwhile effort to keep the Winter and Summer Olympic Games as worthy festivals of youthful endeavour and expression.

The word 'Olympism' is to be found in no dictionary and, for the first time, the International Olympic Committee published a definition in its 1991 Olympic Charter. Olympism is used, written and talked about all over the Olympic World. Few know what it means, or even for what it stands.

This book is an attempt to show how Olympism permeates Olympic life.

Guelph, Ontario   John T. Powell
Canada
1st March 1994

TWO DEFINITIONS OF OLYMPISM

Olympism is a philosophy of life, exalting and combining in a balanced whole the qualities of body, will and mind. Blending sport with culture and education, Olympism seeks to create a way of life based on the joy found in effort, the educational value of good example and respect for universal fundamental ethical principles.

The goal of Olympism is to place everywhere sport at the service of the harmonious development of man, with a view to encouraging human dignity.

Olympic Charter of the
International Olympic Committee, 1991
Lausanne

* * * * * *

Olympism is a harmony of ideas and ideals that affirm the value of Olympic sport in promoting and developing sound physical and moral qualities in individuals and in contributing to a better and more peaceful world by enabling representatives of nations to meet in an atmosphere of mutual respect and international amity.

John T. Powell, 1976
Adopted by the Executive Committee
of the Canadian Olympic Association
18 July, 1986

WHAT IS IT?

It stands proud, leans neither "left" nor "right",
It isn't "cool" but "hot".
It means absolutely nothing,
Or it means a lot.

It's there for all to see when acted upon.
It's not a subject, not a thing, it can't *be* anyone,
But makes possible other things that need no written law.
It's fair, above reproach, it need never ask for more,
It's always ready to receive, like an ever-open door.

It needs co-operation otherwise it can't survive.
It needs fat-free beating hearts, strong and eager hands
To help it constantly revive.

It exists within one's mind and is shown by things now rare
And it can't act on its own because it simply is not there.
It needs unity and amity to make all things so bright
That when there is tense contest and if there really is a fight,
It bides within the rules and things are put to right.

It's a spirit, an attitude, a way to live one's life,
It's not tangible - but for those who know its might
It aids to firm one's spine; to help one stand upright.

There's something in it for us all, for without it sports
                                                      are gone.
The Olympic Games they could be saved but could also linger on.

But, without the practice of this word and for everything
                                                      it stands
And because it's balanced so delicately in 10 million tiny hands;
Which extend to young skilled bodies and educated minds.
Youth can still save this worried world with all its cultural
                                                      demands.

Be that as it may - unless *OLYMPISM* reigns
All formal Games will go;
And our flame will die in cold and withered ash
To be revived no more.
So come to the Academy, go to a Games,
There you'll see and feel the proof
And all you need to do is work along with us.
Your search it will be over, for you'll have found the truth.

                                                      J.T.P.

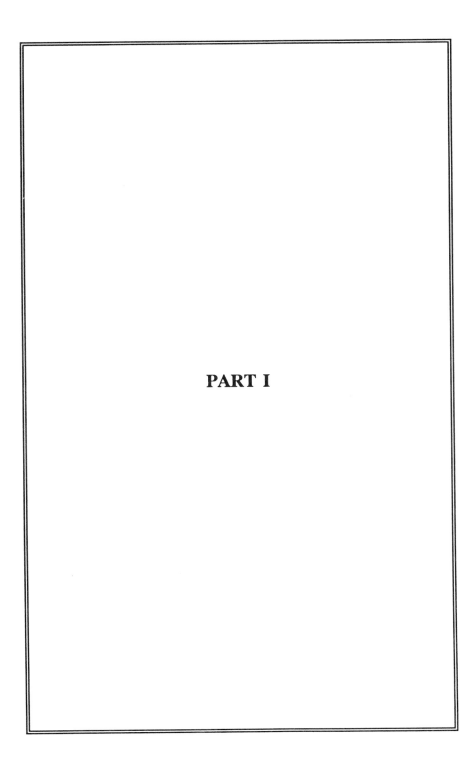

PART I

CHAPTER I

Ancient Greek Athletic Festivals

PART I

CHAPTER I
Ancient Greek Athletic Festivals

ORIGINS

To get rid of one's ignorance, to see things
as they are, and by seeing them as they are
to see them in their beauty, is the simple
and attractive ideal which Hellenism holds out.

Matthew Arnold.

Probably, between 1,500 to 1,200 B.C. a savage and Nordic, blond, fair skinned, long limbed, agile and strong people—the Greeks—surged south from Europe's interior into the Balkan peninsula.[1]

Philologists have found the roots of Greek words similar to those of Persian, English, German, French, Spanish, Russian and Italian. The assumption is that the stock of these races was originally intermingled. The races are Aryan, Nordic or Caucasian.

The Greeks, no doubt came into the Balkan peninsula in three successive invasions for there were found to be three dominant variations of language, Ionic, Aeolic and Doric.

These invaders conquered the highly developed civilization on the island of Crete and absorbed it into their own civilization. They also mixed with those other Mediterranean people they had overrun, and the Ionic and Aeolic tribes lost many of their original characteristics.

This was not so for the Doric tribes. They advanced into the Peloponnesus becoming what we know to be the Spartans.

The Doric advance was the last of the waves of barbarous hordes into the Peninsula. By absorption and settlement the Greeks emerged with a recorded language and an established way of life about 700 B.C.

GEOGRAPHY

Greece is not a large country. Summers are tempered by Mediterranean winds, no part of the country is far from the sea, the air clear, the light vivid. The land is not particularly fertile, there are many valleys locked between mountains. These physical characteristics have produced hardy, independent frugal people epitomising what Robert Frost said in a speech just prior to his death: "What makes a country in the beginning is a good piece of geography."

In the centuries before Christ, Greece was composed of many small and independent states and cities often isolated by the natural barriers. These communities were proud and defensive of their rights and freedom. There were constant feuds and wars, so every Greek citizen had to be constantly prepared for combat. The normal condition was physical and mental readiness. It appears natural that Greeks of all ages, men and women, girls and boys should participate, as a way of life, in physical activity and because cultures have developed on expression through human movement it is automatic that death, birth, marriage, crop success, the winning of a contest, completion of a boat, the triumph in battle, should be celebrated by festival.

GODS AND GODDESSES

Who invented play, who invented competition? No-one. Play is a natural expression of adequacy, freedom, safety, thankfulness, of the biological need to move in a variety of ways, to laugh, to create, to enjoy, to be dexterous, to exhibit. Competition is also natural for prowess, for possession, superiority, fame, adulation or just to be personally better and to exult in bodily and/or mental expression. It is a natural condition of human development shown in very many ways.

The various athletic festivals of ancient Greece developed. No-one originated them so the Greeks gave credit for their origins to their Gods.

When one talks or reads of the religious base of Greek life it must be firmly understood that this religion was in no way similar to our Judaic idea of a God on high. Gods to the Greeks epitomised humans with all the fallibility of the human make up. The Greeks had many gods to whom sacrifices were made and of whom favours were asked. Greek gods left their places on mountain tops, mingled with the populace and had a splendid time abducting humans.[2]

The ancient Greeks were doers. Action was the keynote of their lives, just as it was with their gods, in fact their gods were glorified athletes. To the Greeks their goddesses and gods were playmates made up of the imagery of what the wisest, strongest, most beautiful men and women should resemble.

It was Xenophanes[3] who first wrote that gods were created by men in their own image rather than the reverse.

The Greek gods were idealised athletes who had their own games, sports and festivals. *They* were the national heroes and, gradually, the Greeks brought their goddesses and gods down from the skies into the everyday life of sport, war and other activities. It is easy to understand how they grew to idealise victory making the victors of various contests into national heroes, supplanting to some extent the worship of gods. Eventually this transition brought rational thinking to the Greeks in that they were thus led to glorify the deeds of men and women and to seek perfection in both human form and wisdom here and now, rather than at some distant time and place.

FESTIVALS

It is undoubted that the *formal* Games, the names of which we are familiar, Olympic, Nemean, Pythian and Isthmian, were originated from the *informal* contests of after-dinner and funeral Games.

In Homer's Iliad[4] is a splendid description of Games held for Patroclus by the Thessalian prince, Achilles. It is not known when Homer wrote (it is estimated from the 10th to the 6th centuries B.C.) but it is evident he did so for knowledgeable readership.

In Latimore's vivid translation (University of Chicago Press) of 1951 he tells of Achilles' men spending recreational moments with archery, discus throwing and "casting javelins" (Iliad II, p. 774); of Helen of Troy on the wall, looking for her brother Polyduces, a "skilful boxer" (Iliad III, p. 237) and of how the length of a discus sling and a javelin throw are as familiar measures as are "a furrow's length or a weaver's rod" (Iliad X, p. 351 and Iliad XVI, p. 590).

Also in Homer's Odyssey (VIII, p. 97) translated by R. S. Robinson, is a description of after-dinner Games, which starts:

> Hearken, ye captains and councillors of the Phaeacians, now have our souls been satisfied with the good feasts, and with the lyre, which is the mate of the rich banquet. Let us go forth anon and make trial of divers games, that the stranger may tell his friends, when home he returneth, how greatly we excel all men in boxing, and wrestling and leaping and speed of foot.

These impromptu contests were held by the Phaecians (whomever they were and wherever their land) in honour of Odysseus who, by accident and after years of wandering had landed on their shores.

THE ORIGIN OF THE OLYMPIC GAMES

As time passed and as the Greeks settled in their land so did athletic games become firmly established.

The oldest and most venerated have, through myth and legend, been credited to Olympia.

Legend has it that Mother Earth (Gaea) was worshipped at an altar there and that the Mother of the Gods (Rhea) the wife of Kronos was also honoured by votive offerings made at this altar.[5]

Rhea gave her son Zeus to the Idaean Couretes to rear because her husband Kronos was in the habit of eating her offspring. She substituted the new-born child with a stone.

The Couretes were five; Herakles, Paeonaeus, Epimedes, Iasius and Idas.

The eldest of these Dactyli challenged the others to a race of which he was the winner. The previous night, having rested at Olympia, they made a litter of olive branches on which to sleep and after Herakles won the foot race his brothers crowned him with a wreath of wild olive.

> "The glory, therefore of having first established the Olympic Games, is given to the Idaean Herakles who also gave them the name of Olympic. On this account too, they were celebrated every fifth year, because the brothers were 5 in number. . . ."[6]

Five generations after Pausanias, Eusebius of Caesarea completed his *Chronology* and he records that the Games Olympic were carried on by Clymenus (who also came from Crete) a descendant of Herakles. Next they were held by Aethlios as a proving ground for his sons. From his name the contestants were named "athletes" and the contests "athla".[7]

The son of Aethlios, Endymion, had three sons, they raced and Epeius was victorious, he became ruler of the Epeians. The second brother Paeon founded the land Paeonia and Aetolus made his way to the river Acholous calling his territory Aetolia. Endymion was favoured by Zeus in that he gave him everlasting unaging life. Selene, his wife bore him 50 daughters representing the 50 months of each Olympiad.

Later Oinomaos presided over the sacred festival, then came Pelops who held the Games in honour of his father Zeus. After this the son of Zeus and Alcmena, Herakles continued the sacred sports.

It is then recorded that 10 generations elapsed until Iphitus renewed the Games. Iphetus was from Elis and he wished to do something positive to stop wars between cities. He sent a deputation from the Pelloponesus to the Delphic Oracle. The god replied to the Peloponnesians:[8]

"O inhabitants of Peloponnesus go to the altar, sacrifice and hearken to what the priests enjoin."

Then the god spoke to the Eleans:

Citizens of Elis keep straight to the law of your fathers.
Defend your own country and refrain from war.
Leading the Greeks in impartial friendship
Whenever the genial year returns [?in your ways]

Then Eusebius continues:

"Because of this Iphitus announced the truce . . . and ordained the games with the help of Lycurgus the Lacedaemonian who happened to be his relative, both being descended from Herakles. At this time the foot race was the only contest but later the other contests were added."[9]

Eusebius, who lived around the date A.D. 325, five generations later than Pausanias, listed in his *Chronology* the Olympic Register of Victors from the 1st Olympiad 776 B.C. to the 249th Olympiad of A.D. 217. This register was based upon the compilation made by Sextus Julius Africanus one century earlier; the chronology dates the renewal of the Games to the early 9th Century B.C.

Aristodemus of Elis who lived in the 3rd Century B.C. claimed that it was after the 27th Olympiad that victors began to be listed. Before that time no one had his name recorded.

In the 28th festival of the Games (776 B.C.) Coroebus, variously described as an innkeeper or a cook, of Elis won the stade, the only race. This distance was 192.27 metres yet it was 600 Greek feet.

Pindar in his 11th Olympian hymn relates that the mythical hero, Herakles (son of Alcmena) after killing the then king of Elis, Audeas in a wrestling match, built a temple to his father Zeus in the vale of Olympia, as a thankoffering to his divine benefactor. He then marked out the length of the original Olympic stadium by placing heel to toe, 600 times. His foot therefore was 12.6 inches long and this remained a unit of length, the Olympian foot.

All Greek stadia races were 600 feet but as the length of each measurer's foot was different so the distance run was different. In fact at Delphi for the

Pythian Games the stade was 177.5 metres long and other Greek stadia ranged from 181.3 to 210 metres.[10]

Thus Coroebus was the first victor to be listed. From this event the Greeks recorded their years and 776 B.C. is generally accepted as the 1st year of the 1st Olympiad, which is a period of 4 years, a unit of measure of time used by the Greeks, i.e. the 52 moons that separated each celebration of the Games.

It is also generally agreed that from the founding of the Elean Games by Herakles to the first officially recorded Olympic victory was 419 years.

The King of Elis, Iphitus realising the great advantages which could accrue to Greece, wished to extend the festival from a local one between men of Pisa and Elis to one giving a Peloponnesian character. The strength of the Delphic Oracle's pronouncement lay in the aspect of neutrality, thus Elis, in the peaceful environment of Olympia, an idyllic place framed by the Kronion hill and the two rivers Alphaeios and Kladios, was to become the centre of civilisation, of religion, art and athletic contest. This came about in 884 B.C. when the renewed Games were carried out with grandeur, an agreement was signed which was called EKECHEIRIA (truce) between Iphitus, on behalf of Elis, and Lycourgus, on behalf of Sparta, and of Cleosthenes on behalf of Pisa. This agreement was incised on a metal disc.[11]

It is reported that the disc still existed at Heraeon in the time of Pausanias in the 2nd century A.D.

Olympia became the aesthetic focal point of Greek unity.

In his 1st Olympian Ode, Pindar—at a much later time, was to write "Olympia will cover with her Glory all the Greek land just as the sun covers, during the day, all the stars of heaven."[12]

Thus Elis the old and honoured cradle of civilised intellectualism bred the Games. Furthermore other athletic and cultural Festivals followed the Olympic Games, each being an integral part of the life of the nation, region or place.

Although all of these celebrations have their origin in antiquity their idealism is as pertinent and as desirable, now, as the day they were conceived.

They were based on the theory that the human body is of equal and inseparable importance as is the human intellect and that only through their mutual co-ordination and discipline is Man's potential realized.

It is undoubted that these Games contributed to the greatness of Hellas whose life and conduct were determined in large measure by the populace's attitude to victors in Nemean, Isthmian, Pythian and Olympic Festivals.

The truce (Ekecheiria), also called Therma was a binding institution. The heralds (Spondophori) selected from the officials of Elis, went out 10 months before the start of the next Olympiad to proclaim in their visits to all part of the land that shortly the Games would start.

The truce ensured the inviolability of Olympia, which when not occupied by the throngs of people for a festival was a quiet place maintained solely by a few priests.

The 10-month period is interesting also as it was the period of time athletes who wished to compete had to enter into strict training, it was also the time for the Hellenodikae (judges and/or coaches) to begin their training session. The last month of this period was to be spent in Elis by both athlêtêr (winner of prizes) and Hellenodikae. In his *The Life of Apollonius of Tyana* Philostratus has Apollonius give a speech in which he says ". . . the Eleans train the athletes for 30 days in Elis itself just before each Olympia festival; at Delphi the management brings the athletes together at the time of the Pythian games so does the Corinthian management at the time of the Isthmian and they say "Go to the Stadium and be man enough to win." But the Eleans on the way to Olympia (i.e. from Elis City) harangue the athletes as follows:

> "You who have completed the toil of training in a manner worthy of entering Olympia and have done no loafing and nothing under-handed, proceed with confident heart; you who have finished the training otherwise, depart, in whatever direction you choose."[13]

WOMEN'S OLYMPIC GAMES

Pausanias recounts there is a mountain with high precipitous cliffs, Typeum, from which any woman caught at the Olympic Games or even on the other side of the Alpheius would have been cast down. No woman was caught, except Callipateira, a widow disguised as a trainer. She brought her son to compete at Olympia.[14]

Peisirodus was victorious and his mother jumped over the enclosure in which trainers had to stay, revealing herself as a woman. She was let go and out of respect for her son, her brothers and her father, all of whom had been Olympic champions. A law was then passed that for future celebrations all trainers must strip before entering the arena.[15]

The foot race for maidens was the prime race of the Festival of Hera. This was celebrated, as were the Olympic games for men and boys, every 5th year, i.e. the first celebration of an Olympiad.

Pausanias described these Heraean Games (V,16 2-4)[16]

He stated that the contest was for maidens of three age groups. The distance was reduced by 1/6th of the length of a stade, that they "all ran with their hair down their back, a short tunic reaching just below their knees and their right shoulder bare to the breast."

It is also stated that:

"Originally the prize given to the young girls who were victorious in the foot-race may conceivably have been a pomegranate, which was a symbol of fertility and was also sacred to Hera."[17]

The races were held in Olympia, the winner given a portion of the cow sacrificed to Hera. They also had portraits, and much later, statues made with their names inscribed upon them.

It is said that Hippodamia, in gratitude to Hera, for her happy marriage to Pelops selected 16 women and with them inaugurated these Games to the goddess.

The choice of the 16 women arises from the time when Damaphon, tyrant of Pisa was particularly cruel to Eleans. After he died the people of Pisa and Elis wished only for friendship amongst themselves. So, one woman from each of the 16 Elean cities was chosen to make peace. Later, these same 16 were entrusted with the management of the Heraean Games and with the weaving of the robe for Hera. They also initiated and arranged two choral dances.

When Elis was later divided into 8 tribes, two women were chosen from each to continue to organize the athletic festival for young women.[18]

It appears to be thought that females were barred from spectating at the Olympic Games for men. This according to Pausanias is not so.

. . . now the stadium is an embankment of earth, and on it is a seat for the presidents of the games. Opposite the umpires is an altar of white marble; seated on this altar a woman looks on at the Olympic Games, the priestess of Demeter Chamyne, which office the Eleans bestow from time to time on different women.

Maidens are not debarred from looking on at the games.[19] In another translation[20] the matter is made perfectly clear. "Virgin girls of course are not barred from watching."

EVENTS OF THE ANCIENT GAMES

As Pausanias has recorded in such a detailed way, the events and the dates of their introduction[21] into the Olympic Festival it is only necessary to give some of, what appear to be, most significant features. For 41 Olympiads only the stade was raced. After the 13th Olympiad (dating from 776 B.C.) the diaulos (2-stade run) was introduced. Hypenos a Pisaian won it. In the 15th celebration of the Games (720 B.C.) the dolikos was contested for the first time. The distance of 24 stades, about 4½ kilometres. A Spartan was the victor.

In 708 the wrestle and the pentathlon were added, while in 688 the boxing match and in 680 the chariot races with the four horse chariots, the "tetrippon" and in 648 the pankration, i.e. wrestling and boxing simultaneously. Thenceforth and at different times various contests were added. A point had been reached when there was a total of 23 contests . . .

The Stadium length, the double length, the twenty-four lengths, the wrestling, the pentathlon of men, boxing, the four horse chariots, the pankration, the horse race, the stadium length for boys, the wrestling for boys, the pentathlon for boys were gradually introduced. This latter contest was held only once, as it was considered too strenuous for boys and because time would not allow it.[22]

The Pentathlon for boys was introduced at the 38th celebration of the Games and Eutelidas was the first and only winner for ". . . the Eleans felt it was better from then on for boys not to enter for the pentathlon."[23]

It is reasonable to assume that the maturity the pentathlon takes was not present in the adolescents of ancient Greece. By carefully looking at sculptures of boys in classical times it is obvious from the smooth lines and lack of muscular definition, they could not compare physically with the well-nurtured North American youth of today.

Boxing for boys, the hoplite race in armour, the chariot drawn by two mules (apene), the Synoris (chariot drawn by two horses), the four-colt chariot race (tetrippon polon), the two colt chariot race (synoris polon), the kalpe, a race in which the rider of a mare took the bridle and ran the last curve with the animal, the colt race, the Pankration for boys and, finally, in the 96th celebration, contests for trumpeters and for heralds were introduced.

It is reported that, male athletes competed nude. Lucient (A.D. 124-180) in his work *Anacharis* translated by R. S. Robinson, had Anacharis converse with Solon saying: "Yet, in the beginning, as soon as they had taken their clothes off, they put oil on themselves, and took turns at rubbing each other down . . ."[24] and "tell me why it is that in the Olympic and Isthmian and Pythian and the other games, where many, you say, come together to see the young men competing you never match them under arms but bring them out naked . . ."[25]

Dionysos (in *Roman Archaeology* 7,12) tells that Acanthus of Sparta, who won the 15th Olympiad's dolichos, competed naked but Pausanias tells how

Orsippus ran the stade and let his belt fall so that he could run more freely, both of these instances are recorded for the Games held in 720 B.C.

In Gardiner it states:

> "Thucydides (i.6) states that the use of the loin-cloth had only been abandoned even at Olympia shortly before his own time."

> "Yet the vase-paintings and art prove that absolute nudity had been the rule in Greek sport. Is it possible that an attempt was made at the close of the 6th Century to introduce the loincloth, and that this temporary fashion is the reason for Thucydides' statement?"[26]

My own thoughts on this matter are that as I have noted loincloths only on bearded men, indicating age, it may have been the prerogative, through veneration of those older males to have chosen such a garb.

THE TIMING OF THE GAMES

The Olympic Games, as a festival was always held at the time of the 52nd full moon after an Olympiad thus inaugurating a new Olympiad. The full moon was the second or third following the summer solstice making the celebration fall usually in August, but sometimes, because of the use of the Julian calendar, in September. The central day of the 5 given to the festival was at full moon. The Greek day started when the sun set and all religious ceremonies and sacrifices had to be concluded prior to 12 noon the following day.

The first day was given to preparation, the taking of the oath and the necessary sacrifices.

That is the only certainty except that the last day also contained rituals and, it is assumed that the hoplite race was last because, being in armour it was a reminder of the truce and the need to be prepared. After the heralds had sounded their horns the visitors were encouraged to make haste to their homelands.

The three days between were for contests.

THE OATH

It was just after noon when the athletes with fathers, brothers and other male relations met the judges, and before the statue of Zeus swore they had the qualifications of training, citizenship and had never committee a crime. Everyone took the oath and afterwards registration took place and lots were drawn for dual competition.

> In the afternoon, outside the Bouleuterion, announcements were made regarding the events which would be carried out in the Olympiad and of the contestants who had registered themselves (Dion. Kas. 79, 10). Finally there came to the Great Temple with the resplendent retinue of the Judges, a young lad, garbed in white, an "amphithale" boy (that is whose father and mother were alive). Here at the Temple of Olympian Zeus, close to the south facade of which grew plenty of wild olive, he cut, with a golden pruning hook, so many branches as there were events. These branches were made into garlands, tied with light coloured woollen yarn. These were the unsurpassably valuable prizes (athlon) of which were constituted the magnificent award of these great Games.[27]

HONOUR TO A CHAMPION

Wearing the Kotinos, the Olympic winner could expect adulation, perhaps an ode would be written to commemorate his feat, a statue made and honour accorded on returning home through the breach in the wall of his city. The state possessing such a citizen had no occasion for walls.

To Leonidas of the island of Rhodes fell such particular honour. He won the Triast (3 events in Olympia on the same day) in 4 consecutive Olympiads, the 154th, 155th, 156th and 157th. The events were the Stade, Diaulos and the Hoplite; the prestige and the aura which surrounded him became an apotheosis.[28]

THE TERMINATION OF THE GAMES OF OLYMPIA

The first patrons of the Games were the gods, the last, men.

The internal decline of Kalos k'agathos (the virtuous and the good) was the beginning. Then came the Macedonians, later the Romans who did not appreciate or comprehend the deeper meaning of the festivals. Nero postponed the holding of the Games[29] then when he did compete, fell from his chariot, did not complete the race yet had himself crowned victor not only in that contest but as harpist, a tragedian and in a contest in which only he competed—the 10-horse chariot race.

The last know Greek victor was Varastades who won the boxing crown in the 291st Olympiad, i.e. A.D. 390.

I have dwelt a long time on the origin of athletic games and those particularly at Olympia because it is essential to understand their historic significance in the creation of, and influence upon, the life of a nation. Again, without a truce, in which safe conduct was guaranteed for those visiting the athletic festivals and returning from them, there would have been no unification between the constant warring factions, no intermingling of the people who made up the composition of the Greek civilization and no centre of unification. Thus, through the religious base of human athletic and intellectual expression Greece became a mighty power of idealism and cultural prestige quite unknown prior to that time. That the Olympic Festival lasted—in recorded time—for 1,168 years (776 B.C.–394 A.D.) of unbroken sequence, shows it to be probably the longest lived of man-made institutions.

Reason taught the weakness of power, all of Greece believed in peace during the Olympic truce.

Yet the Olympic gatherings lost their religious significance and became professional circuses, banned by decree in A.D. 394 by Emperor Theodosius I.

The heart-beat which had sounded loud and clear 320 times since Iphitus's time had stopped; the soul of Greece was dead.

The statue of Zeus was taken to Constantinople and later destroyed in a fire; earthquakes in 522, 551 and 580 destroyed the magnificent structures in the vale of Elis; the Cladius overflowed, the Alphaeus deviated its course silting the hippodrome.

The Olympic glory was covered. The gods had shown their anger.

PART II

The Influences of the Other Major Pan-Hellenic Athletic Festivals

Three other main *athletic* festivals at Delphi, Nemea and Isthmia originated later than those of Olympia whose model they were.

To describe in another way, rather than simply recount the history of the origins of Games and competitions at these festivals I have chosen to illustrate them through some of the words and works of Pindarus, no doubt the most graphic of the recorders of deeds pertaining to these pan-hellenic festivals.

PINDAR

One of the greatest of the lyrical poets of Greece was a native of Boeotia. He was born very close to Thebes in the village of Cynoscephalae.

He recorded his birth as the day which coincided with the Pythian festival at Delphi. This celebration always fell on the 3rd of the 4 years of an Olympiad.

According to the lexicographer Suidas the poet was born in the 65th Olympiad which, in its third year corresponds to 518 B.C. However, the most probable alternative is the 3rd year of the 64th Olympiad, 522 B.C. To support this he is reported as "flourishing" (that is being about 40 years of age) at the time of the Persian War, 481–479 B.C.[30] Therefore, had Pindar been born in 518, he would have been only 37 years of age at the start and 39 at the end of that war.

Had he been born in 522 he would have been 40 in 482 the year preceding the expedition of Xerxes. In Gaspar's *Chronologie Pindarique* published in Brussels in 1900, on page 15, Gaspar states there is uncertainty between the dates 522 and 518 for the birth of Pindar because of the corresponding uncertainty between the dates 586 and 582 B.C. as the beginning of the Pythian era.

Were Pindar to have been born at the 17th Pythiad his birthday would be 522; if the date of the 1st Pythian celebration is counted as 586, or, were the reckoning to be from 582, his birth date would be 518 B.C.

It is now assumed that the latter date (518 B.C.) is the date of the beginning of the Pythian era so the assumption of Pindar's birth is in favour of 518 also.

He is considered to be closely connected in heritage with the Dorians and an admirer or Dorian aristocracy.[31] In 498 he received his first commission for an epinician ode (Pythian X).

In September 490, the Persians were defeated by the Athenians in Marathon.[32]

Just days before the battle Xenocrates won the chariot race in the Pythian games. The official ode was composed by Simonides but Pindar who was present at Delphi also wrote praise of the victor's son Thrasybulus (who drove his father's chariot) in his Pythian hymn XII.

It should be noted that only the owner of a chariot was honoured, the drivers, as jockeys of today, received no prize.

As a diversionary note it is of interest that Cynisca of Sparta entered her horses at Olympia, and won but as Pausanias (111 8 1;) states she did not appear there in person for this first victory by a woman. The bases of the statues set for her at Olympia are still there.

A quarter of Pindar's odes are in honour of athletes from Aegina. The first of these was in honour of Pytheas in the *Nemean* Games of 489 B.C. The earliest *Olympia* ode (Olympia XIV) celebrates the winner of the boys race of 488. The *Delphic* chariot race winner in August of 486 was commemorated in 7th Pythian. In the Isthmian ode VI he recounts the pankration winner Phylacidas—also of Aegina.

Of the 17 works of Pindar only the 4 of the Epinician Odes are intact. Each of these was prompted by a victory at one of the 4 Panhellenic festivals. Usually the contest is not referred to and is never described. The skill, previous distinctions won by the victor's family are referred to; metaphors and similies are used to give colour to the victory.

Always the god in whose honour the games were held was referred to and myth played a vital part as did reference to the city state and its traditions from which the conquering hero came.

To me Olympian VII is the most satisfying for it tells of Diagoras, his boxing victory, the mythology of the island of Rhodes and of Diagoras's triumphs at all the great games of Greece.

The bronze of Argos knew him, the caldrons in Arkadia and Thebes, the temperate games the Boeotians keep; Pellan likewise. At Aegina he won six times, at Megara the stone ballot tells no alternate story. But Zeus, father, brooding over the peaks of Atabyrios, honour the set of the song Olympionician.[33]

THE PYTHIAN GAMES

The Pythian festivals at Delphi held in honour of Apollo, the conqueror of the python, were of very ancient origin, but, in the early 6th Century B.C. they changed their character from exclusively musical tributes to include athletic contests.[34]

Initially prizes for the writing of, and the singing of, hymns as well as flute playing were of gold and/or silver but, in accordance with other major national festivals the winner's tribute became a laurel wreath as well as an apple and, to the winner of a heat, the symbolic palm branch held in the right hand. This custom was originated, so mythology said, by Theseus (at Delos) who instituted the Games to the god of truth, a son of Zeus, Apollo.

Apollo was born on the island of Delos, he is associated with beauty, culture and music as well as healing.

The Oracle became his voice.

The contests were, initially held in the Crisean fields in the neighbourhood of Delphi (formerly called Pythia) and the contest area grew to a stadium, the total length of which was 400 metres, a theatre in which all forms of musical contests took place and a massive hippodrome for the horse races.

Initially the athletic aspect, as at Olympia comprised one race, the Stade, but the tragedies, harp, flute, choral and perorations made to the Pythian god took a number of days, as did the horse races.

Until 582 B.C. the whole festival was managed by Delphians and the celebrations took place every 8th year.

After 582 B.C. they were conducted by the Amphictyons and took place in the last year of an Olympiad.

As at Olympia the composition of the festivities was often changed. At Delphi contests were in flute playing, horse racing, chariot racing, athletic events, poetry, music. Later again different types of poetry were introduced named in the form of historical narratives and painting and sculpting contests were popular.

Statues to victors were placed in the Crisean plain and the contests and games were held regularly until the end of the 4th Century.

By that time the stadium had been constructed at the height of over 1,800 feet on the lower southern slopes of Parnassus.

At Delphi, as at Olympia, "treasuries" were numerous—the best preserved to this day is the one honouring the Athenian victory at Marathon over the Persians.

THE ISTHMIAN GAMES

Sisyphus, a mythical king of Corinth is said to have originated the Isthmian Games. He attempted to cheat death and gave offence to both the gods Zeus and Hades. As a consequence he was condemned to the Underworld to roll a boulder to the top of a hill in hell. Just as it reached the summit it, inevitably, rolled down again—his punishment was thus eternal.[35]

Yet the story of the rivalry between the centres Olympia and Corinth is also attributable to the gods. Olympia was celebrated under the divine patronage of Zeus, Isthmia's patron was Poseidon, Zeus's brother. Poseidon was ruler of the sea and the hidden forces within the earth, Zeus was the god of clear air, mountain tops and the sky.

The two entities sun and sea give distinctive character to the Isthmian landscape, and out of these elements was yet another myth built, woven of the anguish and enmity between Helios (the god of the sun) and Poseidon (the god of the sea). They contested the possession of the Isthmus.

One of the Cyclops, Briarios (reputedly the son of Poseidon) gave the land to his father and to Helios the mountain Akronkorinthos—later given to Aphrodite. Professor Oscar Broneer[36] recounts yet another legend in which the founding hero of the Games was the boy Melikertes, (grandson of Kadmos of Thebes) who was drowned when his mother Ino fled from her maddened husband King Athamas of Orchomenos, with the young lad clasped in her arms.

The mother leapt into the Aronic Gulf, was metamorphised into a sea divinity renamed Leukothea (white goddess).

Although Melikertes was drowned, a dolphin carried him to the Isthmus where he was found under a pine tree by the Corinthian King, Sisyphus. The funeral games enacted at the boy's burial founded the Isthmian Games. Melikertes was also given a new name Palaimon and divine honours were accorded him at Poseidon's sanctuary.

By this myth the Corinthians accounted for the origin of the Isthmian Games.

The Festival of Isthmia was held at what is now the village of Kiras Vrysi[37] twice in every Olympiad i.e. in the Spring of the 1st and in the summer of the 3rd year of that Olympiad.

Compared to the Olympic ceremonies, the Isthmian Games were celebrated with splendour, a carnival atmosphere prevailing, for Corinth was the playground of the Pelopponesus. This narrow strip of land which joins the Pelopponesus to the mainland is, on the West caressed by the waters of the Corinthian Gulf and on the East by the Saronic Gulf thus it was easily accessible, particularly from Athens which also had vested interests in Corinth for the Athenians held special privileges and seats of honour (proedria) in the Stadium because they too credited the founding of the Isthmian Festival to their own God Hero, Theseus.

It is recorded[38] that Theseus on his journey from Troizen to Athens destroyed many monsters. At the Isthmus he encountered one, Sinis whose "nick name" was "pine bender", challenging him to a pine-bending contest. Sinis's method was to tie the legs of his victims to two pine trees which he had bent to the ground and then let them spring apart. Theseus inflicted this death on Sinis and celebrated by instituting the Isthmian Games.

These then were three myths purporting to originate the Corinthian Festival.

POSEIDON AND PALAIMON

The worship of Poseidon extends from the eighth century B.C. and the Director of the American School of Archaeology, Professor Broneer states that Poseidon's first temple, being a superb example of Doric architecture, was built around the date 700 B.C. and replaced by a more splendid edifice about 465 B.C.[39]

The second most important centre of cultism on the Isthmus was the Palaimonion containing a circular temple to the human Palaimon at which a black sacrificial bull was slaughtered to inaugurate the Isthmian Festival.

As at Olympia, trainers, judges, parents and athletes had to swear at Poseidon's Altar that they would perform according to the rules.

In the temple of Palaimon the athletes descended into an unlit crypt and stood in water to hear a Priest read them a binding oath such that anyone who perjured himself could not escape punishment. Cheating in the contests was thus very rare.

The Palaimonion was built on the site of the abandoned old stadium—one of the oldest in Greece, probably originating in the 6th Century B.C.

In a communication to the late Avery Brundage on 27th July 1963[40] Professor Broneer states that his:

> Excavations in the Isthmian Sanctuary—the place where the Isthmian Games were held—have revealed the existence of two stadia, both of pre-Roman times. The earlier of the two had an intricate type of starting line found in no other known stadium in Greece. Because of its encroachment upon the second precinct that contained the Temple of Poseidon, this stadium was abandoned probably as early as the 4th Century B.C. Its successor was constructed in a natural hollow some 250 metres farther toward the northeast.

Later he tells of the race course linked on each side by water channels that opened into basins every now and again, indicating that these were to bring water to both spectators and athletes alike. As at Olympia and Delphi the sides of the stadium bulged slightly in the centre. The width of the starting line was 26.23 metres and there were 16 running lanes as in early stadia.

The length of the stade was 181.15 metres differing only a few centimetres from that of the stadium in Epidauros.

The events at Isthmia were different than at other festivals. It is reputed that Jason had won the boat race and dedicated his galley in the Temple of Poseidon. Another unusual contest was the torch relay race.

It was Professor Oscar Broneer who discovered the 16 individual gates which made up the starting gates, known as Balbides in the earlier Stadium and he considers them reminiscent of the starting gates in the Olympic Hippodrome which Pausanias compared to the prow of a ship.[41]

Music, literary works and oratorical contests also formed part of the celebrations as did a variety of athletic events.

The victory symbol was a wreath of pine, in the earliest days, placed upon the head and a palm branch in the right hand; but, by Pindar's time the wreath was of wild dried celery which was also used at Nemea, yet here the celery was fresh.

It has been said that the withered celery influenced St. Paul's reference in his first letter to the Corinthians. "Every athlete exercises self control in all things; they do it to receive a perishable wreath, but we an imperishable life."

THE NEMEAN GAMES:

Little appears to be known about these Games in comparison to, say the Olympic festival to which Pausanias gives two complete volumes yet only a few confusing, almost contradictory passages about Nemea.

There are however 14 odes—to Olympic victors, 12 for Pythian athletic champions, 7 for Isthmian and 11 for those who triumphed at Nemea—all by Pindar.

Nemea (formerly Hagios Georgios) in Argolis is exactly 18 kilometres North, North West of Argos. Five Kilometres east of the town is the Nemean valley in northern Argolis being 15 kilometres South West of Corinth.

The Nemean festival was the fourth of the Periodos—the Circuit, being held biennially.

It is know of the strained relations between the Isthmians and the Olympians[42] and it is thought that this encouraged the Eleans to give support to the Nemeans. No Elean was permitted to compete at the Isthmus but any Corinthian was entitled to take part at Olympia.

An account left by Herodotus makes it clear that in the early years of the 6th Century the Olympic festival management was re-examining its conduct of the quadrennial games.

A delegation was sent to Egypt to have discussion about the rules of the Games Olympic. They (the Olympians) wished to confirm that their Games were ". . . the fairest and finest . . ."

The Eleans' concern about their Dorian management was occasioned by the Pythian Apollo Delphic Games being expanded into a regular Pan-hellenic festival. At the same time the old Games of Isthmia, in honour of Poseidon, promoted by Corinth with support from Athens, concerned them also. The improvements at both Isthmian and Delphic Games were completed by 582 B.C.

This worry was compounded because the lively Games at Isthmia were held twice as often as at Olympia and in a place easily accessible to the Eastern Greek world.

Perhaps then, this is why the sudden emergence in 573 B.C. of the Nemean Games into the Pan-hellenic group and of the Nemean Games being held in the same years as the Isthmian came as a counter force to the new-found Pythian/Isthmian association and particularly the influence of the Ionian festival near the bustling economic centre Corinth.

In the British Museum is a papyrus fragment—the Oxyrthynchus Papyri of 1783—purchased in 1920 in Egypt, containing parts of a victory ode for a Sosibius of Alexandria who entered his chariot in the Nemean Games. The poem shows clearly that Greek athletics continued in spite of political changes.

At Nemea everything remained simple and as Carl Blegen remarks in his article (pages 421–440 in the American Journal of Archaeology, No. 31/1927) "The spectators stood or sat on the ground itself which descends in a regular, and certainly artificially made slope to the floor of the stadium.

It is almost certain that all the athletic events held in Olympia were duplicated in Nemea as careful scrutiny of Pindar's epic hymns of victory clearly show.

To end, I wish to quote extensively from Philostratus—*The Life of Apollonius of Tyana*[43] as this brings the Ancient Athletic Festivals into perspective and clearly shows what they meant in the life of a nation.

There was a man of Thessaly, named Isagoras, whom he met in Olympia and said: "Tell me Isagoras, is there such a thing as a religious fair or festival?" "Why yes" he replied, "and by heaven there is nothing in the world of men, so agreeable and so dear to the gods." "And, what is the material of which it is composed?" asked Apollonius; "It is as if I asked you about the material of which this image is made, and that you answered me that it was composed of gold and ivory." "But", said the other, "what material, Apollonius, can a thing which is incorporeal be composed of?" "A most important material," replied Apollonius, "and most varied in character; for there are sacred groves in it, and shrines, and race-courses, and of course a theatre, and tribes of men, some of them from the neighbouring countries, and others from over the borders, and even from across the sea. "Moreover," he added, "many arts go to make up such a festival, and many designs, and much true genius, both of poets, and of civil counsellors, and of those who deliver harangues on philosophic topics, and contests between naked athletes, and contests of musicians, as is the custom in the Pythian festival." "It seems to me," said the other, "O Apollonius, that the festival is not only something corporeal, but it is made up of more wonderful material than are cities; for there is summoned together into one community on such occasions, the best of the best, and the most celebrated of the celebrated."

REFERENCES

1. Harlan, Hugh. *History of Olympic Games Ancient and Modern* (Los Angeles: Bureau of Athletic Research, May 1931) p. 9.

2. Powell, John T. "The Olympics as a Human Arena" (Pennsylvania, East Straudsburg State College, November, 1972) p. 1.

3. Xenophanes (Frag 2), *Sources for the History of Greek Athletics* (Cincinatti, translated by Rachel Sargent Robinson, 1955) Privately printed, p. 91.

4. Homer, *Iliad* (Chicago: University of Chicago Press, 1951), translated by Richard Lattimore, p. 774.

5. Palaeologos, Cleanthis. "Birth, Establishment and Development of the Olympic Games" (Athens, in Report of the Second Session of the International Olympic Academy, July 1962) p. 132.

6. Pausanias. *Description of Greece* (Cambridge, Cambridge University Press, 1886) translated by A. R. Shillito, V. 7, p. 6.

7. Eusebeus. *Chronology* (Cambridge, Harvard University Press, 1912) translated by W. Schoene, X, p. 192.

8. Eusebius. *Chronology* (Cincinnati, translated by Rachel Sargent Robinson, 1955. Printed in *Sources for the History of Greek Athletics*, Col. 194.

9. Pindar. *The Odes of Pindar,* (Cambridge, Harvard University Press and Heinemann Ltd., 1915) translated by Sir John Sandys, Olympic Ode XI, p. 341.

10. Finley, M. I. and Pleket, H. W. *The Olympic Games, the First Thousand Years,* (Toronto, Clarke, Irwin and Company Ltd., 1976) p. xiii.

11. Palaeologos, *op. cit.* p. 136.

12. Pindar. *op. cit.* Olympic Ode 1. p. 6.

13. Philostratus. *The Life of Apollonius of Tyana.* (Cambridge, Harvard University Press, the Loeb Classical Library, 1912) Translated by F. C. Coneybeare, Book V. Vol 1, XLIII, p. 571.

14. *Pausanias. Description of Greece,* II, Book V, (Cambridge, Harvard University Press, 1926) Translated by W. H. S. Jones and H. A. Ormerod, Elis I, vi 5–8, p. 411.

15. *Ibid.* p. 473.

16. Drees, Ludwig, *Olympia, Gods, Artists and Athletes* (New York, Frederick A. Praeger, Publishers, 1968) p. 29.

17. Pausanias. *op. cit.* Elis I, XVI, 1–4, p. 473.

18. Pausanias. *op. cit.* Elis I, XVI, 7 - XVII, 3.

19. Pausanias. *op. cit.* Elis I, VI, 20.

20. Pausanias. *Description of Greece,* II. Southern Greece, (Middlesex, England, Penguin Classics, 1971) Translated by Peter Levi, Book VI, Eleia II, p. 345.

21. *Op. cit.* p. 217 et sec.

22. Paleologos. *op. cit.* p. 141.

23. Levi. *op. cit.* p. 219.

24. Robinson, R. S. Anacharsis, in *Sources for the History of Greek Athletics* (Cincinnati, Privately printed, 1955.) Translated by the author, p. 62.

25. *Ibid.* p. 76.

26. Gardiner, Norman E. *Athletics of the Ancient World* (Oxford, Clarendon Press. 1930) p. 191.

27. Paleologos, Cleanthis. "The Ancient Olympics" (Athens, in Report of the fourth session of the International Olympic Academy, August 1964) p. 82.

28. Paleologos, Cleanthis - *Legends of Olympia* (Athens, Published privately, - 1962, English Translation) p. 57.

29. Philostratus. *The Life of Apollonius of Tyana* (Cambridge, Harvard University Press, the Loeb Classical Library, Translated by F. C. Coneybeare, 1912. p. 477.

30. Sandys, Sir John. *Life of Pindar* (Cambridge, Harvard University Press 1915), p. vii.

31. *Ibid.* p. ix.

32. Ioannides, Ion, P. in *Olympic Review,* "The True Course Run by the marathon Messenger" (Lausanne, published by the Comité International Olympique, 1976) No. 109–110, November/December, pp. 599–602.

33. Sandys. *op. cit.* p. 22.

34. Herodotus. In, *Sources for the History of Greek Athletics* (Cincinnati, privately published, 1955). Translated by R. S. Robinson, p. 61.

35. Grant, Michael. *Myths of the Greeks and Romans* (Cleveland, The World Publishing Company, 1962) p. 444.

36. Broneer, Oscar. "The Isthmian Games" (Athens, in Report of the International Olympic Academy, tenth session, August 1970) p. 94.

37. Roberts, Steven V. "New-found mosaic reflects glittering Greece" in *The Globe and Mail* - Toronto, Saturday, 3rd April 1977.

38. Broneer, *loc. cit.*

39. Broneer, *Ibid.* p. 95.

40. Broneer - personal communication title "The Latest Stadium at Isthmia", to the late Avery Brundage - permission to quote granted by the Archivist of the Brundage Collection - Archives - University of Illinois - Champaign - U.S.A.

41. Broneer, Oscar. "What Isthmia has taught about Athletics" (Athens, in Report of the third session of the International Olympic Academy, July 1963, p. 183.

42. Pausanias. *Description of Greece,* V (Cambridge, Harvard University Press 1961) Translated by W. H. S. Jones, pp. 2–5 and 9–16.

43. Philostratus: *Life of Apollonius of Tyana* (Cambridge, Harvard University Press 1960) Translated by F. C. Coneybeare. Book VIII, XVIII - Discussion of what makes a festival, p. 375.

CHAPTER II

Opinions of Some Philosophers and Poets Regarding Ancient Greek Athletic Festivals

CHAPTER II
Opinions of Some Philosophers and Poets
Regarding Ancient Greek Athletic Festivals

If the Olympic Games were being held now . . . you would be able to see for yourself why we attach such great importance to athletics. No-one can describe in mere words the extraordinary pleasure derived from them and which you yourself would enjoy if you were seated among the spectators feasting your eyes on the prowess and stamina of the athletes, the beauty and power of their bodies, their incredible dexterity and skill, their invincible strength, their courage, ambition, endurance and tenacity. You would never stop applauding them.

Lucian (2nd Century A.D.)
in *ANACHARSIS*

INTRODUCTION

What cannot be measured is the impact that the thinkers had upon athletes and upon the Festivals. The esteem in which philosophers and poets were held and the quality of expressed thought in the Palaestra, the Lyceum and the Academy must have influenced society. It is known that, in the 5th Century before Christ at least 137 Greek cities all held athletics festivals: this shows how much a part of Greek life was devoted to preparedness, through contest and general physical activity.

Therefore thoughts were turned towards: Homer (850 B.C.), Hesiod, Thales (640–546 B.C.), the first natural Western philosopher, Anaxemenes of Miletus of the 6th Century B.C., Anaximander (611–547 B.C.) to Socrates in the 5th Century before Christ, to two of the greatest pre-Socratic philosophers Heraclitus and Parmenides—the first great mystical metaphysician who denied that any real knowledge is attainable. Then to Plato and to Heraclitus who considered that everything is subject to change and to the last pre-Socratic influence which formed Plato's philosophy—the Pythagorian doctrine of numbers.

Pythagoras was born in Samos early in the Sixth century B.C., and it was he who established the basis and understanding of mathematical knowledge.

It was Socrates (470–399) who turned philosophy away from high cosmological speculations and concentrated attention on man and his moral problems. He was concerned with "what do we know and how do we come to know that which we do know?" He also dwelt upon what is the highest excellence or virtue of Man, thus it is to Socrates to whom reference upon excellence of athletic achievement must be made. It is difficult, however, to distinguish between Socrates as he actually was and Socrates as Plato (427–347) represented him in his dialogues. Plato was, undoubtedly, the greatest literary artist amongst philosophers, the most fertile, the most profound; one who was prepared to change doctrines and yet who knew that degrees of knowledge corresponded to degrees of reality. And so to Plato's pupil, Aristotle (384–322) the founder of formal logic and a marvellous naturalist.

But there are many sources, fragments, implications and recordings about ancient Greek athletic festivals and the temptation has been resisted to recount them, thus limiting the following thoughts to what the philosophers and poets had to say.

FUNERAL GAMES

The description, by Homer in the 23rd Iliad[1], is the earliest description of Funeral Games known. It is not know when Homer lived, or whether the poems he wrote described Games as he saw them, or whether they were of Games held two or three centuries previously.

The blond Achaens, described by Homer, were invaders from the North who later became settlers; they were war-like and to keep them ready for war they exercised and exulted in victory. In the Iliad, Glaucus said:

"My father bade me ever be far the best and far excel all other men and not to put to shame my father's lineage."[2]

Achilles prepared the Funeral Games for his beloved hero friend, Patroclus. The first contest was the chariot race, with a dual first prize of a servant-woman and a tripod, the second prize being "a mare heavy with a mule", a cauldron as third, gold pieces as fourth and a jug was fifth. Achilles judged fairly, arguments were mediated with reason, and each contestant received a prize. Each of the riders presented himself, and when Antilochus stood, his father, Nestor, gave him a long speech of advice insisting that skill in driving and use of tactics were far more important than speedy steeds. He suggested to his son that he hug the turning post without actually touching it—this, he said, was the crucial manoeuvre. The combatants drew lots for lanes and Achilles placed Phoenix at the turning point. A whip was cracked and the chariots moved. Then comes a thrilling description of the race with Eumelus taking the lead, followed by Diomedes, but the God Apollo causes him to lose his whip, which the goddess Athena returns to him, and in turn she breaks the yoke of Eumelus's chariot from which he is thrown, to be badly bruised.

Antilochus rides neck-and-neck with Menelaus but wins, followed by Antiolochus, Menelaus, Meriones and Eumelus, last. Achilles took pity on Eumelus, offering him second prize as consolation but Antilochus objected. Argument ensued but all was amicably settled. Meriones took fourth prize, and the fifth, Achilles gave to old Nestor who accepted, making a speech recounting his victories when a youth, saying that, then in the Funeral Games for King Amarymeus, he won every prize but one—the charioteer's.

The boxing contest is next described where Epeius claims the victor's prize of a mule, having dropped Euryalus with a solid blow to the cheek and then he helps him to his feet. Odysseus and Aias confront each other for the wrestling title. The contest is even and long until, very skilfully, as Aias lifts him, Olysseus hooks his leg behind Aias's knee, drops him and pins him. The second fall also goes to Odysseus, but before the bout continues (3 falls were necessary to win), Achilles steps in, offering equal gifts to each competitor. Some authorities write that the contest was a draw (H. J. Rose in the Oxford Classical Dictionary) but Walter Leaf's translation agrees with the above resolution of the contest[3].

Then followed a foot-race in which Aias (not the wrestler, but the son of Oileus), the youth Antilochus, and Odysseus compete. Odysseus is losing, prays to Pallas Athena, who trips Aias into a dung heap nearing the race's end, and Odysseus won. Then came the armour, shield and sword contest. In this Aias (the wrestler and son of Telamon) has the fight stopped in favour of his opponent, Diomedes, who wins a sword.

Archery is next and Teucer unleashes an arrow without first praying to Apollo. He misses the dove (the target) tied to a ship's mast but severs the cord tying it. Suddenly Meriones grasps a bow, fits an arrow and brings down the flying bird, thus receiving his first prize of ten double-bladed axes.

Four contestants vie for throwing a lump of precious iron furthest. Polypoetes easily wins the contest and the missile, which is the award. And so to the final event—the spear throw which is not contested as, in deference to Agamemnon, Achilles gives him the prize and Meriones accepts, with grace, the consolation award.

Note the power of the gods, their constant presence and how they are called upon in all phases of decision. Note also the spirit in the Games and the awarding of prizes to all. No-one wishes to upset the gods and goddesses, neither to disturb by discord the dead; yet they contest, which was a normal phase of life indulged in naturally and enjoyed.

FEAST GAMES

In Homer's Odyssey[4], a graphic poetic interpretation of athletic events is given. Odysseus—of the seed of Zeus—had landed in the country of the Phaecians (wherever that was; some, today consider it to be the island of Corfu) and landed at the court of King Alcinous. After a feast and music the King said, "Let us go forth anon, and make trial of divers games, that the stranger may tell his friends, when home he returneth, how greatly we excel all men in boxing, and wrestling and leaping, and speed of foot."[5]

First, there was sprinting, then wrestling, long jumping, weight throwing, and boxing. Then Odysseus was asked did he excel in sport, by Laodamas, Alcinous'son. Noting a reluctance in Odysseus, Euryalus rebuked him, "No, truly, stranger, nor do I think thee at all like one that is skilled in games. . . ."[6]. Odysseus responded, in no uncertain terms: "Yet, thou has stirred my spirit in my breast, by speaking thus amiss", and ". . . for all my affliction, I will essay the games, for thy word has bitten to the quick, and thou has roused me with thy saying."[7] He then lifted a weight larger than any previously used in the contest and heaved it with one hand further than any other cast. Then he challenged any in boxing, in wrestling, and even the foot race. He told them of his supremacy in archery and of his only defeat by Philoctetes of Troy and of his excellence with the javelin.[8] Only Alcinous answered, changing the tense situation to one of pleasure again, calling for the dance.

Once again is seen the cathartic effect of human physical prowess and that no excuse was necessary for competition to reign.

HESIOD

Hesiod, a poet, lived in an age innocent of philosophy. Mythology and mythological thinking pervaded his time and the people of that era in mystically determined ways. He was born in Ascra, Boeotia. In his *Works and Days*[9] Hesiod writes that he belonged to the period immediately following the Trojan War (1194–1184) yet most scholars date him after Homer (850 B.C.)

Hesiod's work also allows men to take the centre of the stage but his approach is quite different to Homer's approach. Hesiod deals with Men in their relationship to gods, to social order and to the necessities of life. Although not a philosopher he influenced both Greek philosophy and philosophers. He recounts how he competed at Chalcis at the Funeral Games of Amphidamas and won a "fair handled tripod" which he dedicated to the Muses of Helicon. A later legend asserted that his beaten rival was non other than Homer.[10]

PINDAR

The most illustrious of the Greek lyric poets was born in 518 B.C. Most of his works have perished although 45 of his odes are intact commemorating victories by strength, dexterity in running, speed of horses and mules, skill in music, in wrestling, boxing, and pentathlon. He wrote hymns, paeans in honour of gods, songs in praise of Apollo, dithyrambic verses to Dionysus, drinking songs, dirges and odes on Olympian (14), Nemean (11), Isthmian (8) and Pythian Games (12).

Sometimes his hymns were said, as at Olympia in the evening, by the moon's light after the termination of an event—and at other times on the return of a victor to his native city when the protecting wall had been broken to allow his entrance. This would have been a sacred time, yet a joyous homecoming. The poet would have trained a chorus to recite the triumphal ode usually followed by a banquet.

An explanation is necessary before reading Pindar's odes. Mythology, idealogy, community, social and family genealogical symbols were all enwrapped and enmeshed. His words were enhanced by flute or lyre music, cymbals, or solo and chorus chanting. His hymns were all commissioned, and were ceremonial, flitting between gods and men, infinite and finite and making assumptions difficult for us but, no doubt, commonplace to those who heard the original praises. As an example, Olympian VII, written for Diagoras of Rhodes may explain. The island of Rhodes, in Greek legend, derived its name from one of Aphrodite's daughters who married Helios—the god of Sun who, when Zeus divided the earth between the gods, was absent. Helios was not angry for as he returned he had seen within the sea, an island about to rise which he requested. This was Rhodes.

Diagoras had been a successful local athlete as well as at the four major athletic centres in Greece. In Delphi he won, but had been guilty of some inadvertent transgression yet had, in 464 B.C., won the boxing title at Olympia.

Pindar's Ode is compared to a loving cup given to the bridegroom by the bride's father who is recognised by name. The cup serves two purposes, the pledge of wedlock and the poet's pean of fame. Zeus is asked for his blessing on ode and victor, that his clan be prosperous so that the State benefits; the ode finishes, listing Diagoras's victories.

Here is an extract[11] from *OLYMPIA* 7 p.19:

> . . . and to both strains I keep company with Diagoras, singing the sea's child, daughter of Aphrodite and bride of Helios, Rhodes and give praise, spoil of his boxing, to the onslaught of a man gigantic, wreathed in victory beside Alpheos' water and Kastalia; and to Damagetos his father. . . .

In his 8th Olympian is a firm indication that a typical subject for enquiry at Olympia's oracle was the prospects of Olympic athletes:

> "Olympia, Mother of contests for golden wreaths, Lady of truth, where men of prophecy divine the word of Zeus, white lightening's source, in sacrificial fires and learn what plans he had for men. . . ."[12]

The event was boys wrestling, Alcimedon of Aegina was the winner.

STRABO (63 B.C.–21 A.D.)

About 400 years later than Pindar, Strabo[13], in his book *GEOGRAPHY*, named Oxylus as the founder of the Olympic Games and that it was at the end of the 12th Century B.C. that any Olympic Games, as such, were established.

His great work of geography, in 17 books, has been preserved in its entirety except for aspects of the seventh volume. The Loeb Edition (1925–26) has published the work in eight volumes. Strabo was well educated, well travelled and adopted a stoical philosophy amply shown in the translation of his work. Here again is evidenced the influence of the gods for, on the re-establishment of the Games is noted that ". . . a sworn agreement was promptly made by all, that Eleia should be sacred to Zeus."[14] It goes on to say that anyone who invaded that country would be under a curse, those who failed to defend the country would also be cursed and that those who later built the city did so without a protecting wall, for those who went through the area, with an army, were to surrender their arms to receive them again when leaving. It then suggests that Iphitus celebrated the Olympic Games and Eleians became sacred people.

However, Farnell[15] deals with the founding of the Games very contemptuously and Rachel Robinson[16] also expresses her concern about both omissions and the tenor of Strabo's account, prior to Oxylus.

PHLEGON (about 138 A.D.)

In his philosophical work *Historical Introduction*[17] Phlegon gives more evidence of the oracular power concerning Games:

"Zeus is angry at you for sacred rites which he revealed by oracles because you fail to honour the Olympic Games of all-ruling Zeus. . . ."

Furthermore he also outlined events at Olympia before the 12th Century B.C. and dwells about the length of time the Games were neglected up to the time of the recording of Coroebus's victory (776 B.C.) telling of their revival more than 100 years previously.

EUSEBIUS OF CAESAREA (about 260 A.D. to 340 A.D.)

Philosopher, "a man of many notebooks" and, in 314 chosen Bishop of Caesarea, lived five generations after the great author Pausanias. Eusebius was a noted researcher and in his *Chronology* is recorded the Olympic Register of Victors from 776 B.C. to 217 A.D.[18] The chronology follows Phlegon's account concerning the matter of dating the renewal of the Games to the early ninth century B.C.

It is now generally agreed that from the founding of the Elean Games by Herakles to the first officially recorded victory was 419[19] years. According to the modern scholar Cleanthis Palaelogos[20], ten generations elapsed until Iphitus renewed the Games. Iphetus was of Elis, and, wishing to stop national warring, sent a deputation from the Pelloponeusus to the Delphic Oracle. The god's reply to the Peloponnesians was:

"O, inhabitants of Peloponnesus go to the altar sacrifice and hearken to what the priests enjoin."[21]

The god then spoke to the Eleans:

Citizens of Elis keep straight to the laws of your fathers
Defend your own country and refrain from war

- 35 -

> Leading the Greeks in impartial friendship
> Whenever the genial year returns.[22]

Eusebius continues:

> "Because of this Iphetus announced the truce . . . and ordained the Games. At this time the foot race was the only contest but later the other contests were added."[23]

HEROD THE GREAT (born about 62 B.C. died 4 B.C.)

The first contact the people of Israel had with Hellenistic culture was in the time of the Macedonian, Alexander the Great who, conquering country after country arrived in Jerusalem. Herod had, in 25 B.C., built a stadium near Jerusalem and, in 12 B.C. Herod not only built the city of Caesarea but also had constructed another magnificent stadium in which he inaugurated a festival according to the Olympic Games programme. It was in this same year (the 193rd Olympiad) that he not only acted as President of the Quadrenial Festival, when he stopped at Elis on his way to Rome, but "endowed them for all time with an income big enough to ensure that his presidency should never be forgotten."[24]

LUCIAN (125-180 A.D.)

A contemporary of Pausanias was both philosopher and researcher who spend 20 years in Athens, although a Mesopotamian. He wrote *ANACHARSIS*[25] which is really a conversation about Greek athletics between Solon the Athenian lawgiver and the Scythian Anacharsis who came to Greece in his quest to find wisdom. The conversation took place in the Lyceum in Athens. From the discourse is learned much of athletic practices of the fifth century B.C. and proof that ". . . they compete in throwing the javelin for distance",[26] and, when talking about discus throwing ". . . they throw that high into the air and also to a distance, trying to see who can go the farthest and throw beyond the rest."[27] Many authorities have suggested that the Greeks threw javelins and slung discoi at a target; these assumptions have been based upon no references being found giving times or distances. Further evidence comes in the 8th Ode of Bacchylides wherein he celebrates the victory of Automedes of Phlius in the

Nemean pentathlon.[28] Automedes won both javelin throw and discus as well as the last event, wrestling.

> He shone among the other pentathletes as the bright moon in the middle of the month dims the radiance of the stars; even thus he showed his lovely body to the great ring of watching Greeks, as he threw the round discus and hurled the shaft of black-leaved elder from his grasp to the steep heights of heaven, and roused the cheers of the spectators by his lithe movements in the wrestling at the end.[29]

Again it must be reflected upon the era in which these athletic contests were held and the lack of sophistication in organisation. It was necessary only to give a winner, except in funeral or feast games.

What did the three great Philosophers, Socrates, Plato and Aristotle, note in their analyses of Greek athletic practice?

SOCRATES (469–399 B.C.)

No written word has come directly from Socrates. In *MEMORABILIA*[30] I, II, and III are what Xenophon (430–354 B.C.) nicknamed the Attic Bee, has written in dialogue form, being the words of his noted teacher Socrates.

Socrates meets a poorly developed youth and rebukes him for his underdeveloped body. "Of course, I am not a professional" replies the youth. Whereupon the philosopher gives him a lecture pointing out that no citizen has any right to be an amateur in the matter of physical training, that it is part of his profession simply by being a citizen to keep himself in excellent physical condition ready, at a moment's notice, to serve his State. He then berates the youth, telling him that it is a disgrace for a man to grow old without ever having seen the beauty and strength of which his body is capable and to go, develop his beauty and his strength to the utmost because it is his duty to do so—in this way only will the youth reach the Greek ideal.

In *HELLENICA*, when Xenophon was recording the Spartan war against Elis in 364 B.C. he gives several grounds for complaint against the Eleans. The Eleans were counter-attacking the Arcadians (who had usurped the presidency of the Games) saying that the Pentathlon was proceeding at the same time and that: "They had already finished the horse-race and the track events in the pentathlon and those who had reached the wrestling were no longer in the dromos but were wrestling between the dromos and the altar." Here is yet another clue to the conduct of ancient Games—there must have been some form of elimination as it is known that the wrestling was the final of the five-event contest.[31] In this regard it is strongly suggested that reference be made to the excellent summary of the speech given by Lauri Pihkala, title "The neglected legacy of Philostratus—method of the ancient pentathlon" in the International Olympic Academy Report 1966, pages 126 to 132.

PLATO (born 427, died 344 B.C.)

This great philosopher and pupil of Socrates was a splendid athlete, and it was reported that his original name Aristocles was changed by his wrestling coach to Plato, from the word "platy" meaning "broad shouldered". He competed at the Isthmian and Pythian Festivals. In his *REPUBLIC*[32] Book III, he wrote "After music comes gymnastic, in which our youth are next to be trained." In Book IV[33] ". . . then to sum up: "This is the point to which above all, the attention of our rulers should be directed, that music and gymnastic be preserved in their original form, and no innovation made."[34] He was the leading advocate in his own time for physical activity for women; in his *LAWS*[35] Book VII he, in translation is quoted saying: "I assert without fear of contradiction that gymnastic and horsemanship are as suitable to women as to men" and in *REPUBLIC* V[36] ". . . if women are to have the same duties as men, they must have the same nurture and education." Later, when summing education and what music (being to the Greeks, reading, writing, arithmetic, drawing, poetry, music and harmony) plus gymnastics would accomplish, he writes: "Then let the wives of our guardians strip, for their virtue will be their robe"[37] and ". . . let them share in the toils of war and the defence of their country."

Further to his attitude to women, Plato, in England's translation, states that it is immaterial whether the girl competitors have any clothing on or not but that, "they are, however only to run on the race-course, not across country."[38] and "But for girls who are over 13 and are still unmarried the contests are to go on to any age between 18 and 20."[39] Here he insists that this latter group be properly clad when they compete in races. He is quite firm stating that: "As in the case of the human runners, the horses are to be arranged in three classes"[40] and that all contests in athletics are to be arranged at particular intervals: ". . . it will be settled . . . to take place every two years or every four years, or in what ever way or manner the gods may suggest as to their order."[41]

In Bury's translation of *Laws* in the conversation between Clinias, an Athenian Stranger and Megillus of Lacedaemon, Plato gives advice on the training for war stating that men should box daily and, even when there is no-one with whom to contest shadow boxing should be done alone.[42] When discussing gymnastic training he has the three conversants agree on the priorities that, first in importance is running and running for speed, then hand to hand combat at close quarters to build strength and sturdiness.[43] As for women he advocates races for females, the furlong, a 1/4 mile, a 1/2 mile and a 3/4 mile for all girls under the age of puberty and ". . . who shall be stripped and shall race on the course itself."[44]

A further reference to Plato's athletic knowledge is again recorded in *LAWS*[45] wherein he contrasts the methods of wrestling used in the pankration (in which kicking and leg-holds were allowed) and those of upright wrestling. This latter form he defines so clearly as "the disentangling of neck and hands and sides." He continues stating that in his ideal state only this type of wrestling would be allowed.

In *MEMORABILLIA* III[46] is interesting comment that travellers and athletes from Athens to Olympia regularly walked the 519 kilometres. Socrates questions a tired traveller asking, did he have an attendance and if so, what did he (the traveller) carry? The answer was ". . . my cloak." Socrates asked what did the servant carry and how he fared. The answer was that he carried everything else and ". . . appeared to come off better than myself." Socrates had a ready answer: ". . . how can you think that it becomes a man trained to exercise to be so much less able to bear fatigue than a slave?"

ARISTOTLE (384–322 B.C.)

What is the attitude to and the physical condition of the parents? That was his concern in *POLITICS* IV for he said that few boy victors in athletic festivals distinguished themselves as men. He criticised the unbalanced development of the body and in his book *RHETORIC* i, 5 he was especially enamoured of the union, strength, mobility and beauty of the pentathlete. Aristotle condemned all exaggerated unilateral development whether mental or physical.[47]

It was Aristotle who expanded and revised the previous century's work of Hippias of Elis bringing up to date the victor lists of ancient Olympia; he also is said to have named the oldest athletic festival as that held at Eleusis where grain was awarded to the winners.[48] In Plutarch's *LYCURGUS* Book I is mentioned that Aristotle had seen the discus at Olympia with the name Lycurgus still easily able to be read inscribed upon it. Pausanias (V, 20, I)[49] also saw it and wrote:

"The discus of Iphitus has inscribed upon it the truce which men of Elis announce at the time of the Olympic Games. . . ."

THE DECLINE OF ATHLETIC FESTIVALS

Pindar praised the glory of the Games as did other lyric poets such as Simonides of Ceos (about 556 to 466 B.C.) and his nephew Bacchylides (507–428 B.C.) whose works have been translated by the brilliant scholar Sir Richard Jebb. Philosophers have commented and recorded athletic scandals at Isthmia and Olympia as well as distaste at the gluttony and indulgence of athletes, and professionalism, as well as at the inequality of rewarding mental as against physical ability.

The brilliant philosopher from Colophon in Asia Minor and founder of the Eleatic school, Xenophanes denounced the biased honouring of athletic prowess ". . . this is a most unreasonable custom, and it is not right to honour strength above excellent wisdom."[50] At the close of the Fifth Century B.C. Euripides, the youngest of the three tragic poets also reviled athletes who had, as a class, deteriorated, feeding, training and living solely to compete.[51] Furthermore he echoes Xenophanes: "We ought to crown with garlands the wise and the good. . . ."[52] But it is from Diogenes (404–323 B.C.), called by Plato "The Mad Socrates", that the greatest criticism and scorn arose. Talking about athletes he said: ". . . do you fancy these pot-bellied men are of some use, men who ought rather to be sacrificed, cut up and served at a banquet."[53] He even put a wreath on a horse's head and proclaimed him an Isthmian victor and once he placed a wreath of pine on his own head until warned by the Corinthians to do nothing more illegal. Diogenes made fun of "so-called" athletes.

What is decline?

The Palaestra and gymnasia were the only places boys and young men gathered and, the age of philosophy was advancing fast. Nevertheless the garland of a victor was still prized. Youth was more and more attracted by the eloquence of the famous philosophers and poets than by participation in athletic endeavours. The older people saw the trend; Socrates was accused of corrupting youth by introducing new ideas, different theories, and questioning older concepts. The new trends finally prevailed, it was not over-eating or over-specialisation by athletes which destroyed the Festivals.

In 338 B.C. in Cheronia the Macedonians defeated Greece but, under the conqueror Alexander, all nations up to India, bowed before his forces. He absorbed the Greeks into his army but by each victory, traditions, habits, customs, gradually had their way. Modifications, different ideas, pastimes were seen and indulged in. Competitions were still enjoyed but their character was rather that of the conquered rather than the conqueror.

Alexander died in his early thirties and the Roman eagles followed the Macedonians.

Attitude to festivals was different and when Greece was overrun men fought beasts, slaves were sacrificed, professionalism was rife and the simplicity of the Greek athletic Games was transformed into inhuman spectacle.

The Romans first came to Olympia during the 177th Olympiad (72 B.C.) and Gaius was the dolichos race winner. Nero postponed the Games of 65 A.D. in order to take part in them at Olympia two years later as well as at Delphi, Nemea and Isthmia. He always won, there were no other competitors. His "victories" in lyre, in the 10-horse chariot race and in poetry were never contested—the mystical, simple and symbolic athletic festivals were made into a mockery.

Victory could be bought, competition lost its essence, competitors their prestige, and spectators their interest.

Nothing begins in an absolute manner, nothing ends directly or completely, things change; new things grow out of old. The slow development of the unsophisticated life changed in Greece through different religious patterns supplanting the powers of gods and goddesses, and through Eastern influences, political repercussions and restructuring. During the last 200 years of the four major Festivals, winners were either Roman or Alexandrian, but not Greek.

The old world was changing—the Roman State became politically bankrupt, the appearance of Christianity also swept away the glories of statuary and works of art. There was endless change.

The beauty of being "kalos kagathos" was not prized, the mixing and mingling of races, the whole social structure little by little altered; and gods and goddesses had become "old".

The degeneracy of athletics was only symptomatic of "progress", then in 394 A.D. Emperor Theodosius the Great, murdered the Games after a long and lingering illness. But what a glorious history remains.

Those who have struggled so patiently, pay tribute, make effort, give affection and belief and co-operation in order to, once again, make Olympism a living ideal and a force for peaceful struggles amongst unified peoples. There is no better ending that by quoting from Alan Harrington's *The Immortalist*, where he wrote:

Games— that is, formal sports and pastimes—may be the best simulators of eternal life that humanity has at its disposal. They take place in their own special time, and no other, on the playground of immortality.

Alan Harrington,
The Immortalist.

REFERENCES

1. Homer, *Iliad,* (New York Monarch Press, 1964) Translated by David Sider and David Konstan, Book XXIII, pp. 81–85.

2. Homer, *Iliad,* (Cambridge, Harvard University Press; The Loeb Classical Library, 1960) Translated by A. T. Murray, Book VI, p. 271.

3. Leaf, Walter. *The Iliad of Homer* (London, MacMillan and Co., 1895) Vol. II, Book XXIII, p. 540.

4. Homer, *The Odyssey of Homer,* (New York, The Modern Library of the World's Best Books 1950) Translated by S. H. Butcher and A. Lang, p. 383.

5. *Ibid.* p. 103.

6. *Ibid.* p. 104.

7. *Ibid.* p. 104.

8. *Ibid.* p. 105.

9. Hesiod. *Works and Days,* (Cambridge, Harvard University Press; The Loeb Classical Library, 1914) Translated by Evelyn White, p. 655.

10. Robinson, J. M. *An Introduction to Early Greek Philosophers,* (Boston, Houghton Mifflin Coy, 1968) p. 3.

11. Pindar, *The Odes of Pindar,* (Chicago, Phoenix Books, University of Chicago Press, 1947) Translated by Richard Lattimore, 7, p. 19.

12. Parke, H. W. *The Oracles of Zeus,* (Oxford, Basil Blackwell, 1967) p. 143.

13. Strabo. *The Geography of Strabo,* (Cambridge, Harvard University Press; The Loeb Classical Library, 1961) Translated by H. L. Jones, VIII, 3, p. 30.

14. Strabo. *The Geography of Strabo,* (H. G. Bohn, Bohn's Classical Library 1856) Translated by H. C. Hamilton and W. Falconer, Vol. II, p. 15.

15. Farnell, L. R. *Greek Hero Cults and Ideas of Immortality,* (Oxford, at the Clarendon Press 1921), pp. 125–127.

16. Robinson, Rachel S. *Sources for the History of Greek Athletics,* (Printed by the author, revised and renewed 1955) p. 36.

17. *Ibid.* p. 41.

18. Eusebius. *Chronology* (Cambridge, Harvard University Press, 1912) Translated by W. Schoene, X, p. 192.

19. Powell, John T. "Ancient Greek Athletic Festivals", paper presented at the first session of the National Olympic Academy of the U.S.A., University of Illinois, Chicago Circle, 20th June 1977, p. 5.

20. Palaeologos, Cleanthis. "Birth, Establishment and Development of the Olympic Games" (Athens, in Report of the Second Session of the International Olympic Academy, July 1962) p. 132.

21. Eusebius. *Chronology,* (Cincinnati, translated by R. S. Robinson, 1955), printed in *Sources for the History of Greek Athletics,* Col. 192, p. 54.

22. *Ibid.* Col. 194.

23. *Ibid.* Col. 194.

24. Yekutieli, Joseph. "Herod the King of Jerusalem", (Athens, in Report of the sixth session of the International Olympic Academy, August 1966) p. 156.

25. *Ibid.* p. 47.

26. *Ibid.* p. 47.

27. *Ibid.* p. 48.

28. Jebb, Richard C. *Bacchylides, the Poems and Fragments* (Georg Olms, Verlagsbuchandlung, Hildesheim, 1967) pp. 205 and 305.

29. Harris, H. A. *Greek Athletes and Athletics,* (London, Indiana University Press, 1964) p. 79.

30. Xenophon. *Memorbilia,* (H. G. Bohn's Classical Library 1848) Translated by J. S. Watson, Book III, p. 13.

31. Xenophon. *Hellenica,* (Cambridge, Harvard University Press; The Loeb Classical Library, 1961) Translated by L. Carelton, from L. Brownson and Others 1886 edition. Book VII, 4, p. 29.

32. Plato. *The Republic,* (Oxford University Press, 1883) Translated by B. Jowett, Book III, pp. 403–404.

33. *Ibid.* p. 424.

34. *Ibid.* p. 425.

35. Plato. *The Laws of Plato, History of Ideas in Ancient Greece,* Vol II, (Arno Press, The New York Times Company, N.Y. 1976) Translated by E. B. England, p. 336.

36. Plato. *The Republic* (Cambridge, Harvard University Press, The Loeb Classical Library 1963) Translated by Paul Shorey, p. 424.

37. Jowett, *op. cit.* p. 452.

38. England. *op. cit.* Book VIII, note 833c, p. 336.

39. *Ibid.* d. 3, p. 336.

40. *Ibid.* 834 b, p. 338.

41. *Ibid.* 834 d, p. 339.

42. Plato. *Laws* (London, William Heineman Ltd. 1961) Translated by R. G. Bury, Book VIII, p. 131.

43. *Ibid.* p. 139.

44. *Ibid.* p. 148.

45. England, *op. cit.* p. 349.

46. Xenophon. *Xenophon's Minor Works* (London, G. Bell 1878) Translated by J. S. Watson Book III, 13; p. 6.

47. Aristoteles. *The Rhetoric of Aristotle* (London, MacMillan Coy 1886) Translated by J. E. C. Welldon, p. 188.

48. Foucart, J. "Bulletin de Correspondance Hellénique", Paris, 1884. p. 199.

49. Pausanias. *Description of Greece,* (Cambridge, Harvard University Press, 1926) Translated by W. H. S. Jones and H. A. Armerod. V, 20. I.

50. As quoted in Robinson, Rachel S. *Sources for the History of Greek Athletics 1955,* privately printed. p. 90.

51. *Ibid.* p. 116.

52. *Ibid.* p. 117.

53. *Ibid.* pp. 138 and 259.

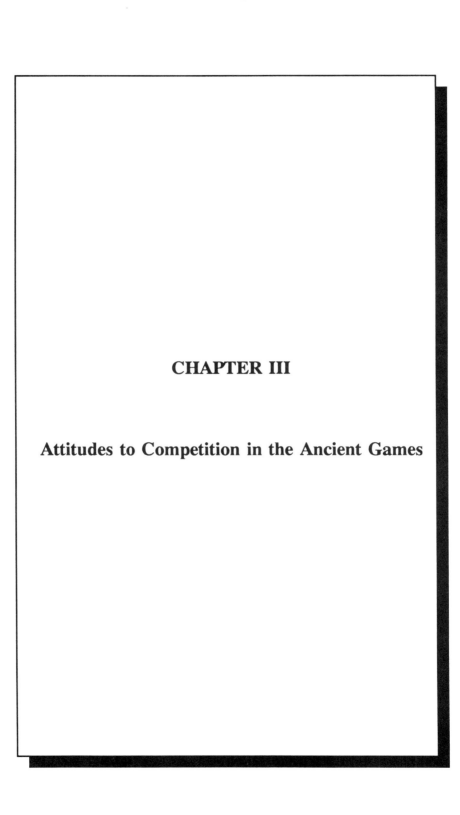

CHAPTER III

Attitudes to Competition in the Ancient Games

CHAPTER III
Attitudes to Competition in the Ancient Games

Custom is lord of everything of mortals and immortals, king. High violence it justifies. . . .

Pindar[1]

INTRODUCTION

The Greeks, although the most humane of the peoples of ancient times have had, throughout their history and in their mythology, a characteristic of struggle, tumult and violence. To analyze, to understand a people and a culture, one must rule out reverence, no matter how great the human achievement of that culture, and yet one must be careful not to judge. It is quite impossible to think as the ancient Greeks thought or to really know the conditions which led to the circumstances of forging a nation.

VIOLENCE IN MYTHOLOGY

When primitive peoples have been asked why a particular thing was, and is, done in a particular way, the response has always been "it is the custom".[2]

Arguments have been advanced to explain why there is so much killing in the ILIAD—that Bible of Greek culture. One argument claims that the killing is a remnant of the barbaric past—a description of a culture, and cultural values, that no longer existed when Homer sang. Another viewpoint holds that the killing is merely a metaphor for courage and heroism; it is not to be taken literally.[3]

As an example, if one is to understand the violence in the ILIAD, one must attempt to comprehend the then Greek cultural values, just as the idea of force and effort is the very essence of ancient athletics as the Greek understood the term. For the Greek word from which "athlete" is derived has two forms, a masculine ($\hat{\alpha}\theta\lambda o\varsigma$) meaning a contest and a neuter ($\hat{\alpha}\theta\lambda o\eta$) the prize for the contest. The idea of contest is the root-meaning and this form is used by Homer (in the ILIAD) to describe the 10-year struggle of the Trojan War. This term is also used in the labours of Herakles. The meaning of the word is most clear in the adjective ($\hat{\alpha}\theta\lambda io\varsigma$) formed from it, which ". . . from meaning "struggling", "contesting", comes to mean "miserable", "wretched". We find this same feeling in Homer when he describes boxing and wrestling as "grievous"[4], an epithet he uses to describe battles or war. The Homeric warrior delights in these "grievous" contests and Pindar describes the athlete as one who ". . . delights in the toil and the cost."[5] Why should an athlete delight in a grievous contest? Any athlete enjoys a hard contest, the athletic spirit does not exist when conditions are soft, neither can this Spirit exist when conditions are too hard and where energies are exhausted in the constant struggle for food or existence. In ancient Greece, power was vested in military skill and the physical prowess to sustain it. The love of fighting and the love of winning were carried into the origins of boxing, wrestling and other contact activities. These were fostered amongst the Homeric Achaeans and led to fierce competition in every aspect of Greek daily life. The results are known, but often the motive became uncontrolled, thus dangerous. Success was worshipped, there was no feeling of generosity extended to those who were defeated, there were no seconds, or thirds, there was only one winner. The means of achieving victory were often dubious and, over-competition spread into over-specialization and professionalism which proved fatal to the essence of victory where once the most coveted prize in the Greek world was the wreath of wild olive.

GODS AND GODDESSES

It was Xenophanes[6] who first wrote that gods were created by men in their own image rather than the reverse. The ancient Greeks believed in action, action was the key note of their lives just as it was with their gods and goddesses. In fact, their gods were glorified athletes. They were the national heroes epitomising humans with all the frailty and fallibility of the human make-up. There were many gods to whom sacrifices were made and of whom favours were asked. Gradually the goddesses and gods were brought down from the sky into the everyday life and particularly into contests. It is easy to understand how the Greeks idealised victory making the victors supreme, supplanting, to some extent, the worship of the gods. Yet in early times, simply to win, assistance from the gods was asked and expected.

FUNERAL GAMES IN HONOUR OF PATROCLUS

In Homer's Iliad the Thessalion prince, Achilles, sponsored games in remembrance of his friend, Patroclus. Prizes were given from the possessions of the deceased in order that he might be better remembered because the contestants had been his friends and were princes. These aristocrats competed with no spectators but their own compatriots and, in spite of bitter words during exciting moments, the contestants accepted victory or defeat with courtesy, remembering their dead comrade. Even here the aid of divine intervention was involved.

In the foot race, three runners took part, Aias, son of Oileus, Odysseus and Antihochus. Aias immediately went to the front with Odysseus just behind, he offers a prayer to Pallas Athena who trips Aias near to the end of the race into a pile of dung and Odysseus was proclaimed winner.

In the chariot race, where five nobles contested the race, Tydeides's stallions were outstripping the others when Apollo intervened by pulling the whip from Tydeides' hand but the goddess Athena returned the lash to him then: ". . . in wrath after the son of Admetos was the goddess gone, and brake his steeds' yoke and the mares ran sideways off the course, and the pole was twisted to the ground. As Eumelos was hurled out of the cart beside the wheel, and his elbows and mouth and nose were flayed, and his forehead bruised above the eyebrows; and his eyes filled with tears and his lusty voice was choked."[7]

Then in the boxing match Epeius is challenged by Eruyalus, the son of an old boxing champion who defeated all comers at the funeral games for Oedipus held at Thebes. Well-cut thongs of ox-hide are bound around the fists and the match is on. "Noble Epeius came on and as the other spied for an opening smote him on the cheek, nor could he much more stand, for his fair limbs failed straightway under him". Epeius helped his opponent to his feet and "led him through the ring with trailing feet, spitting out clotted blood, drooping his head away". This courtesy of Epeius is touching because prior to the fight he shouted he would "bruise his adversary's flesh and break his bones".[8]

And then there was Wrestling which has been wonderfully described. After two falls Achilles stood and restrained Aias and Odysseus with the words "No longer strain ye now, neither be worn with pain. Victory is with you both; take then equal prizes and go your ways, that other Achaens too may strive".[9]

These contests show that the Greeks did not distinguish between the secular and the sacred, that there was no inconsistency between worship and fiercely contested games as part of a religious celebration. Gods and goddesses were respected and feared but they were not loved. Meekness and humility were not virtues in the pagan world. Success was achieved by self-reliance and hard work and it might be better gained by being assisted by divine favour.

The gods were patrons of success and this applied with fair play and ethical behaviour. Thus, in sport, as in war the hero intends to be best "My father," says Glaucus, "bade me ever be far the best and far excel all other men, and not to put to shame my father's lineage".[10] From Hesiod comes this glimpse of early sport in Boeotia from the mainland of Greece in *Theogony*, page 435, when writing of the Goddess Hecate: "Good is she also when men contest at the Games, for there too the goddess is with them and profits them: and he who by might and strength gets the victory wins the rich prize easily with joy, and brings glory to his parents". Victory alone brought glory and honour, there was no virtue in playing for its own sake, defeat brought shame but these attitudes were subdued in the funeral games in deference to the memory of a friend and because all received handsome gifts.

In Homer's *The Odyssey*, Prince Odysseus was shipwrecked on the shores of Phaeacia and after minimal rest the King Alcinoös calls his people together to help Odysseus. After a feast it was decided to contest in various events. Footraces were first, then wrestling, following by long jumping, weight throwing and boxing. Then Laodamas said ". . . let's ask the stranger what he has learned about games in his schooldays. He's not bad to look at, good thighs and calves, a good pair of arms, a strong neck, hefty and not too old. But he's broken down with hardships . . . ".[11] Laodamas said to Odysseus "Come along, father, have a try at the games yourself, if you ever learned them. A man ought to know about games. Games are the best way to fame while you are still alive". Odysseus was rightly upset by this patronizing attitude and although worn out sprang up, seized a hugh weight throwing it farther than any of the prior contestants. He then challenged any—except his host, to box, wrestle or run and ". . . as for javelines, I'll throw one as far as you can shoot an arrow".[12]

Once again the impromptu athletic sports show how much a part of life these activities were in that time and in that culture. It is, however, thought that the Phaeacians were not Greek, neither is it know where Phaeacia was located.

All through the body of ancient writers' works there are allusions to traditions which concern athletic gatherings attended by forefathers of those who fought at Troy in the 10-year war, 1193–1184, B.C.

The extant literature is studded with references to competitions and contests held at the shrine of Zeus in Olympia.

When did the ancient religious rites at Olympia first become tied to athletic games, games destined to be so important that Greek history revolved around them for twelve centuries? The answer is not known; even the ancient writers were not agreed because so much rested on the uncertain echos of folk tradition and memory.

The ancient literacy evidence begins with a Pindaric poem, in the 5th Century before Christ, extending through the chronology compiled by Eusebius in the 4th Century of the Christian era.

After Pindar, many wrote of the origins of Olympia but in the full account by Strabo, 400 years later, he indicates that Olympic Games may have been in existence in the 13th Century, B.C. but states that it was at the end of the 12th Century that Olympic Games of note were established.

One hundred years after Strabo, lengthy fragments from the introduction to a Register of Olympic Winners have been found, written by Phlegon of Tralles. He tells the most detailed story of the revival and reorganization of the Games after an indefinite period of neglect and he joins other ancient scholars in placing the date of this revival more than 100 years prior to the 776 B.C. date when official records are noted. And this is somewhat confirmed by Allimachus (3rd Century, B.C)[13] who wrote that 13 Olympiads elapsed without any victories being listed and in the 14th Coroebus won, and this is accepted as 776 B.C.

It is from Pausanias, the author of *Description of Greece,* a guidebook, written 50 years after Phlegon's work *Historical Introduction* that his on-the-spot observations and interviews reveal the fullest account of traditions and athletic observances.

Just after 594 B.C. from the writings of Plutarch is learned that Solon passed a law to allow the giving of cash prizes to winners in the major festivals. The sums of money were large and an immediate result of this law was that athletic competition in the major centres became less exclusively the privilege of the wealthy. The inducement allowed a person to undertake training, the long journey to Olympia and to take part in the compulsory one-month training there. Athens from that time began her rise to first place athletically in the nation.

In an account left by Herodotus—between the years 592–589 B.C.—it is evident that, in the early years of the 6th Century, those who organized the Olympic Games were critically examining themselves. At that time the Olympic festival was said to have the "Games with the finest and fairest of rules."[14] So, to enhance this, a delegation was sent to Egypt to receive affirmation from their wisest of men. The opinion given was that either the administration be handed over to others or that the Elians themselves should never enter a race. It is interesting to note that after an Elian judge was victorious in two equestrian events in the Games of 364 B.C. it was ruled that no judge should again compete. Pausanias tells the story of the 218th celebration of the Games when Appolonius, a boxer, nicknamed "the Sprinkler", arrived late saying he had been delayed by adverse winds in the Aegean. The true explanation was that he had been competing and getting cash prizes in Asia Minor.[15]

The Hellanodicae disqualified him and gave a fellow Alexandrian the olive wreath, without contest. Appolonius bound his hands and rushed at the announced winner Heraklides and punched him. The fine was heavy.[16]

VIOLATIONS OF THE RULES AND THE PENALTIES IMPOSED

Throughout the known unbroken sequence of 1,168 years, or 292 Olympiads, the Olympic Games saw few rules broken or penalties imposed. Sometimes, because of an illegal blow in boxing or hold in wrestling, an athlete was killed. One such incident is that of Diognetos of Crete who killed his boxing opponent Herakles in a bout. The Hellanodicae refused to grant the wreath of olives and drove Diognetos out of Olympia.[17] There were three types of penalties, a fine, a banishment from the Games and flogging. The last was the least severe and was carried out during the Games.

From the fines, money went to the treasury of Zeus, to the sanctuary and to the wronged opponent—if there was one. In one case the Spartans captured two small towns, Lepreon and Phyrkon, during the truce. The organizers of the Games, the Eleans, fined the Spartans 2 minae for each soldier involved in the sacking of the towns—there were 1,000 soldiers involved. The Spartans said they did not know of the truce (Ekecheiria) so the Eleans asked for the return of Lepreon and they would then abandon their claim, except for the share to give to the god. The Spartans, upon their refusal, were excluded from the Games.[18]

A portion of the monies from fines was used to make bronze statues of Zeus. These statues were 13 in number and the plinth of each may still be seen in the Altis, after the Metroon, below the exedra of the treasuries and on the left as one is about to enter the crypt leading to the Stadium. The first six were erected during the four years after the 98th Olympic Festival with fines paid by the Thessalian Eupolos and the three boxers he had bribed.[19] Pausanias then tells of another instance:

> After Eupolos they say that the Athenian Kallippos, who had taken part in the pentathlon, bought off his potential opponents with money, and this happened during the 112th Olympiad. After a fine had been imposed by the Eleans on Kallippos and his opponents, the Athenians sent Hypereides to persuade the Eleans to absolve them of the penalty. When the Eleans refused, the Athenians treated them very haughtily, and did not pay the money, or take part in the Olympic Games, until the god of Delphi told them that he would not give oracles to the Athenians under any circumstances unless they paid the fine to the Eleans. When they had therefore paid it, statues of Zeus were made, six on this occasion also.[20]

On each statue, Elegiac verses were engraved, the name of the athlete and his village. The verses said that an Olympic victory could not be won by money or unfair means but only by fleetness of foot and strength of body.

Philostratos, in his book, *Life of Apollonios,* writes about the stringency of the Coaches/Judges and their discipline during the one month that coaches and athletes trained immediately prior to each four-yearly festival in Elis:

> There, the method of preliminary training and the kind of exercises are decided by others, and it is not the trainer, but the Hellanodikes who, entirely on their own initiative and without being bound in any way, organize everything in accord with the particular circumstances pertaining from time to time. And the Helanodike has the whip at his disposal, not only for the athlete, but also for the trainer, and he uses it in case of any contravention of his orders; and all have to conform with the orders of the Hellanodicae, since those who violate them may be immediately excluded from the Games.[21]

Further:

> When the season for the Olympic Games arrives, the Eleans train the athletes for 30 days in Elis; and when they have gathered them together and trained them and examined their general condition, they say to them:
> You who have completed the toil of training in a manner worthy of entering Olympia and have done no loafing and nothing under-handed, proceed with confident heart; you have finished the training otherwise depart in whatever direction you choose.[22]

A Syrian Greek named Lucian (125-180 A.D.) lived 750 years later than Solon and wrote a supposed conversation between Solon and a legendary figure, Anacharsis of Scythia. The conversation took place in the Lyceum at Athens. Anacharsis speaks:

> And why are your young men doing all this Solon? Some of them, locked in each other's arms, are tripping one another up, while others are choking and twisting each other and grovelling together in the mud, wallowing like swine. Yet, in the beginning, as soon as they had taken their clothes off, they put oil on themselves and took turns at rubbing each other down very peacefully—I saw it. . . .
> I want to know, therefore, what good it can be to do all this, because to me at least the thing looks more like insanity than anything else and nobody can easily convince me that men who act in that way are not out of their minds. Solon answers ". . . it is not insanity, and it is not out of brutality that they strike one another and tumble each other in the mud, or sprinkle each other with dust. The thing has a certain usefulness, not unattended by pleasure, and it gives much strength to their bodies."[23]

Here is clearly evident the lack of understanding of one culture by a person of another culture.

CONCLUSION

Human frailty was not absent in ancient Greek society or at Olympia but, it is highly unlikely that the Games could have retained their pre-eminence for more than 1,000 years if flagrant abuse of rules and regulations were repeated or common.

The early Greek attitudes towards physical activity as an integral part of life and the necessity of always being ready for action have fashioned our own interpretation of what is fair, what is good and how contests should be conducted. Cheating and abuse were frowned on in ancient Greece just as they are disapproved of by us today, although the ways of dealing with them have somewhat changed.

REFERENCES

1. Pindar, "The Power of Custom", translation by C. M. Bowra, *The Oxford Book of Greek Verse in Translation* edited by T. G. Higham and C. M. Bowra (Oxford: Clarendon Press, 1938), p. 330.

2. Harlan, Hugh. *History of Olympic Games, Ancient and Modern,* (Los Angeles: Bureau of Athletic Research, May 1931), p. 9.

3. Sagan, E. I., *The Lust to Annihilate a Psychoanalytic Study of Violence in Ancient Greek Culture,* (New York, Psychohistory Press, 1979), p. 6.

4. Gardiner, E. Norman, *Athletics of the Ancient World,* (Oxford, The Clarendon Press, 1930), p. 1.

5. Pindar, "*The Odes of Pindar*", translated by Sir John Sandys, (Cambridge, Harvard University Press, and Heineman Ltd., 1915), Olympic Ode 1, v., p. 10.

6. Xenophanes (Frag. 2), *Sources for the History of Greek Athletics,* (Cincinatti, translated by Rachel Sargent Robinson, 1955), Privately printed, p. 91.

7. Homer, *The Iliad,* A. T. Murray, Cambridge (Harvard University Press, and Heineman Ltd. 1967), Book XXIII, p. 545.

8. *Ibid,* p. 549.

9. *Ibid,* p. 92.

10. *Ibid,* p. 93.

11. Homer, *The Odyssey,* translated by W. H. D. House (A Mentor Book, Scarborough, Ontario, 1937), p. 91.

12. Robinson, Rachel Sargent, *Sources for the History of Greek Athletics,* (Cincinatti, 1955, Privately printed), p. 32.

13. Callimachus, *Fragments,* translated by C.A. Trypanis (London and Cambridge, Loeb edition, Harvard University Press, 1965), p. 35.

14. *Herodotus* II, translated by A. D. Godley (London and Cambridge, Loeb edition, Harvard University Press, 1922), p. 160.

15. Pausanias, *Description of Greece,* translated by W. H. J. Jones, Book VI, (London and Cambridge, Loeb Classical Library, 1933), p. 5.

16. *Ibid,* p. 6.

17. Dress, Ludwig. *Olympia, Gods, Artists and Athletes,* (New York, Frederick A. Praeger, 1968), p. 52.

18. *Thucydides,* translated by W. Smith (London and Cambridge, Loeb Classical Library, 1923), v., p. 49.

19. Pausanias, *Description of Greece,* translated by W. H. J. Jones, Book V, (London and Cambridge, Loeb Classical Library, 1933), p. 21.

20. *Ibid,* p. 122.

21. Philostratos, *Life of Apollonios,* quoted in *The Olympic Games Through the Ages,* Ed., Iris Douskou (Athens, Ekdotike Hellados, S.A. 1976), p. 126.

22. Philostratus, *Life of Apollonius of Tyana,* V 43: quoted in R. S. Robinson, *Sources for the History of Greek Athletics,* (Cincinatti, 1955, Privately Printed), p. 110.

23. Lucian, *Anacharsis,* translated by A. M. Harmon, (London and Cambridge, Loeb Classical Library, 1933), p. 40.

CHAPTER IV

Some Thoughts About Ancient Olympia

SUMMER MORNING
06.27

We started early, to walk and run with hope,
    To see this morning's rising sun.
We mount the Kronion hill to be present
    At the birth of yet another day.

We know the sun will rise as always it has done,
    And yet we wait, expectantly, for nature's smile
In its inevitable style, to warm us
    On our selfish, smug, contended way.

One day the sun it will not rise
    And our damage will be done.
We'll have killed environment, and each other
    By ignorance and by gun.

J.T.P.

CHAPTER IV
Some Thoughts About Ancient Olympia

Leaders of Elis, who rule by the laws of your fathers.
Safeguard your own land and do not have recourse to war.
Instead be the leaders of Hellas in individual concord.

(Lucian, *Anacharsis* (Fischer, p. 211)

INTRODUCTION

Really great truths are invisible and the realms of knowledge are as few as islands in a vast uncharted sea of ignorance.

MAN is the one recalcitrant creature which strives to force forward from the tangible to the intangible, from the known to the unknown and inaccessible realms, in search of knowledge and truth.

MAN is not content just to eat, to be warm, to sleep. MAN thinks, MAN innovates, MAN moves. Civilisation is not composed solely of shelter, clothing, food, warmth and industry, but of the human spirit and its persistence to create and survive.

Homer's songs, once passed along by word of mouth alone, have survived longer than the civilisation which produced them, and the wealth of things undiscovered is infinitely greater than those things already discovered.

Endless invention, endless experiment
Brings knowledge of motion, but not of stillness;
Knowledge of speech, but not of silence;
Knowledge of words and ignorance of the world;
All our knowledge brings us nearer to our ignorance.

Christopher Dawson, 1936

We come, we go, doors open and shut. Entire nations and civilisations have existed, flourished and gone; but MAN continues. It is not possible to convey everything, it is impossible to know much. Here, therefore, are some thoughts of one aspect of moving MAN—the essence of bios, which is life, the basis of Biology—the study of life.

CONCEPTS IN THE HISTORY OF MOVING MAN

This chapter is really not about the Olympic Movement but about a concept—one which I have identified and you may have done so too, and which still pervades much of Greek thought and action. There is an Olympic Spirit which cannot be compressed into a set of rules, neither is it solely concerned with taking part and trying to win.It seems to stem from unwritten laws of decency, of fairness, of chivalry, things which may appear to be outmoded today but were very much alive and operative in Ancient Greece.

To the Greeks we must attribute many of our organised physical activities and the very names by which we designate them. From the Greek word "Athlon" (meaning prize) comes "athlete" and "athletics". From the Hellenic word for "unclad", "Gymnos"—gymnast, gymnastics, gymnasium". "Diskoi" gives "discus". From "Stade" (a measure of length equalling 600 Olympic feet, depending upon whose feet were used for measuring) the name of the Olympic short race of 192.27 metres—comes "stadium". The race, twice the course length, was termed the "Diaulos" (the two-handed flute); the longest race of 24 times up and down the stadium was the "Dolichos".

To understand the concepts in the history of moving MAN one must have studied deeply many aspects which impinge upon MAN. How did MAN come to be in the land now terms "Greece"? What kept MAN there? Was MAN free or enslaved?

Climate, composition of the soil, type of nutrition, proximity to water, hilly protection: these features could give MAN economic security or could contribute to moving from one place to another, these then, in the chain of circumstances determined how humanity survived and, eventually, progressed. The late American poet, Robert Frost, said, in a speech just before he died ". . . What makes a country in the beginning is a good piece of geography". How correct he was.

Look at a map of Greece . . . where did "they" come from? The Greeks then were blond Nordic people who adjusted to the environment and flourished in the sun-drenched land. They surged in five different linguistic bands into a new country claiming all they saw and also capturing the island of Crete.

We are all familiar with Greek Statuary, but were the Greeks really as they were depicted in stone—were they idealised?

THE ARTISTIC ENVIRONMENT

As the Ancient Games progressed, there was a closer relationship between athletic events and the architectural or sculptural works of Greek artists.

Leonidas from Rhodos or Milon from Croton could have been used as models by Phidias, or Praxiteles, or Lyssippus. But statuary depicting motion happened only one thousand years after the Games were first recorded as being contested. Only then was achieved a measure of peace; peace gives leisure and leisure gives time for aesthetics to express itself.

Could there have been a better environment for the Ancient Games than in Ancient Olympia, especially when added to this the declamation of Pindar's verse, the hymns of Simonides, the peans of Bacchylides, the reading of Xenophon's history, the reflections of Platon (or Plato), or the later presence of Alexander the Great (a non-Greek) who wished to participate in the Games in order to pass the Helleens' test? Be it athletes, sculptors, chroniclers, historians, philosophers or politicians, what dominated above all was the wish to express muscular life which was, in those times, a song and expression of hope and certainly in the mind, of "the most beautiful of all wonders" as the dramatist has declared—MAN.

Sports were for Ancient Greeks a necessary institution which made it possible for Hellenism to develop (concurrently with the flexibility of mind, in its constant pursuit of universal equilibrium) the strength of arms, legs and body, the skill, endurance, the beauty of human movement, and the preparedness for conquest. From all the regions of Greece, the islands and distant colonies, young men of true Greek birth came to Olympia to compete initially for the olive wreath. Not initially, but eventually, when they ran, wrestled, threw the discus and javelin, they were nude. So, when artists who hurried to these national and other meetings had before them the spectacle of the movements of the human frame, this complex and intricate show of muscles curved under the tanned skin, flayed, hardened by scars, glistening in the sun, but smooth, efficient, beautiful and graceful through use, they used the clear Greek light and fashioned what they saw.

Greek sculpture was born in the stadium. It needed time for artists to leave the grassed banks and for their products to flourish on the pediments of the Parthenon and of Olympia and to become the silent teachers of poets and the encouragers of philosophers. They came to nourish their minds with the sight of the more and more subtle relations sculpture creates in the world of form and movement. There has never been a more glorious, a more striking example of the unity of ART and SPORT since. In short, physical activity, through sculpture and verse, became the father of philosophic thought about movement.

Unfortunately, three major earthquakes in the 300's A.D., the washaways of the Alphaeos and Kladeos, and the destructive spirit of Christian man, pulled down this complex of unique interrelationships which for many years, in the heart of the Greeks, had expressed the deeper language of their society. Because this Altis, this monument to movement, to peace and influence had created a country, its culture and a language.

The fate of ruins is moving, as long as the ruins are respected, not over-renovated; as long as, after having asked for their secret, the ashes of the centuries, the bones of the dead, the accumulated remnants of vegetation and races, the eternal garment of leaves will bury them again. Then time will preserve them from MAN and for MAN. It is through ruins that we are able to reach the depths of our history, just as we are tied to the roots of our life by joy, sorrow and suffering which have formed us. A ruin is a painful sight only to those who are unable to participate, with their intellectualism, and their presence, through humility, in the conquest of the present appreciating the glory that once illuminated life. There is no stronger pleasure than to ponder the prints and clues left by those who prepared their dwellings, to reveal to us from what came the reason for their very existence, and to surmise our own, because of theirs.

A statue which is unearthed nude, an oxydized jewel, a piece of earthenware still bearing traces of paint, all are pieces of evidence which bring more information about ourselves than about those who have gone and who originated this evidence. All forms of art live in the future. It is the fruit of the pain, struggle, death, hope of the people who lived, which will only come to be realised much later, and very slowly, through the process of the needs of society and of what was really depicted by the artists' vision and innovation telling us the story of then, which becomes history, only now. Thus, the heritage of marble which has been bequeathed to us in the valley of the Alphaeus by the "architects of the absolute" and by the sculptors who had learned to catch the breath of life, has acquired, for ever, an eternal dimension.

Is proper gratitude extended towards those Greeks of the 5th century B.C., who succeeded, through their struggles in the stadium, by sculpting, by writing, by songs, creating buildings, works of all kinds, in giving true shape to the future of Western humanity?

These are a few thoughts expressed on the artistic environment of the athlete during the Ancient Games—and the consequences of this on our appreciation of form, symmetry and grace.

THE DAILY ENVIRONMENT

Next to ruling and fighting, the Greeks loved the various forms of sculpture, poetry, music, acting and athletic contest. What was sought was imperishable honour, that immaterial prize of a wreath of Olympic olive leaves placed upon a victor's head, with dangling ribbons on thighs and arms.

By the 4th century the Olympic Games were drawing Greek competitors from all over the Mediterranean and to almost similar festivals at Delphi, Isthmia and Nemea. Here the athletes were competing for honour; they were people less anxious to simply live, but to live well, people not fearful of death by battle, but anxious that they would be eulogised in song or verse, anxious to excel and have their excellence recognised and recorded—particularly in statuary, lyric verse and daily acclaim.

Participation in Isthmian, Nemian, Pythian and Olympic Games dominated the agricultural, mercantile, and waring lives of the Greeks. It is known that as many as 173 athletic contests of a formal type were organised all over Greece, each year, by various communities. In order that athletes might travel to the Games, they were allowed to pass through areas under seige and, in fact, it is thought that local wars were sometimes stopped in order that athletic festivals could take place. To see this in perspective, it is essential to realize that communities were, at the most, inhabited by about 3,000 people. All cities were walled and when an Olympic winner returned home, that wall was breached and left open, the people secure in the knowledge that they were strong, and not likely to be attacked; all because they had a champion in their midst. The Greek philosophers, Greek music, poetry, sculpture, pottery, sea power show a life built from leisure and industry.

Why did Sparta—of which we believe we know so much—become, from its geographical position the centre of Greek pottery-making exporting its products as far away as Cyrene? In addition, why did Sparta play a considerable role in the Olympic Games? From 615 to 580 B.C. the names of 40 Spartans appear on the lists of Olympic victors. In vivid contrast, from 580 to 516 only two names appear. Was it because of a change in educational philosophy? Was it a change in athletic professionalism? But to show the insularity of the Greeks (to them the centre of the world was Delphi where stood a conical stone, sacred to the God Apollo, designated the "navel of the earth", the Umphalos), it is necessary to understand that wandering bands of professional athletes were spoiling the "local" character of the Games which had helped to fashion the unity of a country. Some communities stopped sending their representatives.

ANCIENT OLYMPIA

The Grecian ideal of sports was exemplified in the Ancient Olympic Games. The remarkable vitality of this ideal, as expressed in the purest form of sportsmanship of the participants as well as the art and literature of the Golden Age of Greece, is without parallel in recorded history.

Olympia, the scene of the Ancient Olympic Games, is 352 kilometres by road from Athens, located in Elis on the western fringe of the Peloponnesus; is 17 kilometres east of the Ionian Sea and nowhere near Mount Olympus, the permanently snow-covered home of the gods and goddesses in Northern Greece. Ancient Olympia was a veritable garden for the gods. Even today the terrain is exquisite. The floor of the valley is flat, wide, fertile and surrounded on three sides by tree-clad hills sloping into a natural amphitheatre. To the north of the plain of Olympia is a pine-covered conical hill, about 200 metres high—*Kronian Hill.* It was sacred to Kronus. At the base of the hill, as well as an oracle, was a sacred grove which gave Altis its name.

The date of the full moon, the 52nd moon of the Summer Solstice, was the central day of the Olympic Festival, one which lasted five days every fourth August or September. The women held their own Games until the 1st century B.C., called an Heraeon, under the patronage of the Goddess Hera on the 51st moon of the Summer Solstice. Girls competed in their races, women in theirs. For the victors, portraits were allowed to be placed in the Temple of Hera, later a statue was erected to a victrix in Olympia, and later again the wreath of olives was conferred.

Thus, by set standards of attitude and behaviour applicable to women and men, Greece grew to establish the mores and attitudes of the Western world.

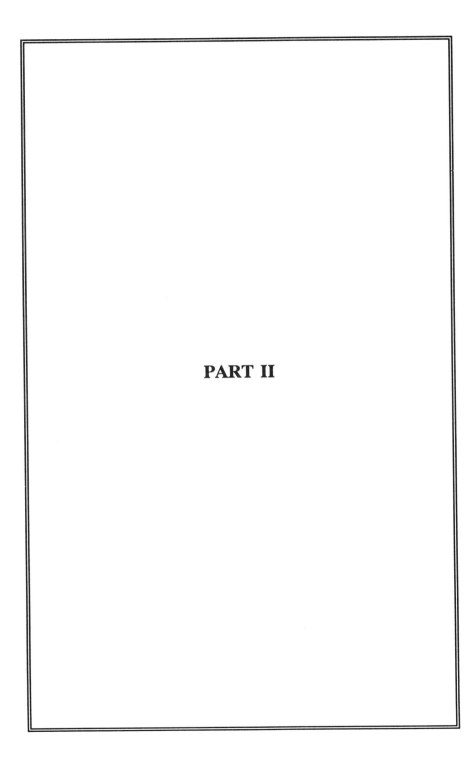

PART II

CHAPTER V

The Contribution of the International Olympic Academy to the Understanding of Olympism

OLYMPIA'S QUIETNESS

Great things come quietly to earth
Sunrise is silent, and life itself
Comes like a breath indrawn
As still and quiet, as the dawn.

All tides wax and wane
Moving on a soundless plane
Answering to the pull and draw
Of some undisputed law.

The seasons come and go
Like a moving show
Across the stage of time and space
With quiet dignity and, sometimes, grace.

A snowflake falling to the ground
Doesn't make the slightest sound
Stars come out rank upon rank
As do wild flowers on a roadside's bank.

The giant trees, many a towering pine
Live in their own peaceful silent time,
Yet there is neither noise nor sound
'Neath the outer roughness of the ground.

So we to Olympia's vale have come
And in silent rapture we will go,
Quieter than when Alphaeus river's flow
Meets the far deeps of the sea.
Both river, and ourselves,
Are held through some magic harmony.

J.T.P.

CHAPTER V
The Contribution of the International Olympic Academy to the Understanding of Olympism

> ". . . the I.O.A. is the educational
> centre of world Olympism."
>
> (H.E. Juan Antonio Samaranch,
> Address: Hill of the Pnyx,
> 6th July, 1981)[1]

INTRODUCTION

It was in Ancient Olympia on the 17th of April 1927 that the late Baron Frédi Pierre de Coubertin first spoke of the idea he had to create an institution which would have as its purpose the teaching and propagation of the idea, and the ideals of, Olympism amongst the youth of the world. Were he to see the assembly each year at the various educational sessions at the Interntional Olympic Academy in Ancient Olympia, he would realise how well that purpose has been achieved.

BARON PIERRE DE COUBERTIN

The Baron had come, in that April of 1927, to Olympia to see the erection of a stele, by the Greek Government, in his honour. This same marble monument is now in the de Coubertin Grove to which place it was moved from the original site just opposite the entrance to the Altis. It was in the Grove, on the 26th of March 1938, that Crown Prince Paul of the Hellenes placed de Coubertin's heart housed in its blue box, inside the column. His heart is placed in the column's base in accordance with his wish, that on his death his heart be removed, then laid to rest in the home of the origin of the Olympic Games.

JEAN KETSEAS

It was on that same day (17th day of April 1927) that Jean Ketseas (then permanent representative of the International Olympic Committee for Greece) heard the reviver of the Games express his doubts and his fears regarding the future of the Modern Olympic Festival and the concern he felt that the educational and moral aspects of this creation would not be taken seriously. In the famous radio "Message to the Sporting Youth of All Nations", issued by de Coubertin that very April day, one reads this passage:

> In reviving the Olympics for you, the last thing my friends and I wanted was to have them turned into a museum piece or a subject for the cinema, or for commercial or electoral interests to use them for their own purposes; what we wanted, when we revived an institution dating back twenty-five centuries was for you to become, once again, followers of the religion of sport as conceived by our great ancestors.[2]

Ketseas was inspired and on his return home to Athens for two weeks he held a series of meetings in his office at the Athens Lawn Tennis Club. It was here that the Baron, Ketseas, Professor Chryssafis (Jean Ketseas's old athletics coach) and the then Minister of National Education, Mr. Argyres, discussed the best ways of establishing an academic Olympic centre. The planting of a seed of a special intellectual centre, of an organism which would grow and, through that growth, disseminate the Olympic ideology and the teachings of Olympism were very much the focus of their discussions, just as they had always been in de Coubertin's thoughts and intentions.

CARL DIEM

de Coubertin had discussed with Dr. Carl Diem (then Rector of the Cologne Sporthocschule) in 1931 the same concerns he had previously discussed in Athens in 1927, and, on the occasion of the Session of the International Olympic Committee in 1934 held in Athens, the friends, Diem from Germany and Ketseas from Greece, met. From that moment they worked together to establish an Academy. This joint collaboration was broken by the death of Dr. Diem in December 1962. Jean Ketseas died in early 1965.

In 1937 on 16th March, Pierre de Coubertin wrote a letter to the German Government stressing the need for an international educational centre ". . . I believe that a Centre of Olympic Studies would aid the preservation and progress of my work more than anything else, and would keep it from the false path which I fear."[3]

In 1939 Carl Diem wrote to the Greek Government suggesting guidelines for the establishment of the Academy. ". . . like the sportsmen of that great classical age they (the students at the Academy) will live together in tents, live on the simple foods of Sparta" and, he continued ". . . they will revel in the experience and study the noblest treasures of art which Olympia has kept for them." "They will enjoy the great treasure of the spirit, which has been the code of Old Hellas; they will experience the harmony of physical, spiritual and cultural discipline which is immeasurably valuable, if combined with the duties of serving the community of MAN."[4]

KETSEAS AND DIEM

Political strife and the Second World War did not stop their work and plans for the establishment of the International Academy were drawn up and adopted by the Hellenic Olympic Committee. It was on 19th June 1947, during the I.O.C. Session in Stockholm that Jean Ketseas made the then Vice-President of the International Olympic Committee, Avery Brundage, aware of the plans. Brundage was not only interested but placed the matter on the Agenda of the ensuing I.O.C. Session. So, in London, in 1948, Ketseas presented the then President J. Sigfrid Edstrom the Report which he and Dr. Diem had prepared. Carl Diem was in attendance at the 1948 Summer Games, *in-cognito,* because of the banning of Germany from the first post-war Games. Privately he confirmed agreement of the initial Report and on the 28th of April, 1949 at the Rome Session of the I.O.C. the final Report of the International Olympic Academy was submitted and unanimously accepted; the headquarters were to be in Greece.[5]

The Hellenic Olympic Committee undertook the task of establishing the Academy and sent invitations to the 80 Olympic Committees of that year. Only four replied and each said "No" to the request to send representatives to what was to have been the first session. Diem and Ketseas were disappointed but not disillusioned. They worked on, and so did the Hellenic Olympic Committee which acquired 100 acres of land to the east of Mount Kronion in 1961 and established the site for the Academy. With one notable exception, financial support from other Olympic committees for this international experiment was singularly lacking.

THE OPENING OF THE ACADEMY

In 1961 the German Archaelogical Society under the direction of the scholars Ernst Curtius, Georg Tru, Wilhelm Doepfield and Adolf Furtwaengler, had just completed the excavations of the ancient stadium in Olympia and the hand-over to the Greek authorities was to take place in June. It was thought an excellent idea to combine this ceremony with the inauguration of the Academy which set its first session from 15th to 24th June.

The monies for the excavations had been provided by the German Olympic Committee as a 75th birthday present for Dr. Diem through the initiative of its President, Dr. Willi Daume who, for the joint celebration said, ". . . as far as the German side can contribute to it, we will help to create the Academy."[6] This they did, the money being matched by the Hellenic Olympic Committee.

Dr. Carl Diem was determined that, right from the beginning the success of the Academy would be assured were the best publicity to be given to all its endeavours. That is why he brought with him one hundred men and women student gymnasts who, with a matching one hundred Greek students under the direction of the late Dr. Cleanthis Palaeologos, worked for one week together and gave a splendid gymnastics display to all the Greek and foreign dignitaries present, despite the rain. The Academy had been launched well, seen and noted by international representatives and was to be enjoyed by 31 delegates from 24 different countries for the next ten days.

Concepts are only sound if they survive. The concept of de Coubertin, brought to reality by Ketseas and Diem fostered and forwarded by Dr. Palaeologos and Dr. Szymiczek is like the light of the Olympic Torch which, on being handed on, illumines the way, enabling it to show the Olympic world what the International Academy of advanced thought has for its benefit.

Truly the Academy has become the principal memorial to Baron Pierre de Coubertin embodying the educational principles basic of his reasons for re-establishing the Olympic Games.

MEANING AND PURPOSE OF THE ACADEMY

In the Report of the 1st Session of the International Olympic Academy, the late Carl Diem spoke about the meaning and purpose of the Academy. He saw it as a ". . . continuation of the Ancient Academy—an Elis of today—and the realisation of de Coubertin's plans to lay a scholastic foundation for the Olympic idea."[7]

In de Courbetin's opinion, a centre for the exchange of ideas and for research into the sciences upon which performance, teaching and technique rest, was as necessary as was the practical expression of endurance and physical prowess exhibited in the Games.

Out of the Ancient Olympic Festival grew that which came to be a unified country. At Olympia the Greek world met with its different tribes, tongues, customs and attitudes for five days every four years where talk, discussions, trade, arranged marriages, meetings, ultimately focused on one feature, the watching of one's own champion compete. This unifying aspect became allegiance and pride, a common language (written and spoken) and, through time, a nation.

So far as recorded facts go, it is known that the Ancient Olympic Games were continuously in operation for 1,276 years, from 884 B.C. to 394 A.D. In our own Modern Series we are now in the second year of the XXIth Olympiad having seen only 21 celebrations of the Summer Games now in their 98th year. Have we yet formed a unified approach to Olympic participation, as did the Greeks?

THE PRESENT

The International Olympic Academy is situated in a beautiful vale with its man-planted 160,000 trees and aesthetically sited and designed buildings. They are not there by accident. It was in a letter to Jean Ketseas in 1964 that architect Peter Zannetos described his concept for the development of this Academy. He realised his responsibility, because the Academy is close to the Sacret Altis, and he wished to develop designs, colours and materials in a sensitive and subdued way. "All buildings are fashioned in the Doric spirit, this is to blend with the austerity which fits everything together when dealing with the Olympic Spirit."[8]

In our quiet moments those of us who know this place thank the originators for their belief, perseverance and patience and applaud those who continue to work for, and through, the Academy for the propagation of the Olympic Movement.

The intellectual energy generated in Olympia, the seeking after truth, the vigour and enthusiasm of youth, all help clarify, better understand, put into perspective, the identified excesses of the physical expressions of the Games themselves. Because those who value the Olympic Movement must be most critical of it, the Olympic Movement must be subjected to stringent analysis, exposed to every facet of objective criticism, bared to every argument with intensity and reason.

The Academy is a symbol as well as a tool. The symbol is identified through its ideas and beliefs which translate into communication. The tool is the means by which this communication is converted into action. The symbol becomes understood through an abiding by the principles of the Movement, and the tool identified by the work done in the cause of Olympism. Each must use that instrument, keep it sharp and ready so that, through understanding and effort, Olympic ideal becomes reality.

The Academy is the academic arm of the Olympic Movement. Each arm has a hand. Aristotle described the hand as ". . . the tool of tools" and the hand as an extension of self. Arms and hands are outgrowths of the body; in this case the body is the Olympic concept and the limbs are the expression of that concept. Thus, through the Academy and its extensions, the teachings of Olympism can reach out and touch many persons and organisations.

The Academy will remain strong and be the fountainhead of innovative ideas and action, but only as long as young people are willing to share in the progress by giving leadership. There must be no pause; the process dares not stop, the leaders must be vigilant and show concern through effort. Today there are as many dangers to the Olympic Movement as were foreseen by Baron Pierre de Coubertin. This was also identified by the Dean of the Academy, the late Dr. Otto Szymiczek. "The solution is that of finding a means of educating and imparting culture to people, at least to those who are utilised as leaders, so that they may become carriers of the genuine Olympic ideology and of the principles of the true Olympic spirit."[9] We are all of the Olympic family irrespective of our language, colour, geographic location, culture, sex or age. When in Olympia at the Academy we sit, talk, walk, compete, eat, dance, sing as members of one organisation. We have differences of religion and belief, customs, attitudes, loyalties and expectations, yet we accept each other for what we are. We respect each other and are eager to hear opinions, we are tolerant and wish to learn from each other.

Through our education and through the intellectual stimulation caused by being there, we are able to bring concerns and problems which bear on Olympic matters to the front, and with fresh and vigorous ideas search for solutions, just because we wish the Olympic Movement to keep on, keeping on.

The Academy has been, and will continue to be the catalyst which enables all kinds of exciting things to happen. One such superb outgrowth of the energy generated here has been the blossoming of National Olympic Academies. Since Dr. Nina Pappas hosted the first United States Academy in Chicago in 1977, another 75 have been established all over the world, with Spain being the first National Academy founded more that 27 years ago. What a remarkable example of international understanding the Greek Academy's influence has generated. What an influence it has been.

In the Academy in Greece, all participants gradually come to appreciate one another. All have travelled far, have met and started to live as a family; but the best thing is that all have talked. Communication is the surest way to break barriers and to build understanding. The I.O.A. has enabled everyone to do these things and through its graduates, this understanding has grown and will grow to permeate thoughts and actions in relation to matters Olympic. The Olympic Movement has made it possible for all to know something about the countries which belong to the Movement; the more each knows, the easier each feels; the more confident everyone acts and the greater trust is shown. We always fear the unknown. But in Olympia are echoed the words of de Coubterin himself. "The foundation of real human morality lies in mutual respect—and to respect one another it is necessary to know one another."

The first I.O.C. Commission for the I.O.A. was appointed by Avery Brundage in 1962. Jean Ketseas was its first Chairman, in 1969, the late Ivar Vind of Denmark was the Chairman of the Commission and then the Academy had the privilege of having the Prime Minister of Tunisia, Mr. Mohammed Mzali at the helm; followed by Mr. Nikos Filaretos as its leader and now Mr. Freddy Serpieris. This liaison between the Academy and the International Olympic Committee is a vital link in international understanding. The results of the deliberations made though 14 groups' discussions at each General Session are transmitted directly by the President to the I.O.C. in the form of a Consolidated Report so what is said in discussion-groups matters very much. The opinions of delegates from the more than 80 nations represented guide future actions, and future Olympic educational policies.

The Academy has been instrumental in assembling members and staff of National Olympic Committees, prominent lecturers, educationists, and, in particular, the youth of many countries. But other groups use the facilities in Ancient Olympia and fall under the spell of its beautiful valley. In recent years, the Academy has been host to international seminars and conferences and, more recently, because of the opportunies offered by the partial scholarships available to members of the Olympic Movement by Olympic Solidarity, greater numbers, and more countries have availed themselves of the chance to participate. As late as 1977, however, only 64 of the then 133 N.O.C.'s had sent representatives to the O.O.A. This situation was changed; latest figures show that more than 100 countries of the 178 nations presently recognised by the I.O.C. have sent participants to the Academy. In 1993, 85 countries were represented. This is one area where greater efforts have to be exerted. It is possible to have one female and one male member of each Olympic country attend a young people's General Session, through Olympic Solidarity funding, each year, for 16 days.

In 1981 in memory of the late Academy President Epaninonidas Petralias the Hellenic Olympic Committee instituted an essay competition. Eighteen papers were received and awards made. Here is yet another opportunity to spread the academic aspects of the Olympic spirit amongst the youth of the world as this practice still holds. More scholarships are now made in the name of the late Dean of the Academy, Dr. Otto Szmiczek.

The International Olympic Reports have been published since 1961, except for 1974, containing the perfect history of the Academy. Articles, consolidated reports, attendances with names and addresses and countries represented, are all faithfully shown. Each National Olympic Committee has a complete set of the Reports as do many libraries. These excellent Proceedings are no good looking beautiful on a shelf. Everyone is encouraged to use them showing what has been done, confirming one's own ideas by what has been written and discussed and to be amazed at those who were in Olympia, what they said and what was discussed.

A King, Princes, a Prime Minister, a Cardinal, Ministers of Church and State, four Presidents of the International Olympic Committee, 40 I.O.C. members, all the women represented on the I.O.C. executive, numerous N.O.C. members, a President of Greece, lawyers, Press and Television representatives, Radio personnel, authors, dancers, innumerable Olympic champions of Winter and Summer Games, military persons, representatives of all academic disciplines and hundreds on the threshold of interesting and influential careers have been to the Academy. In fact, this Academy—the first and only Olympic University, has touched, in all its dimensions, all levels of society.

Films have been made at the Academy by Bulgarians, the IOC, Hungarians, and North Americans; the Academy has its own film. Theses and books have been written about the Academy and its work. But, what has become of those who have studied in Ancient Olympia? Education cannot be measured in terms of numbers of people or their success noted by status and money. Education can only be experienced through ideas which have become reality and which have influenced thinking; to measure ideas translated into action is impossible. The accumulated thoughts and actions of the thousands who have passed through the Academy's portals have influenced the attitudes of millions towards a fuller understanding of the Olympic Movement and Olympism.

Whilst it is important to be thankful for what has been done by others and through their efforts to have enabled those who have had the privilege to be at the I.O.A., it is appropriate for others to make a contribution. Regrettably, some go to the Academy to have a holiday, but the vast majority go to learn and to refresh ideas, hone thoughts to enable one to continue to contribute to all that is Olympic on returning to one's homeland. There is still much to work on, to inform the general public of what has been done in Ancient Olympia, what the Academy stands for and of what will forward its objectives. What of the inequalities within the Movement which restrict opportunties to train, travel, compete, to have suitable equipment? What of the problems of drugs and doping, inadequate nutrition, of other forms of unfair and unethical behaviour? National Olympic Committees need help to combat these evils and each needs to be aware, vigilant and prepared to act in the Olympic cause of fair play. Each person knows why he or she came to be in Olympia. Each knows how fortunate and privileged one is. The privilege is to repay by being exemplary members of the Olympic family and being graduates of the unique Olympic Academy. The privileged community which has been fashioned with its similarities and disparities is just a microcosm of our world.

This symbiosis of mind and body experienced by some, for the first time, is what those who have experienced the I.O.A. have become. It is to be hoped that every person will carry this union into the Olympic life all wish to lead, so that others might benefit.

The Academy's influence towards international understanding through Olympism, not only in the Olympic world of thought and action, has been great. It can be even greater through necessary and continued efforts.

What better way to end this Chapter than with the words spoken at the 21st celebration of the International Olympic Academy by the President of the I.O.C., His Excellency Juan Antonio Samaranch:

What a beautiful example for you participants of international understanding and co-operation. Here is a Greek institution operating in Greece under the auspices of an international organisation founded by a Frenchman with headquarters in Switzerland and which welcomes participants and lecturers from all over the world.

REFERENCES

1. Juan Antonio Samaranch, *Address.* Hill of the Pnyx, Report of the Twenty-first Session of the International Olympic Academy at Olympia. (Athens, 1982), p. 26.

2. Pierre de Coubertin, *Olympic Memoirs,* Olympia (1927), International Olympic Committee, Ed. Geoffroy de Navacelle (Lausanne, 1979), p. 133.

3. Carl Diem, *Introduction,* Report of the First Session of the International Olympic Academy, 2nd Edition (Athens, 1973), p. 7.

4. Willi Daume, *Closing Address,* Report of the Fourth Session of the International Olympic Academy (Athens, 1964), p. 35.

5. Xenophon Leon Messinesi, *A Branch of Wild Olive,* Exposition Press, (New York, 1973), p. 94.

6. *Ibid.,* p. 95.

7. H.C. Diem, "An 'Elis' of our Times", Report of the First Session of the International Olympic Academy, 2nd Edition, (Athens, 1973), p. 18.

8. Letter to Jean Ketseas from Architect Peter Zannetos, 1964. In Avery Bundage Collection (University of Illinois, Urbana, U.S.A.). Permission granted to quote.

9. Otto Szymiczek, "The International Olympic Academy, its History, Achievement, Objectives." Report of the Fifteenth Session of the International Olympic Academy (Athens, 1975), p. 47.

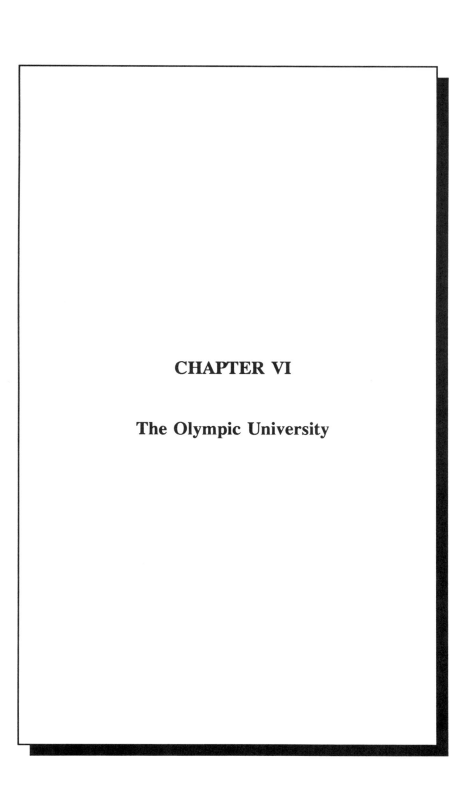

CHAPTER VI

The Olympic University

BIOS

I do not know what life is
For no-one yet has it defined.
I only know that life is what each has
The same as all of human kind.

I do not understand how flowers draw
Their precious fragrance from dull brown earth.
Yet, when I gently touch soft petals wet with dew
I DO know they've not been made by me, or you.

I do not understand how butterflies are born of lowly grubs
And wonder how do swallows know
That Spring is coming to our Northern world
When all is covered, white, with snow.

I do not know how a bulb of common glass
With filament of fine wire, by touch of distant switch
Can flood a room with instant light to push dense
Horrors back into the night.

Because I cannot understand these things
That swamp each ordinary day,
How may I hope to grasp the vast eternal truth called life
By which clock and calendar notch up yet another day.

So, with you I just use life's common things
Hoping I'll understand something—some day.

J.T.P.

CHAPTER VI
The Olympic University

The Olympic Movement is eternal, it is addressed to all ages, to all levels of athletic ability, to all social layers, to all men and women and includes all types of events and sports. The aim of the Olympic Movement is to realise the pursuits of Olympism with, as its ultimate purpose, the harmonious development of MAN.

Otto Szymiczek
"The Olympic Movement and
The Olympic Games"
30th June, 1976
16th Session, I.O.A.

INTRODUCTION

The essence of the Olympic Movement lies within Olympism. What is Olympism? It is the spirit of and the way in which all things Olympic are conducted. Yet Olympism is not solely connected with Olympic Festivals. Olympism is all pervading, it is life and the way that life is lived by one person, a group, or a country and is best shown in international relationships. These principles of living are epitomised in the pageantry, panoply, contest and atmosphere of spectator and athlete alike at the celebration of an Olympic Festival.

Olympism enables things to happen for good—but one must believe in it, work for it and allow it to be the driving force within every person. It is easy to believe, for a moment; it is much more difficult to believe, to justify one's belief, to be known for it and to be an example of it.

Many people join in but few lead. Each has to be imbued with the essence of all that is done through study and action—and then, and only then, can Olympism be realised. It is time to pay tribute to the persistence that has enabled the International Olympic Academy—in truth the Olympic University, to prosper, not only through the vision and generosity of the Hellenic Olympic Committee, the International Olympic Commission for the I.O.A., the Academy itself, but Hellas. The Academy is in the land of leadership, in the land of those who, emerging through the ages of, and influence of, myth, led MAN to intelligent consecutive thought, the power of intellect and concept, and the whole expression of music, poetry, drama and human movement; to life, rather than existence, to humanity rather than barbarism.

The flowering of genius in Greece was a result of the impulse given when clarity and power of thought were added to great spiritual force. That union made all that was Greek: writings, statuary, temples, festivals, sports and games, love of fact and beauty, reality and idealism. It enabled Greeks to hold tight to things seen and unseen, and to leave the foundation for modern education to express—science, religion, art, philosophy, physical contest and the constant search for truth.

No one can recapture the ancient Greek point of view—the simplicity and directness of that vision is, unfortunately not for us. Time does not stand still but the deep integration of the concept of the individual will never be lost. The great tragic poets of old warned and told that that which is of any importance within us is that which we share with all.

". . . we are not against flesh and blood but against principalities and powers", wrote St. Paul.

Something within each of us will not let us rest—each needs to find the truth. Each generation has attempted to reconcile the truth the spirit knows, with the truth the mind knows. We could do well to consider the successes, through adjustments achieved in the past. The Greek way was the most complete. It did not abstract away the outside world to choose the inner world; the Hellenes harmonised the things seen and unseen. The Greeks saw the paradox of truth, accepted it and created clarity, completeness, harmony, law and freedom, beauty and goodness, the objective and subjective—the result was balance. In Greek art there is an absence of struggle, a calm and a serenity something the world has yet to see again.

Can Olympism achieve, once again, this balance? Can the pursuit of truth, via the study and practice of Olympism become a viable area of study within universities?

THE OLYMPIC UNIVERSITY

. . . search all of history and you will find nothing that has ever remotely approached, either the speed with which the Olympic Movement has swept the world, or the extent of its capture of the attention and the participation of mankind since 1894. 75 years is a very short period and, in the restless search for new records, there is sometimes a tendency to forget the real objective of the Olympic Movement:

1. to develop the complete man, physically, mentally and morally strong in the sense of the Golden Age of Greece;
2. to teach the value of amateurism or devotion to the task at hand rather than the reward;
3. to encourage the practice of fair play, and,
4. to create international amity.

- 82 -

When these Olympic ideas are extended from the fields of sport into the greater fields of business and politics, we can be sure of a happier and more peaceful world. This was the glorious idea of the Baron de Coubertin 75 years ago!

> Avery Brundage, on the celebration
> of the 75th Anniversary of the
> International Olympic Committee.
> Helsinki—29th October, 1969.

All who meet these objectives are potentially members of the Olympic University, ideally sited in its rightful home. The very concept of this Olympic University, (where many study and those who have come before have done so, as will those who come after will search to seek the truth) was a dream made reality by those devoted to belief, virtually unhelped or internationally unsupported, thoroughly Greek, believed in and persisted with. Now, one sits in comfortable chairs, not on benches beneath trees, in internationally mixed sleeping quarters, not in tents—solely because a succession of devoted men and women believed and acted in the spirit of Olympism.

Those who study enjoy the benefits of this faith—persisted within the face of vicissitudes which would have broken less determined people—and it becomes a privilege and a necessity to keep this energy of Olympism active, alive and known. By example, conviction, belief and work Olympism is another stone on which this Olympic University has been built.

Through National Olympic Committees, many educational programmes have been instituted and encouraged. Also, leaders and educators have met the responsibility—wishing the Olympic ideal to flourish—introducing courses, lectures, films (such as the Canadian series of 30 films shown on Educational Television, fashioned especially by Dr. Maureen O'Bryan to encourage youth and not eulogise champions) stressing Olympism. Excellent educational texts from the National Olympic Committees of Australia, Canada and the United States of America. Olympic Solidarity, formed in 1972, encourages and sponsors, amongst other services offered, courses in leadership, coaching, sports medicine. Many universities conduct credit courses in the study of the Olympic Games and the Movement. Some have had study sessions in Greece. One such area of concentration is headed by Dr. R.K.Barney, Director of the Centre for Olympic Studies at the University of Western Ontario in London, Canada. This is but one, of few focii, into the Olympic World within a university. Others are—

a. the Centre d'Estadis Olympics at the Universitat Autonoma de Barcelona, Edifici "B", 08193 Bellaterra (Barcelona) Spain under the direction of Professor Miguel de Moragas;

b. Dr. Karl Lennartzis Carl-Diem-Institut e.v., Deutsch Sport-hochschule Koln, Postfach. 450327, 5000, Cologne 41, Germany.

Then there are the two aspects concerning Olympic studies in Lausanne, Switzerland.

c. the Olympic Research Department under the direction of Dr. Karel Wendl at the Chateau de Vidi—1007, Lausanne, and

d. Mrs. Fani Kakridis-Enz's Centre for Olympic Studies in the Olympic Museum, 1006, Lausanne.

As I write, two other centres are being created:

e. Dr. Garth Paton is to head the Centre for Olympic Studies at the University of New Brunswick in Fredericton, New Brunswick, E3B 5A3 in Canada, and

f. Dr. Ian Jobling will be the Director of the Olympic Studies Centre at the University of Queensland, 4072, Australia.

In 75 countries, National Olympic Committees have taken remarkable initiatives instituting and conducting Olympic study through National Olympic Academies and by holding official reunions of those who have had the privilege of study and contemplation in the Academy of Ancient Olympia. There is also an Alumni Group formed for those who have studied in the International Olympic Academy. It would be a mark of true international Olympism were all other nations to follow such examples.

Each knows what is going on in her or his country to prepare for the next celebration of the Olympic Festivals in Lillehammer in 1994 and in Atlanta in 1996, and the plans being made for national competitors in those Olympic Games, but who is aware of what is going on in one's own colleges and universities concerning Olympism?

Departments of Classics, Philosophy, History, Languages and Human Movement have scholars and enthusiasts teaching a variety of aspects concerning classical mythology, Ancient Greek philosophic thought, ancient Games such as funeral, feast, Nemean, Isthmian, Pythian, Olympic as well as other Pan-Hellenic Festivals and Modern Olympic celebrations. Then there are various and progressive coaching schemes, Junior Olympic programmes, national championships, the formation of national training centres, physiological and psycological testing centres. Ministries and Ministers of Sport are common in many countries.

There are tens of thousands of books in libraries all over the world about the Olympic Games, hundreds of films, thousands of ex-athletes who have been Olympic competitors, and millions who have been touched by the concept of the Olympic Games, BUT, is it know where there is one consolidated area of study, one Department of Olympic Studies in any university, in one's own country, devoted to OLYMPISM, except in Elis, that hallowed ancient spot? Of course, there are many, some of which are quoted, but how well known? The task is to introduce the spirit of the Games, to discuss the essence of Olympism, not necessarily the winning of a title; to take out of the media the unofficial point-scoring for a victory, the pitting of one nation against another bred by biased reporting, to eliminate the sensationalism, the stress on unfair advantage through drugs, other ergogenic aids, through sponsorship and appearance money, and substitute these by objective reporting, unbiased television, radio transmissions and through an enlightened attitude to competition within the rules.

How are these to be done? Through an understanding of Olympism, which is another word for "education", or even the word "enlightenment". Because Olympism is subjective, many feel it is not tangible. cannot be measured in an objective way thus is better left alone. It is the only aspect pertaining to the Olympic celebration, not dealt with in university courses as a specific subject. In many parts of the world, universities have aspects of their academic structure devoted to the preparation of teachers, and teachers eventually teach children. It is in the children that the concept of Olympism needs to be fostered.

Sport has become a manipulative political tool—well understood by politicians. Athletes must be made aware of this trend; but Olympism is the spirit, however intangible, of the attitude towards participation and each other; fragile in some hands, a weapon in others. Youth can be exploited through its own idealism and athletes, who devote their lives to the attempt to achieve excellence, are often used as nationalistic symbols, sometimes for fine example for other youth, but often as instruments of political ambition. Despite the evils which can result as a consequence of using athletic excellence—the athlete must remain supreme because it is the athlete, by competing, who creates the spectacle. The spirit of pure competition transcends—at that moment—all other thoughts, feelings, ideologies. The essence of Olympism, the equality of striving, devotion of mind over matter is epitomised in a smile, an extra surge of effort, a dream realised, the handshake of a beaten opponent, a oneness within oneself. That is Olympism.

Can it be taught, is it worthy of being fostered, it is realisable, can it transcend national barriers, the communication difficulties of speech, language, custom, cultures, rivalry? The essence of Olympism lives wherever idealists congregate, who are the examples of this practical idealism.

The International Olympic Academy in Ancient Olympia is the world university of Olympism. It is the rightful place, the fountainhead of the essence of this nebulous intangible. Where else in this world but in Greece (the mother of formulated recorded language, the bearer of the great historians, poets and thinkers of the Western world for 25 centuries), should the studies in Olympian knowledge be fostered and persisted with?

Where are the sources? They are in every library, in every, and any issue, of the *Academy's Reports* printed by the I.O.C. annually since 1961, each filled with articles espousing Olympism. In any library; go, look, refer, read. There stacked in unparalleled sources are materials for courses on Olympism. Note the modern history of the Games in that excellent monthly magazine *Olympic Review* and the quarterly *Olympic Message* issued from the I.O.C. Headquarters. Read one's own nation's publications.

However, all these sources, all these expressions lie dormant if one does not interpret them and unless one sees that the principles of Olympism are taught. Belief, knowledge, enthusiasm will be given the sparks which will light the Olympic flames of knowledge and give the light by which others can see the essence of Olympism, which must burn bright and be kept kindled, if the Olympic spirit is to be kept alight, visible and viable from Olympiad to Olympiad.

Some scholars have devoted their lives to the Olympic idea. The late Dr. Cleanthis Paleaologos (and his work) is worthy of study: read him, note his research, identify his knowledge bred through his pride of being Greek and giving, for all the world to see, a living example of Olympism. This is as it was with Academy Dean, Dr. Otto Syzemicek. His ideas of Olympism, his writings, speeches and international example are to be drawn upon. And so it is with many scholars present and past who live Olympism. Draw on them, be sustained by their example and use their works from which to teach and gain inspiration. Only in this way will universities see the need to include Olympism within curricula. Of course, it is mentioned—referred to but only as an incidental. It should become a deliberation, for it is more important than ever today to stress the fundamentals of the Games (rather than the Games themselves) and what intellectual aspects lie behind them. Athletic festivals, and how they are conducted, are the direct, visible sign of the philosophy which created them.

Young blood is vital to the survival of any movement—vigorous life is the real Olympics and each young Olympic enthusiast throbs with life, each heart eagerly pumps blood to enable the brain to seek and search. That is the sole purpose of a university—to give those who attend the challenge to think—and thinking leads to the way of finding knowledge and truth. What are these truths concerning Olympism?

Life is what the spirit is concerned with—the individual. Abstractions from life's experience are the concerns of the mind. The ancient Greeks were concerned with both mind and spirit. They wished to know what things are and what do these things mean; but they did not lose the individual and what he/she represented. Greek education was the result of Greek balance; individuals who sought truth for all of humanity in every human being—of mankind within man, womankind within woman. The Greek mind never saw anything in and for itself but always connected it with that which was greater.

The Greek spirit saw beauty and meaning in each separate thing but, although individual, with significance to the universal. This was an expression of the Greek ideal, beauty, absolute, form everlasting—the irradiation from the particular to the general. But what is different today? The Greeks who taught us how to think espouse the same principle: from individual to the society, from the particular to the general.

It was in front of the monuments dedicated jointly to Jan Ketseas and Karl Diem that General Papathanassiadis, then President of the Hellenic Olympic committee said in 1968 at the 8th Academy Session of the International Olympic Academy:

"Olympia is once more becoming the spiritual centre of the world."

It is only by returning to the sources of Olympism that MAN is able to restore equilibrium where there is centred unity of body, mind and spirit. Also, it is solely in the Greek language that there is a word summing physical vigour and intellectual excellence; "Kaloskagathos". This should be the University's motto, for it assumes that all who attend desire wisdom and on hearing the words of Sophocles, "there are many marvels in the world, but the greatest marvel is MAN", will understand. So, if MAN, whose brain has allowed hands to work, can also create, why cannot this universal university dream also become a reality? But is it not already in existence?

WHAT IS A UNIVERSITY?

A corporation of scholars and teachers, studying and researching in the higher realms of learning, and having power to confer degrees. Each receives a diploma on leaving the International Olympic Academy and has the blessing and the support of the Greek Government. Is it not, then, already a university? For a person to benefit from a university education he/she should be educated, not trained.

The university is a place of converse, of depth as well as breadth of study, of liberalism in thought and expression—but the essential factor lies in balance—the blending of excellence in intellectual and social endeavours, in sports, games, dance, exercise with mental and spiritual discipline; of courses of study built upon holism; involving touching, questing, challenging, upsetting, demanding, stimulating and through these processes preparing both mind and body, yet satisfying the spirit. A university is a privileged place and anyone attending is a privileged person destined for leadership by virtue of having been there. The university serves society and yet it fashions it. It is devoted as much to the élite as it is to the mass, fulfilling every need, at every turn in every way. A university is an example of Olympism, for it feeds soul, body and mind. It is not a building, but a collection of scholars at all levels on the academic ladder which is unending, there always being another rung to climb.

WHAT IS AN ACADEMY?

It is an institution of learning, the expression derived from the Academy founded in the garden of Akademos where Plato established the first university. Thus, by right, in every sense, the Academy is already the Olympic University; the only one in the world which propounds one subject, and which has as its driving force, Olympism. It is known that throughout the world, important things are being done in the name of Olympism, but when something Olympic cannot be clearly labelled, it is also put under the title "Olympism". This is not good enough. Many talk of "Olympism", few know what it really means.

Who are to be the students of this International University? It is to be hoped that those who are entitled to be present at an Academy have been prepared, as it is so clearly stated in the Hellenic Olympic Committee's brochure (page 5):

"Participants should have shown particular interest in the aims of the Academy and the subject to be studied and are therefore expected to take an active part in the discussions."

Also,

"They are also expected to contribute, upon return to their countries, in the spreading of the Olympic spirit and the fulfilment of the aims of the I.O.A. in general."

Nothing could be more clear.

Were one to read the Report—*Canada at the Olympic Youth Camp*, 12th July to 4th August, 1976, prepared by Captain James A. Murray, one would see, and sense, exactly the same spirit. Within the Report is a letter of recommendation to the International Olympic Committee from the Canadian Olympic Association advocating, amongst other things:

1. ". . . for the inclusion of such camps into I.O.C. regulations".
2. ". . . the meeting of young people from all over the world is instrumental in the furtherance of the objectives of the Olympic Movement . . ."
3. "The Olympic Youth Camps are an essential contribution to better understanding among peoples of the World".
4. ". . . the I.O.C. make a proposal to the Organizing Committee of the Games of the XXIInd Olympiad in Moscow to arrange officially a Youth camp".
5. . . . that the I.O.C. member in Canada convey this motion to the I.O.C. at the earliest date possible."

But many have never heard of Olympic Youth Camp. Could not participants at the International Academy become the undergraduates of the Olympic University and, in Ancient Olympia, would eventually become the graduates of programmes of this, the Academy for Advanced Study?

Already two doctoral dissertations have been written about the International Olympic Academy:

1. L'idee Olympique de Pierre de Coubertin et Carl Diem et son Abouttissement dans L'Academie Olympique Internationale—Norbert Müeller (Graz);
2. The Greek Concept Realized in the Founding the International Olympic Academy—Nina K. Pappas (Illinois).

Next should be compilations of the work already done there and presented by individual scholars, such as those two stalwarts of Olympism already mentioned. Furthermore the collections and translations of works by the late Professor Liselott Diem in Köln; the Archives at the I.O.C. Headquarters in Lausanne; the Avery Brundage Collection at the University if Illinois, Urbana, and careful work published by the Pierre de Coubertin Committee, should all be studied.

There are excellent books, thousands, in fact, about the Olympic Games' Festivals, but one must take care that Olympism is sought and its essence understood.

Films are made, but what is the theme: articles are written, but what is their message; speeches are made, but what really is said? We look, but what do we see: we read, but what do we comprehend; we listen, but what do we hear? University education and Olympism is the theme. The ideal place for the study of this subject is within a university, but who is prosecuting the subject? It is plainly difficult, the settings are often wrong, the atmosphere antagonistic or apathetic. How many think of Olympism until just before or just after an Olympic celebration? What happens in between, where does the Olympiad go, how is its time spent? This is the time for study, for putting new courses into curricula, for preparing candidates and reaffirming Olympism's goals. Professors of Olympic programmes and themes have learned well from those of ancient Greek times, from the modern prophet Baron Frédi Pierre de Coubertin; a man of vision, a conceptualiser, Jean Ketseas, another visionary and Dr. Carl Diem, friend and worker for Olympism. Here are some extracts of what they said and wrote:

PIERRE DE COUBERTIN

Humanist, educated in the Classics, devoted his life to the proposition and realisation of a complete intellectual system based upon sport, physical education, intellectual education, plus study in spheres of aesthetics, culture, history and sociology. His Hellenism (considered to be the epitome of perfection in philosophy, art and literature achieved by Greece) gave him clarity of vision identified within vigorous physical activity, biological, moral and character-forming values.

Baron de Coubertin, the educator, was influenced also by the English public school system and how games and sports were applied in the United States of America. But it was his vision, his clarity of thought, his conceptualisation—so far ahead of his time—that made him misunderstood and yet so convincing that his revival of the Olympic Festival became fact:

> In wishing to renovate not so much the form as the spirit of this age-old institution, because I saw in it a pedagogical orientation which had become necessary for my country and humanity. I was to try to restore the powerful intellectual and moral buttresses which have shouldered it in the past.

Extract from the French Pierre
de Coubertin Committee tribute and
presented in *Olympic Review,* 80–81,
July–August 1974, p. 303.

His statements, even when taken out of contest, ring true. It was he who coined the word "Olympism".

"Olympism strives to gather, in a radiant beam, all the principles which contribute to the improvement of man", and
"Is not emulation the mainspring of all exertions, whether mental or physical?"

Speech in Athens, 7 April 1896

"Before laying claim to "Olympism" therefore, your "complete athlete" should begin by completing himself."

Olympic Letters—20 December 1918

"Olympism is a huge noiseless machine whose cog wheels do not grate and whose movement never stops, despite the handfuls of sand which certain persons throw into it, perseveringly but unsuccessfully in an effort to sabotage its operation."

From: *LaRevue Sportive Illustrée*
Belgique, July 1920

"Ancient Olympia was a city of athletics, art and prayer. It is a mistake to reverse the order of these 3 terms. . . . The sacred and aesthetic character of Olympia were consequences of its muscular role. The city of athletics was intermittent; the city of art and prayer permanent. It will be the same with the modern Olympia."

Offered by the *Review Olympique* to
participants in the International
Architectural Competition, Paris 1910

"I have seen fifty years pass since the day in 1886 when I put aside every kind of preoccupation and dedicated my life-effort to the preparation of an educational revival, being convinced that no political or social stability could be obtained henceforward without a previous pedagogic reform. I believe I have accomplished my task, but not in full."

Published by the author, Pierre de
Coubertin. A speech given to the
bearers of the Olympic torch from
Olympia to Berlin, 1936.

The principles enunciated by Baron Pierre de Coubertin are those of recognised university disciplines. It was so well said by Rene Maheu, the then Director General of UNESCO on 28th October 1963 at the International Congress celebrating the centenary of de Coubertin's birth:

"His notes on public education are a complete treatise on modern education, putting forward practical solutions of such astonishing topicality that even today they could serve as the basis for all teaching reforms."

JEAN TH. KETSEAS

Were one to go to the Modern Olympic Museum in Ancient Olympia, one would see the smiling photographic likeness of Jean Ketseas; when entering the O.I.A. library, one would be told that the first 500 books were donated by him. He was variously Secretary General of the Hellenic Olympic Committee, permanent representative of the International Olympic Committee to Greece and President of the Board of Trustees of the International Olympic Academy. It is in the last of these capacities that he wrote a report to the I.O.C. in 1949:

Already in 1927, the Baron de Coubertin, while in Athens, expressed to me his fears that the mechanisation and training to the hilt of the athletes would have an outcome detrimental to the necessary equipoise between the body and the mind.

In 1938 Jean Ketseas, and his friend Dr. Carl Diem, evolved a plan to establish an international centre for research into matters Olympic, in Ancient Olympia. On the 19th of June 1947 in Stockholm, Jean ketseas spoke on the matter at the I.O.C. Assembly. He did so in London in 1948 and in the first month of 1949 presented a report to the I.O.C. specifically recording his close collaboration with Carl Diem. The establishment of the International Olympic Academy was approved by the I.O.C. on 28th April 1949; almost 45 years ago.

Negativism, lack of international understanding, simple indifference thwarted their idea. They persisted, and in Athens in July 1961 at the I.O.C. congress it was agreed that the first Session should be held, in Olympia, 15th June to 21st that very year, on ground (100 acres) purchased by the Hellenic Olympic Committee.

In a report submitted to the I.O.C. in 1964, Mr. Ketseas outlines, most clearly, the historical progression on the way to the establishment of the International Academy and how it was that, in 1961, the Carl Diem trust of the Deutsche Olympische Gesellschaft provided the money for the holding of the experimental 1961 Session. Thereafter the Greek Government and the Hellenic Olympic Committee have sponsored and financed this Academy of learning.

CARL DIEM

He was devoted to the "Olympic Idea" and, with friends, laid the foundations of the German sports movement. He was the head official of the German Olympic teams of 1912, 1928 and 1932 and, in his capacity as General Secretary of the German Reich Committee for Olympic Games, ordered the construction of the first great stadium in Berlin where, in 1936, he saw his ideas and organisation materialise in the 1936 Olympic Games for which he originated the running of the Flame and its ceremony.

At Baron Pierre de Coubertin's request, he took over the direction of the International Olympic Institute in Berlin, publishing 24 issues of *Olympic Review,* the official organ of the I.O.C., continuing de Coubertin's editorship of *Revue Olympique* (1901-14). He was a friend of the Baron; organised youth tours to Greece, excavations at Ancient Olympia and not only coordinated with Jean Ketseas in 1934, the initial organisation of the first torch relay to be realised in 1936, but together they conceived the plan for the first International Olympic Academy meeting in 1961.

> Coubertin might be called an Olympic Academy in himself, so rich are his writings and proposals . . . so wide is their range of still valid teachings, so full is their store of sporting insight, practical realism, shrewd psychology and social vision.
>
> "An Elis of our time" from *The Olympic Idea*—
> Carl Diem, Carl-Diem,Institut, 1979, p. 114.

> . . . we are on earth to perfect our human nature. In youth this can most suitably be done in the field of competitive sport, which is to man what the blossom is to the tree. With further growth the striving for high attainment is transferred to more serious fields. The blossom falls, the fruit remains behind.
>
> and
>
> "The true sportsman finds his standard of behaviour within himself. Let us make ourselves worthy in our own eyes of the Olympic ideal."
>
> From *Sport und Leben,*
> Heidelberg 1948, No. 1, p. 22.

Writing about Olympic Art in *Olympic Review* in April 1939, No. 5, on Page 18, he stated:

> Only in so far as they make us thrill inwardly with awe before man's nature, do they deserve an Olympic award. Only in so far as the architect achieves in his sports building a meaningful and arresting nobility of form, is the olive branch his due.
>
> We can say simply that the "Olympic Academy" which is to arise here will be on the one hand a continuation of the old academy—an "Elis" of our times—and on the other hand the fulfilment of Coubertin's plans to put Olympism on a scholarly basis.
>
> So this Academy is dedicated for all time to the ethics of sport, i.e. to an exemplary sporting morality as a training for the whole of life. And keeping before our eyes this path to our goal of a higher humanity, let us begin our work.

Paper given at the First Session
of the I.O.A. 1961. Published by
the German Olympic Committee,
Dortmund 1961, pp. 17–20.

These, then, are some of the forebears of modern Olympic heritage. Men who practised Olympism as well as having studied it. It should be now quite clear why the International Olympic Academy ought to be named the first Olympic University and why the study of Olympism is so worthy of the best minds and the utmost devotion of scholars in established centres of learning.

CONCLUSIONS

1. In the way the term Olympism has been outlined in this chapter, no course of study is known which uses Olympism as its theme, in any university.
2. It is proposed that the International Olympic Academy be considered the Olympic University.
3. Undergraduates should proceed a) via Youth Camps and b) selection by national Olympic Committees before returning to the International Olympic Academy in Ancient Olympia, for advanced study and c) having attended a session of the I.O.A., and d) their own National Academy.
4. That the term "Olympism" be understood as being of the spirit; as that which builds harmony, symmetry and balance of body and mind and, that it is integral of the Olympic Movement, because it is its essence.
5. That Olympism is worthy of study in its own right and that scholars should be enabled to devote time and effort to collate works of those known to be, by their writings, belief and by their very lives, Olympists.

Olympism has many aspects. It pervades the whole Olympic Movement and is shown to the world as a moral/physical expression in élite contest known as an Olympic Games.

Every human act is a physical and mental test. The Games are the elevated effort of the individual to combine the regeneration and improvement of bodily powers with a moral and intellectual education, an essential factor contributing to overall development.

Dr. Cleanthis Palaelogos.
"Olympia, the Great Centre of
Ancient Greek Civilization"
15th Session, I.O.A., July 1975
Olympia, p. 61.

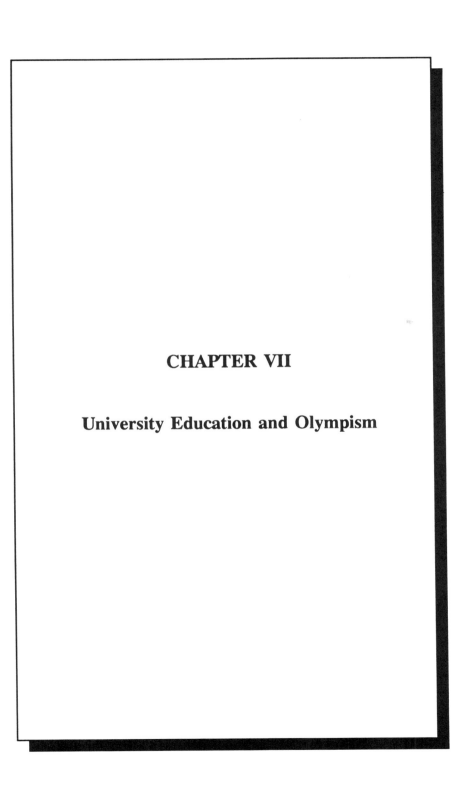

CHAPTER VII

University Education and Olympism

CHAPTER VII
University Education and Olympism

The safeguard of the Olympic ethical principles as the solid foundation of Olympism is as imperative as is the necessity to take into consideration the dynamics of modern development. This would imply to cultivate traditions alongside with changes which occur in conformity with social conditions and the progress of science and technology.

Nadajda Lekarska
Essays and Studies on Olympic Problems
1973, p. 122.

THE PURPOSE OF THE UNIVERSITY

Is the main function of the university teaching—that is, the transmission of knowledge and the values of culture to future generations? OR, is the main function of the university research—the discovery of new knowledge?

These views come from different ways of looking at the university. From the time of Plato until the end of the 18th Century, the educated person was the one best conversant with Western civilization's classics. This person sought to discover the rules for correct action by careful scrutiny of the past—this is the picture of a traditionalist.

Markedly in the 19th century, the concept of the nature of an intellectual made a dramatic turn. Socially and mentally, through defying the rules of schools of thought, transcending the limits of convention, perhaps by dressing in an unconventional way, introducing novelty into work and through personality quirks the intellectual became the one who was "original", different and non-traditional. In Plato's thought, it was believed that in copying there was no originality but that the individual genius, unencumbered by past convention or society's demands, was the source of originality, of truth and of beauty. Thus, the classical idea of learning as the absorption of, and the preservation of what was good in the past gave way to the modern idea of learning, as that way of discovering what is new. Faculties in universities are still involved with this concern about the meaning of knowledge and the meaning of education. It is realized we are all products of history and the virtue of study of the past is to make us more sentient, more vitally aware of the problems of what went on before we were born, and of how those concerns affect us today.

Those of us who were, or are, privileged to teach in universities attempted then, and now attempt to, contribute to new knowledge. I am privileged having created a new concept—after 32 years of work and deliberation—that of human kinetics, an holistic approach to the biologically scientific study of MAN moving. There have been few to be so privileged. Most faculty members attempt to force into new frontiers, to strike out in new directions which they hope will lead by originality of thought into new areas, vistas and visions. There are those who are not "original" who are content to express what has been learned, how to think, and how thought bears upon the present. These scholars take delight in what is done and what has been done and what can be learned from the process.

The word "amateur", which is no longer used in relation to physical activity's expression, (I even hesitate to use the word "sport" because it has almost gone the way of "amateur") is derived from the meaning "to delight in". The word "amateur" has become a "dirty word" but it really means "one who is in love with something". Are we able to say candidly that our society would be the poorer were more or us to take pleasure in things of the mind and those things of our imagination rather than with science's devotion to fact? We know the state of the world today, we know that the past is no sure guide. We realize that we must face the demands of new experience and new situations which require new ideas and new ways of response. That double allegiance, on the one hand, the idea of the university as the preserver of tradition, particularly in teaching, and on the other hand, the explorer of the new in research, takes us to the heart of the matter. This is the tension of the very nature of a university, as well as the tension in the existence of the life of an individual. To define this tension one has to define "conformity". We are frightened of conformity, we never see ourselves as conformists, it is always someone else and we would hate to be that other person. Yet one of the reasons why universities came into being was to shape the present generation to accept the morals and attitudes of society as well as to fashion that generation to the expectations of society thus conforming because the university is a function of its own society.

The oldest universities were initially devoted to human medicine; their purpose was to train medical practitioners—not educate them. At Cambridge University in England in 1316, a college was founded for the purpose of training secretaries for the King's society's needs in veterinary medicine and agriculture; but not in computer technology, the mechanical arts, liberal education, physical activity. Today society needs business people, architects, physicists, chemists, linguists, engineers, computer designers, and so universities will continue to flourish because of the need to provide those with the skills necessary for work and to meet the needs of society.

But there is a deeper way in which the university, in fact all of education, should act, and this is through the avenue of conformity. Education throughout, from the earliest possible moment to the latest possible years of life, is an agent, an initiating agent to encourage on-coming generations to accept the skills. The process of advancement throughout university is to ceaselessly bring young people into society through systems of thought and imagery which underly the values, objectives and aim of culture. The professor in a university is paid to encourage students to think, to formulate, fashion, express and to have new ideas. In these ways, students are brought into intimate relation with intangible loyalties, the feeling for, and the principles by which organisations exist and productive life is lived.

Yet again, when one is privileged enough to have a young man or woman think, many delightful and exciting things happen. The thinker starts to question, to identify conflicts and contradictions within systems of values and in the things which society knows, acts upon and cherishes, as tradition. The young intellectual makes society uncomfortable because he or she demands that society should make new choices and that it should query its own values. Each of us loves freedom and equality, but the historian reminds us that it is only through special circumstances, both social and economic, that we are able to enjoy both. In fact, at different times one may have to surrender one in order to retain the other. So, in this way, by reviving tradition, the intellectual person realizes that our way of life is no simple unitary thing through which we can measure conformity with, or deviation from, tradition. We all realize, sooner or later, that we have to devote serious commitment to the present as well as to the past. So the young intellectual accepts the responsibility and inevitability of plunging into the concerns of today, conscious of the efforts made by those who lived in the past, who did what they did, for the future.

OLYMPISM

It is vital that thought be given to the foundations of the Games, why they have persisted in modern times—except for curtailment by wars—since 1896. Within this framework, the question must be asked, "what have universities done about fostering understanding of the Olympic Movement?"—virtually nothing. Young intellectuals should question this and if thought worthy of one's endeavour do something about it; for without young brain power and involvement the Games are doomed.

The academic aspect of the whole Olympic Movement lies within the area of Olympism—something which most people talk about, seems to understand, about which whole books have been written[1], the definition of which is in no encyclopedia and yet it is the absolute essence of the Movement. This definition was published in 1976:

A harmony of ideas and ideals that affirm the values of Olympic sport in promoting and developing sound physical and moral qualities in individuals, and in contributing to a better and more peaceful world by enabling representatives of nations to meet in an atmosphere of mutual respect and international amity.[2]

This concept should be analyzed, dissected, discussed and, if necessary, re-written, but it should be studied and questioned, as should the 1991 Olympic Charter's first expression of what is deemed to be Olympism. From discussion will come agreements and disagreements and perhaps better understanding of what force it is which makes the Olympic movement flourish. This intellectual approach is fundamental to the understanding of the purpose of the Movement and of the Games. If fundamental principles are not thoroughly understood and acted upon the actual physical expression of the Olympic Movement which is the Olympic Games—will be unmanageable. It is this academic vigour which is needed within university curricula to appreciate the past and plan for the future. That is why this subject is always for discussion in Olympia at the International Olympic Academy.

Without strict study given to the problems, the concerns of ethics, political influences, financial dominance, gargantuanism and commercialism, which pertain to the Games, the Olympic Festivals are destined to dissolution through violence to physical organisms by drugs, unbalanced nationalism, unequal professionalism, materialism and by out-of-proportion devotion to the necessity of winning. Here one must look to the past.

The best brains are needed to discuss these vital matters for the very survival of the Olympic Games is at stake. Universities do sponsor courses, train athletes, promote athleticism, teach coaching methods, conduct experiments and tests on athletes, recommend training schedules, study dietary factors and teach, within some physical education and nationally sponsored and organized courses about the Olympic Games, but the majority of this devotion is to the wise, proper and best expression of athletes in Olympic-like competition. Essentially, it is the spirit of, and the way in which, all things Olympic are conducted which are of fundamental importance, and yet are little studied. Olympism is not solely connected with the Olympic Festivals. Olympism is a way of living, a way of dealing with fundament concerns, of principles put into practice. It is these principles which are epitomised in the whole of the attitude to pageantry, contest, and to the atmosphere of athlete and spectator to each other, as well as to the actual contest. These principles must be firmed and fully comprehended.

Thus we must look at tradition and ask, does it satisfy, is it adequate for today? If it is found to be inadequate, what is the substitute, what is suitable and how long will that last? It is easy to criticise adversely, it is much more difficult to criticize constructively. Look carefully at the past, analyze the present, prepare for the future. Through one-to-one conversations, group discussions, interchange and exchange of ideas will come suggestions for the future of the Games and for the ideas and ideals of the Olympic Movement.

Earnestness, intellectualism and vision will become the pathways to the road which the Olympic Games will move upon. We who read this come from different cultures, different terrain and climates, different educational backgrounds, different idealogies, and thus contribute different attitudes, different experiences and different moral persuasions to the consideration of the future of the Olympic Games. Only through discussion is there the opportunity to benefit from such divergent opinions in such amity. Diversity is strength and it is this strength which will enable the vigour of the Olympic idea to remain alive and well, simply because the Olympic Movement is for all; all over the Olympic World.

Through interaction and communication the International Olympic Committee benefits, for by communicating the results of deliberations and individual thoughts one contributes to the work at the Headquarters of the I.O.C. in Lausanne. You, therefore, determine what the Games will be, or whether they will even continue. Of most importance is that through individuals' actions and influence how the Games are, and will be, perceived internationally will be determined. Also, expressed thoughts and feelings will determine the future pattern and perception of the Olympic Movement. In fact, because of devotion, interest, energy and intellect, every interested person will be able to recommend a better, and an even more appealing sequence of events for the improvement of the Olympic ideal.

CONCLUSION

So the intellectuals, and by extension, the university, come to be critics of society, not only by insisting that the study of the past raises problems for understanding in the present, but by saying that the traditions of the past may be a hindrance to the present, the origin of our confusion and a blockage to the wish for what is adequate Olympic understanding and participation. The intellectual individual, therefore in formulating the meaning of tradition, is led to imagine alternative lines of development that did not take place and that, whether aesthetically, politically or ethically seem to be more admirable.

The intellectual becomes the critic of tradition and a critic of society and, in an attempt to present systematically the fundamentals of values and beliefs, the intellectual becomes not only the conveyor of traditional values but the critic of the very values he or she wishes to convey. So, those in universities are caught in the difficult position of being both in and outside of society, although committed to it, one is yet alienated from it. Because of this, society is suspicious because those in universities cannot easily say whether the main purpose of the university is to preserve the old or discover the new. What may seem to be opposites turn into one and the same activity. They are not opportunities but poles which define the energy we name intellectual life—this is the field of power which we call the University, and the power in the International Olympic Academy is that which entitles and enables scholars to consider change in thought to the true Olympic University, the Olympic Movement, and to its outward expression, Games, and whatever that may mean and may cause.

REFERENCES

1. Jeffrey Segrave & Chu, Donald. *Olympism,* Human Kinetics Publishers Inc., Champaign, Illinois, U.S.A., 1981, p. 392.

2. Powell, John T., "Development of Olympic Athletes". *Olympic Review,* Lausanne, Switzerland, No. 193, 1983, pp. 748–753.

CHAPTER VIII

Olympism and its Ethics

CHAPTER VIII
Olympism and its Ethics

In this year 1894 and in this city of Paris . . . electricity transmitted everywhere the news that hellenic Olympism had re-entered the world after an eclipse of several centuries.

Baron Pierre de Coubertin at the Paris
Congress 1894 in the new Sorbonne.

OLYMPISM

The first reference to the word "Olympism" is noted in the quotation heading this Chapter.

What does "Olympism" mean? Bob Paul, of the U.S.A. Olympic Committee, wrote to many authorities around the world in 1987 asking them to define "Olympism"; he received few answers. Six responses were published in the National Academy Newsletter of U.S.A. later that year.

ETHICS

The word comes from the Greek—ethos. It means character, nature, disposition. It is the science of morals, oral principles and rules of conduct.

One division of philosophy is the philosophy of values with its main branch being moral philosophy, or ethics. However, the word "ethics" is used in two different senses, sometimes relating to psychological or sociological investigations about the actions of human beings. In this sense ethics is empirical scientific investigation as in the opinions given concerning the testing, taking and using of ergongenic aids by those accused of using them, to enhance physical performance. Ethics in this sense really belongs to empirical science rather than to philosophy.

In the other sense, ethics is the philosophy of moral values or moral norms. This aspect does not investigate facts but gives opinions only, as to what is good, what is evil, what is correct to do and what is wrong to do. Ethics thus expresses standards or judgements about moral values relating to human actions. Ethical reasoning examines the problems of good and evil in life and is concerned with questions of conduct and ultimate objectives. Ethical choices are factors in our existence. Each of us faces certain situations which may be called ethical, although often one is not sure whether a situation is ethical—or not. In which of these senses does ethics apply to Olympism? Both.

The ethics of Olympism are absolute. Olympism is the expressing of, and the practising of ethical principle. Thus, ethics and the practice of Olympism are one. Olympism condemns unethical behaviour and practice, and condemns the use of unethical means by which one takes advantage of another. Furthermore, it advocates fairness, applauds sound actions and permeates, through its own subtle communication and rises above cultural, linguistic and ideological barriers, shows, through gentleness, the ease of a smile, the touch of a hand, the congratulations of one who has not been identified as a winner, although successful in behaviour and attitude. Everyone can 'win"—yet few receive the medal. The medal is the symbol of recognition of observable and identified success; on that occasion. To win is to have overcome oneself and all other competitors, or to be generous in defeat and to know that one has given all that one is capable of giving—at that time. Winning is a constant—it is the victory of one's own self over one's own self, and sometimes—over others.

While it is important to be idealistic, it is also necessary to be practical. It is easy to talk of ethics, it is a matter of the application of ethics which matters. The influence of home, school, example of educator and the whole process of education, the national attitude towards responsible behaviour and to people in general.

Whilst laudable it is a pity that the International Fair Play Committee, centred in Paris, finds it necessary to make awards annually for deeds of fair play in sport—when decency, thought for others, and action to help should be part of normal behaviour and living.

INEQUALITY

There are many dangers for the Olympic Movement. All of them stem from greed or deprivation.

There are dreadful inequalities in the Movement; the "have" and "have not" countries. There are more countries (178) in the Olympic family than there are in the United Nations, yet representatives of about 40 countries achieve one of the first three places in Olympic Games Finals in the Summer Games. Winter Games are games of exclusion and this must be rectified. When will Africa be in a financial position to hold an Olympic celebration?

Olympic Solidarity does a splendid service but even through its coaching schemes, other aids, and its publications cannot hope to raise competitive standards to be comparable to some other nations.

And yet these and other inequalities do not stop nations from competing in Olympic Games. This is proof that medal-winning is not the prime reason for representation at an Olympic celebration, and that the Games are still contests between individuals and not nations.

Millions have tried, trained, sacrificed, and progressed with worthy aims and ambitions of being chosen for a team—at whatever level—all with the hope of eventually achieving national recognition and choice for a nation's Olympic contingent.

The honour, the opportunity, the chance to meet others who have striven just as hard; the identification of different cultures, different languages, different attitudes and standards and the chance to be part, to take part, to compete in an Olympic Festival, all these things are worth the sweat, strain, deprivation, effort, exhaustion, the years of devotion just to "be there".

There will always be inequalities—the genus MAN was not born equal. The Olympic Games are great levellers, attempting, at one time, in one place, to have people on that same level under similar rules. There is much to do to bring greater equality to eager, striving nations and their peoples; and to involve more people in the pursuit of excellence with reasonable hope of success.

ETHICS AND ERGOGENIC AIDS TO PERFORMANCE

The fundamental objective of games and sports has always been to win—to be superior, to score, gain more points than another, to jump or to throw farther, to leap or vault higher, to hit longer with force, to run faster and, finally to be victorious over oneself, or an opponent, and to strive to beat an existing standard or record. All these objectives through the way they are achieved are concerned with ethics.

We realize that ethics involves the study of ideal human character, actions and ends. When applied to a particular controversial situation the queried behaviour is either right or wrong, ethical or unethical, moral or immoral and the decision may lie entirely upon an individual's interpretation and judgement and have nothing to do with established regulations and rules.

It may be a criminal act to smash someone down to the sidewalk but perfectly acceptable to do the same sort of thing in a boxing ring, because that kind of action is accepted by the performers, judges, referees, spectators, and appears to be within the rules. But there are certain actions which are blatantly against the rules. Athletes have always looked for the "magic potion", anything which will help one to be bigger, stronger, faster, have more endurance, and greater capacity for work.

Performers have rationalised the use of an "aid" into two categories:

1. *The direct influence*—advantageously—of the *physiological* capacity, of one, or more of the body's systems which will contribute to greater performance.
2. *The indirect influence*—the "aid" should remove psychological restraint thus enabling the physiological capacity to be extended.

It is the search to find and to use the substance which will exert both psychological and physiological effects which drives some athletes and their advisors to find this "magic portion".

THE USE OF DRUGS—SOME INSTANCES

Plato revealed that in the Pankration and in boxing, athletes used opium. The Vikings used certain mushrooms to enable them to ward off fatigue. Dutch swimmers in 1865 were known to use "certain substances" to increase endurance. Cyclists have been know to use both ether and caffeine; in the 1960 Rome Olympic Games two Danish cyclists died as the result of taking a patent vasodilator; in 1968, a French basketball player died having taken an overdoes of amphetamines at the Tokyo Olympics. Four weight-lifters from Canada were sent home from Seoul having been tested positive for having taken anabolic steroids, two other weight-lifters on the 1988 Olympic team were left in Canada because they had been tested positive for anabolic steroid use. The greatest modern disgrace is that of Ben Johnson of Canada and those who advised and administered to him. He cheated, knowingly, then and more recently in the hopes of winning a gold medal—but even more, to bring the adulation, fame, renown, visibility, acclaim, the prestige and money—through cheating.

TRUST AND INFLUENCE

When a young person enters the sphere of athletic endeavour, ideas, earlier and easier absorbed, are strengthened. "Honey gives quick energy", "use of wheat germ oil"; then later again the training room is loaded with Ginseng, Vitamin C tablets, dextrose tablets.

Attitudes are being formed, success is hung out like a carrot on a stick to a donkey. The coach, who administers "harmless" aspirin tablets, salt tablets, sugar energy tablets to young athletes may be eliciting the placebo effect. This may not be doping but it may affect young athletes' attitude and subsequent behaviour.

THE ATHLETIC HERO

It is important that the term "hero" be put into perspective again. Heroes today are often not the same kind of heroes as those of twenty years ago. Then, usually a hero was admired for worthy deeds. Naturally this may still be so in some quarters, but today's hero seems different because the attitude to winning seems different also.

Fans, coaches, administrators, players, their parents often believe nothing could ever be more important than winning (or more disgraceful than losing) and that cheating, in victory's cause was therefore commendable.

In more naive times adulation by small boys and girls was earned by worthy sports-men and sports-women and the example they set. What has changed? Is it that youngsters have been looked after, all the way from junior school if they have shown potential as skilled athletes, that they have never been pressed to work academically or to work things out for themselves? In the early days of playground and high school leagues one of the key issues was moral obligation; children made the rules and abided by them. Later, one indulged in sports with principles inherent in the way the activity was conducted or played. Now it appears that what seems to be taught is performance.

Are human athletic-machines being produced without a moral sense that might prevent sniffing cocaine, taking performance-enhancing substances, i.e. drugs, to complement the thirst for victory?

EDUCATION

What are the answers to unethical behaviour and practice? Education? But what is education? It is not only knowing, but understanding and applying. The criterion inherent in education being that something worthwhile should be achieved in an acceptable manner.

Education allows and encourages innovation and creativity based upon knowledge and understanding. What is the solution to the use of dope in athletic activities?

Popeye's spinach, energy-loaded cereal, power candy bars, superman sneakers, multi-vitamins? All these give eager young television watchers suggested ways of being better, more energetic, more attractive and capable, in a very short period of time, of being strong, big, tough and aggressive.

Education should begin at home and continue through school years and beyond.

Knowledge and wise attitudes about moral values and the dangers of drug-taking may help to make people aware of the devastating mental, emotional, psychological, physiological, social and health hazards brought about by taking of drugs—even though they are taken for a short time.

TWO EDICTS CONCERNING DOPING

In January 1963, the Council of Europe, at a special meeting of medical experts in Strasbourg defined doping:

> Doping is defined as the administering or use of substances in any form alien to the body or of physiological substances in abnormal amounts and with abnormal methods of healthy persons with the exclusive aim of attaining an artificial and unfair increase of performance in competition. Furthermore, various psychological measures to increase performance in sports must be regarded as doping.[1]

The subsequent meeting of the Committee, in November 1963, held in Madrid passed an amendment:

> where treatment with medicine must be undergone which as a result of its nature or dosage is capable of raising physical capability above the normal level, such treatment must be considered as doping and shall rule out eligibility of competition.

Also attached to this latter amendment is a list of drugs regarded as doping substances, including certain hormones, respiratory aids, narcotics, amine stimulants, and such alkaloids as strychnine and ephedrine and *all* analeptic agents.

The first routine tests were made at the Grenoble Games and the Mexico Games of 1968. Over 1,000 tests were conducted. In 1956, a hundred substances were identified,[2] then two hundred substances were banned in 1963.

In 1984, 700 drugs were listed which were considered to be ergogenic aids. Today there are more than one thousand banned drugs.

ERGOGENIC AIDS

To give *one* example of the concerns about the future of the Olympic Games, it is vital to consider the ethical and health uses of the therapeutic Anabolic Steroids.

The Greek word *Anabole* means a heaping up and the term *Anabolism,* in biology, means constructive metabolism. *Metabolism* literally means "change" and refers to all the chemical and energy transformations which occur in the body. The word "ergogenic" refers to the tendency to increase work ability. Androgens are the hormones that exert masculinizing effects, they promote protein anabolism and growth. Androgens increase the synthesis, and decrease the breakdown of protein leading to an increase in the rate of growth. They also cause the epiphyses to fuse in the long bones, thus, eventually stopping growth. Secondary to their anabolic effect, androgens cause moderate sodium, potassium, calcium, sulphate, phosphate and water retention. They also increase kidney size. Testosterone from the testes is the most active androgen and doses of exogenous testosterone (which exert significant anabolic effect) are also masculinizing and increase libido.

All androgens are steroids and can be synthesized from cholesterol and acetyl coenzyme A, but testosterone is secreted in such quantities that it is regarded as the primary androgen responsible for the male characteristic effects. Testosterone exerts a number of physiological influences; one is to increase protein synthesis primarily in skeletal muscles, thus testosterone may be used to increase body size, through the greater capacity the protein synthesis gives for hard work.

In the male, increased agitation and aggression are noted; there is a tendency to have high blood pressure, become impotent and the testes shrivel.Some of these afflictions are irreversible. In the adult female, androgenic changes give heavy arms and body hair and an enlarged clitoris; the voice is also deepened.

The rationale against drug-taking revolves about two issues:

1. sports ethics;
2. medical reasons, these are the pharmacotoxic dangers of taking certain drugs.

From a neuro-psychiatric point of view overdoses of anabolic steroids act upon the nervous system and the psychotoxic effects are identified in habit formation. The use of drugs to improve athletic performance is unethical in the extreme, is morally wrong, physically dangerous, socially degenerate, legally indefensible and an expression of an inferiority complex. It has become a social disaster. yet, many athletes take drugs. Is the taking of ergogenic aids an indication of a refusal to live within one's own natural limits? Does it represent a refusal to be individually responsible for one's own success, or failure?

The paradox arises from the fact that many medical authorities have concluded that no pharmacologic preparation can enhance human athletic performance. It has been shown that the performance of first-class athletes was improved significantly after taking placebos (inert substances) provided that the athletes concerned believed them to be effective drugs. On the other hand, the administration of a potent compound gave no positive results when the athletes believed they were being given placebos.

Athletes are always looking for the "secret for success". Anything which will help one to be bigger, stronger, faster, to have more endurance and to possess the capacity to work. Performers have often rationalized the use of an "aid" from Alcohol to Zygote into two categories:

1. advantageously, the direct influence of the physiological capacity of one or more of the body's systems which will contribute to performance, OR
2. the capacity of the "aid" to remove psychological restraint, thus enabling the physiological capacity to be protracted.

It is this search for the substance which will give advantage through both psychological and physiological effects that drives athletes to try to find the "magic potion". So it is often that they turn to the chemical compounds of anabolic steroids, which are similar to testosterone, to aid in the building of muscular tissue through nitrogen retention and hard physical work.

COMPETITION

Competition is such that the merest fraction of a centimetre, a minute error of judgement, or a momentary mental lapse, are enough to destroy the amount of immortality, that crowning of years of sacrifice through work and devotion to a cause—the fulfilment of the Olympic dream. What can an athlete do to ensure success? What is success? What is the purpose of competition?

Is it to achieve personal excellence, to take part, to have fun, to provide maximum participation for the great majority of people at all levels and ages, or is it simply to win? The analyst must be prepared to probe deeply into those elements which make up these different attitudes. There may not be a solution but analysis will lead to reflective thought by others.

SUMMARY

Is Olympism worthwhile? Do the ethics inherent within Olympism stand a hope of success in open competition? Has the cheating for monetary advantage and personal prestige overpowered the efforts of the many, the striving, training, and devotion given to normal progress and honest success for its own sake? Have the use of drugs destroyed the essence of the Olympic Games? Remembering, of course, that the taking of drugs is only one of the social evils which afflict the Movement.

QUESTIONS TO ASK ONESELF

a. Is it essential to be first—is it necessary always to win?

b. Is there value and worth in being a good loser?

c. Drugs - who takes them?
       - who gives them?

d. Is that which happened at the IXth Pan American Games a scandal and a warning? Is what happened in the XXIV and XXVth Summer Olympic Games the pattern for the future concerning drug abuse?

e. If it is known that one's team-mates or one's opponents take ergogenic aids to improve performance, should I take them?

f. Is it fair if one knows that one is to compete against those who take anabolic-androgenic steroids?

g. Does drug-taking aid in masking injury?

h. When one has finished with competition, should one continue to take drugs?

i. Are drugs addictive?

j. Concerning marriage, social obligations for female and male athletes. Have drugs after-effects?

k. Politics, anabolic steroids, patriotism, T.V. coverage, terrorist activities, publicity, violence, excellence, fame, "No. 1" . . . and the future of the Olympic Games. How is each of these affected by taking ergogenic aids?

l. Some "aids" are soda loading, blood doping, Benzedrine, tranquilizers, Stanozolol (Winstrol), Dianabol or Orabolin, testosterone, alcohol, caffeine, amphetamines. In 1972 there were more than 600 androgenic and anabolic agents banned by the International Olympic Medical Commission—how many drugs are banned now?

m. Is it worth it? How does one feel about all this ethically?

n. Is there anything to be done to stop the rot in physical activities, particularly in the Olympic Games?

REFERENCES

1. *Doping.* Published by Medical Commission of the International Olympic Committee, Lausanne, 1972, p. 33.

2. John T. Powell, "Theoretical Implications of Tranquilizers and Energizers", VIGOR, Sept. 1965, p. 39–53.

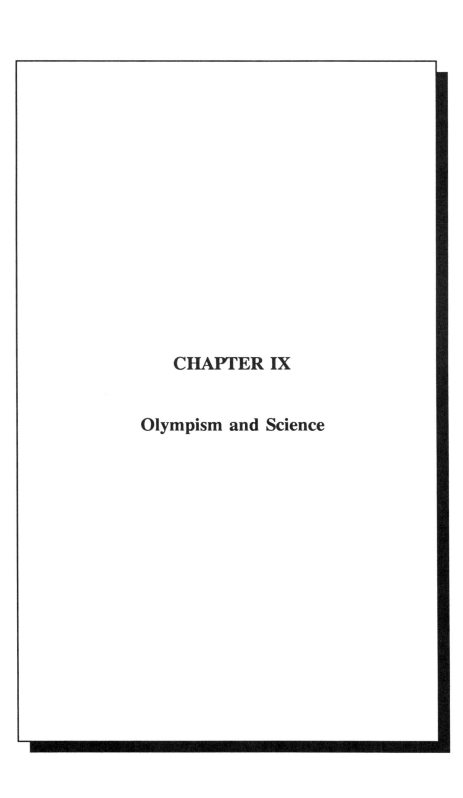

CHAPTER IX

Olympism and Science

CHAPTER IX
Olympism and Science

No intelligent man will ever be so bold as to put into language those things which his reason has contemplated, especially not into a form that is unalterable . . . which must be the case with what is expressed in written symbols.

(Plato)

INTRODUCTION

Olympism is a philosophy, it is one's attitude adopted toward Olympic involvement and participation and it is the intellectual approach, rather than the applied approach, to the study of the Olympic Movement. Furthermore, Olympism is a subjective assessment of the ideals which allow the Olympic concepts to be understood and to be spread. It is both a theory and a doctrine; because Olympism being a philosophical enquiry as well as an attitude, it is also true to say that science has influenced it and may have even reduced its scope because it is often thought that Olympism is not realistic enough to cope with modern scientific trends and attitudes.

SCIENCE AND ART

Science may be identified as:

The knowledge of facts and laws arranged in an orderly system. There are natural sciences, social and applied sciences. Science is also the pursuit of knowledge, or truth for its own sake.[1]

Art is any form of human activity that is the product of, and which appeals primarily to, the imagination.

THE ACADEMY AND ITS WORK

Much criticism has been levelled at the International Olympic Academy because, over the years, lecturers have presented theoretical concepts and have not always presented facts. What has been completely consistent is that the workings of the Academy, its expressed aim and its administration have been direct and never divergent. The Academy has been a free forum for ideas from different cultures, backgrounds and tongues allowing for the better understanding of the ideals of the Olympic Movement, and in particular, the study of Olympism.

Gradually applied science, and its impact upon the thought and action of human physical and mental performance, has come to be discussed in Ancient Olympia because scientific knowledge has become the launching pad for philosophical analysis. Philosophers are analytical and critical of the assumptions and concepts of others. The analyst's intent is to clarify, elucidate and explain the thoughts of scientists, so it is at Olympia that historians, philosophers and scientists tolerantly express ideas and mix freely. The Olympic Movement has room for all—provided each is a contributor.

HISTORY

History is an important determinant for philosophic thought, either directly or indirectly; however, the contemporary scene also offers much more opportunity for scientific analysis and expression. Olympism can learn much from its past and from its modern presentation and, at the same time, Olympism must be constantly vigilant, alert, and remain aware of modern changes in attitude which will affect understanding of its idealism.

True Olympism is realistic, it is the force of conscience as well as the approved way in which all matters Olympic are to be operated. Olympism is the process through which competition is to be conducted and contested, its essence lies in fair play, for fair play allows things to happen; it is thus, neither restricted nor restrictive because it proceeds within the established rules of Olympic conduct.

SOME QUESTIONS FOR SCIENCE

It is suggested that Olympic competition is a laboratory for democratic living and it is here that Science and Olympism become one. But what has science done to deter MAN from using scientific findings and methods for unfair advantage? Science should not only be the watch-dog of actual human conduct but, by its precise nature should establish, for itself, ethical practices and behaviour. The process of scientific investigation is such that truth is sought through exact and precise replicable procedures, recording and observation.

Science has been used to create equipment and machines from anemometers to ergometers, from electrical timing devices on track, in pool, on fencing strip to long-jump measurement by electronic ray, and through computers, and the whole range of communication technology, to record and reveal accurate and instantaneous results of just-seen performance. Science and its applications, have revolutionized the participation in, and the observation of, the Olympic Festivals of Winter and Summer. Even though science, and its application, has changed almost every aspect of Olympic participation, from travel to the most minute measuring aid, there are still two most important areas to which scientific endeavour should be applied:

1. the judging of subjectively assessed events;
2. the control of the use of substances concocted by science.

SUBJECTIVELY ASSESSED EVENTS

It is time for science to come to the aid of judging in the arts of diving, boxing, gymnastics, ice skating, synchronised swimming and rhythmic gymnastics. A questions which must be asked is "what is perfect?". Is a "6" in ice dancing "perfect", a "10" in gymnastics "perfect"? What is perfect? Is any performance "perfect", even though one may not have seen every performance? Is any performance "perfect" only in context to the present? Was the performance of Jane Torvill and Christopher Dean, with its judged "perfect" scores perfect, and will that "perfect" be good enough for another year and will their performance of the recent past now become the base for all other "perfect" scores? The performance was beautiful to see, it had vigour, flow, colour, interpretation, power and peace, symmetry, harmony, order and proportion. The performers displayed their joy and satisfaction, the judges their awe and appreciation, awarding 13 perfect marks. Are all these enough? Will science's intrusion into the aesthetic appreciate or destroy what is considered to be "good enough", or, to be absolutely fair, must there be absolute facts that cannot be confuted?

It is salutary to remember that after the 1948 Summer Olympic celebration the international competition for medals and diplomas in the various arts depicting sport, was cancelled because it was adjudged too difficult to judge what was best amongst excellence. Will science be able to preserve the aesthetic potential of viewing and doing by reducing every detail of performance to fact? If so, will physical expression become sterile? Or will unpredictable and irascible MAN preserve proportion? Is it possible for performance to be judged without relation to the physical environment, climate and altitude, pageantry, flags, music, partisanship, person preference and bias, state of health of the judge and the personality of the performers? *Anything* pertaining to the unpredictable human is difficult to judge.

Only when those scientific instruments which eliminate the human factor are used is there an ability to equalise measurement. Even though times are taken, distances measured and each athlete comes under almost similar conditions, the other circumstances of physique, training and coaching opportunities, cultural and religious influences and observance, nutrition, the "luck of the draw", sudden illness, a broken skate, are amongst the innumerable other factors which cannot be controlled. That is why rules are established, conditions are regulated and standards are set to equalise circumstances, as far as possible.

Some Ideas:

What are these ways in which scientific knowledge can either replace or assist subjective judgment

1. In diving events there could be a squared screen placed opposite the judges and around the diving platform; this screen would also be shown on each judge's computer. As each dive is performed so it is photographed and reproduced on the judge's computer screen from the angle at which the judge has seen the dive. Then, superimposed over the grid would be shown the "ideal" dive, *exactly* depicted. The judges could then compare the ideal to the actual and, also having seen the performance prior to its reproduction on the computer screen, would be enabled to assess the dive more objectively. This system could also be applied to each of the events in gymnastics.

2. In ice skating a computerised model of each recognised move could be established against which the seen and executed "trick" could be gauged, irrespective of the order in which it was done, as the performance proceeds. The continuity, expression, mood, atmosphere and interpretation would all be identified by the judges as the various phases proceed. This would be particularly useful in the set compulsory short programme where all pairs complete the same moves in a stipulated time. Video pictures of the execution could be shown over the *perfect* model to which all judges would refer.

3. A device to measure the splash magnitude for water entry in tower and springboard diving events would also help in assessing verticality. This could also be used to advantage in aiding marking in the complete viewing of team synchronised swimming as well.

4. Is it not time that the target in boxing be electronically wired so that direct blows on the target can be recorded? Fencing contests, in two weapons, have electronic scoring yet still under surveillance of a Chief Judge(President).

Still the question remains, does one wish to eliminate "artistic merit"; if so, what are the criteria for doing so? If the spontaneity of performance, its flair and vitality are considered integral of its composition then perhaps applied science's aids will help referees and judges who will be enabled to give more attention to the spirit and over-all impression than to recordable and measurable technical skills. Applied science will thus aid in assessment.

ETHICS AND SCIENCE

Many athletes are prepared to sacrifice the future for the present moment's satisfaction. To achieve, over all others seems to be worth the risk of ostracism, censure and ignominy. It is here that the work of the International Olympic Academy comes sharply into focus as the world centre for the academic approach to the study of Olympism. The intellectual endeavour which is spent by lecturers and delegates to instil the ethics of the Olympic Movement into the youth of the Olympic fraternity and sorority is essential to the understanding of the balance, so necessary when even discussing about, or performing in, any aspect of an Olympic Festival.

What is ethics? The study of morality and moral principles; but what is a moral principal? It is a settled rule of action towards what is right or wrong in conduct, by which a person's life is guided. What have all, or any of the sciences, done to firm and confirm these principles and deter MAN from using scientific advances and findings to gain advantage outside the accepted rules of ethical behaviour?

Sperm banks are established and Nobel Prize winners have been asked to contribute to create and maintain genetic lines of superior intelligence. Will this method be used to selectively choose physical structures, speed genes, strength, mobility, size, balance, height and endurance factors in order to establish specific qualities demanded in certain sports? This experiment has been attempted. Hitler's obsession to create "ein volk" of blue-eyed, blond(e) Aryan youth was thwarted. Is the importance of winning so utterly dominant that such measures will be resorted to, to create species so superior that the title of Olympic Victor will be supreme?

The use of scientific method to assess and predict at an early age; the constant testing of athletes to determine adequacies and inadequacies, have already changed, for many, the purpose of sport. Will these and other scientific uses lead to the creation of a few super gladiators who will compete for the rest—the spectators? Science has been used to improve all types of performing surfaces, has controlled temperature and pressure, created aerodynamic javelins, weight-graduated pole-vaulting poles and myriad other features. Is it too much of a stretch of the imagination to conceive that Olympic superiority will demand and accept genetic tampering with the human entity? As each Olympiad passes, technical advances and advantages often enable vast numbers of athletes to surpass standards set only four years previously. Herein lies a warning.

CONCLUSION

Is that which happened at the IXth Pan-American Games[2] a scandal and a warning? Is what happened at the 1988 Summer Olympic Games, concerning doping, an indication of the future? How many or how few athletes will be eliminated from Olympic competition because they have been identified as having taken drugs? In the International Olympic Commission's booklet[3], it is stated that the responsibility of the Medical Commission is to assume the moral responsibility for the different kinds of controls. Any athlete who refuses to undergo doping control or who is found guilty of doping will be eliminated from the Games, and yet athletes use drugs to increase the potential for winning. Is competing never enough, is it essential to win, not matter the cost in status or health? Would these controls be necessary were the principles of the Olympic Movement[4] to be abided by and the concept of Olympism to become a living force? Is science responsible for creating drugs and for creating such ethical dilemmas as are caused by their use? Is science to be held accountable and responsible for the correction of drug abuses?

Because Olympism is an attitude and that attitude carries weight, importance, meaning and strength, it should influence behaviour. Can Olympism influence science just as science has influenced Olympism and can scientific discovery be moderated by MAN's rationality, for the benefit of the Olympic Movement?

These are questions for National Olympic Committees and their National Academies to set, for delegates to ponder, answer and act upon.

REFERENCES

1. *Canadian Senior Dictionary* - Gage Publishing Ltd., Toronto, 1979.

2. *Caracas: A Scandal and a Warning,* Sports Illustrated. August 26, 1983, pp. 18–23.

3. *Doping,* Published by the Medical Commission of the International Olympic Committee, Lausanne, 1972, p. 64.

4. *Olympic Charter*. Lausanne, Switzerland, 1992, p. 6.

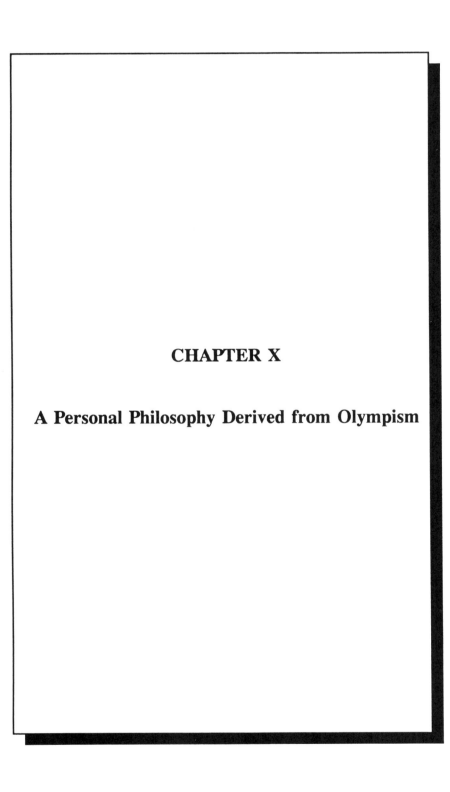

CHAPTER X

A Personal Philosophy Derived from Olympism

BLAST!

You invited me here I'm happy to say
And I'll thank you in this rather unusual way.
We can't adequately reflect the joy we feel
Because we're always on this whirling wheel
That nature rides upon, spinning us from hopes,
Moments just begun, when thoughts, feelings,
Wishes ideas began to run, or started to
Flow into another receptive ear or eager
Mind—then he or she, who hears is gone;
And that wonderful surge is left behind,
And that happy moment has just flown.

Here we're all of one like mind.
Some have come for fun, some far, some near,
But in every case some sacrifice was made.
"Will it be worth it?" "Will we see, meet or make
Friends or deepen friendships once again?"
"Will the speakers' talks be trite?" "Or will
My friend again, be 'tight' tonight?"

We never know—we hope, we make the effort
(And on occasion we steal the hotel soap),
We dress as well we can to attract and hold
The lasting moment that means to much.
And sometimes even that puts us back upon our butts.

Take time. *MAN*'s enemy is time, use it well.
Let it not use you, for fruitful moments
Of watch-time are too few.
A lecture here, a coffee there, a vital question
Never asked, another never answered well—
Time, you see, is taking its toll—ah well!

J.T.P.

CHAPTER X
A Personal Philosophy Derived from Olympism

"The virtue of each thing whether body or mind, instrument or creature when given to them in the best way comes to them not by chance but as the result of the order and truth and art which are imparted to them."

Plato—Gorgias

INTRODUCTION

To be effective in the Olympic Movement one must understand the objectives of Olympism—some consider them too idealistic to be workable in this strife-torn political world in which we live. However, it is of no use having an aim and objectives if they are not realisable; those of us concerned should create a nucleus of intellectual energy and influence to keep Olympism working.

Gone are the days of pure theory. The Modern era of Olympiads is upon us and soon we will enter the XXVIth in Atlanta. Our modern experience is enough, but our influence has been too ineffective to keep pace with nationalistic aims of victory at any cost, blatant commercialisation, the unethical and demeaning use of drugs, the selection and isolation of infant athletic prodigies solely for the hopes of achieving a gold-plated medal and even worse, the eventual sacrifice of youth on the altar of a debatable "religion" of that which is called "sport". The essence of this disgrace is that often very young humans are being exploited for a given time and then cast off. Then what happens, how do they fit into society, how will they adjust to ordinary life, for what have they been prepared, what of their hopes, ambitions and aspirations?

On the other hand, there are many people who, because of reaction to what they identify as excess, seemingly necessary for athletic prowess, seek to eliminate all competitive aspects. Is not one excess as bad as the other? The classical example of a purely theoretical conception of philosophy is provided by Aristotle (Metaphysics, Book I, Chapter 2, Renford Bambrough edition, New American Press, 1963, p. 44) who talks of philosophy as being studied for its own sake. "So, if it were to escape ignorance that MAN engaged in philosophy, plainly they were pursuing science for the sake of knowledge, and not for any practical purpose" and:

Plainly, then, we do not study it for any use beyond itself: rather, just as a free MAN is one who exists for HIS own sake and not for anyone else's, so we study this science as the only one that is free, since it is the only one that is studied for its own sake.

In contradiction one notes the activistic philosophy exhibited when one system, by careful selection of a few individuals, trains and rears them to the exclusion of the thousands of others who, by natural maturation, education, encouragement and competition, might have enjoyed a full and active life. That system defies Olympism.

However, excellence is a worthy aim and should be a part of every life. Olympism's essence lies in the opportunity to excel; not at the expense of others but as a fulfilment for the majority which will bring to the top the very best in man, woman, boys and girls.

True sport is worthy and through it lasting benefits, physical, mental and social can accrue, lasting friendships are made, tensions released and pleasure takes the place of mistrust and unhappiness.

ANCIENT GREEK THOUGHT

Is it too much to expect, in this modern age, to take our example from the ancient Greeks where the conscious predominance of their Games lay in the elements of poetry and art? The Greek, an artist by nature, elevated the strenuousness of sports with an air of fine sentiment, touched them with poetry, legend, and grace of art and song. The most brutal of Greek contests even imparted an atmosphere of beauty through such works as were expressed by the lyric poets Bacchylides, Simonides and Pindar. Yet, artistic contests have now been eliminated from Modern Olympic Festivals.

We know the Greek educational ideal lay in the attainment and maintenance of balance. A favourite watchword with the Greeks was "mean" of "middle", the exact point of rightness between extremes. "Nothing in excess" was a motto inscribed over an arch in Apollo's Delphic inner temple—nothing could be more characteristic of the ideal of these adherents of proportion. The "mean" is that which adapts itself, in due proportion, to the requirements and circumstances in every case; thus Aristotle, whilst blaming a man who is unduly passionate, blames equally one who is insensitive; the aim being to be angry ". . . on the proper occasion and with the proper people in the proper manner and for the proper length of time".[1] Aristotle gives a subtle and shifting problem the solution of which must be worked out by each individual in each particular case. To him conduct is free and living, not a machine controlled by fixed laws. Every life is a work of art shaped by the one who lives it. There is neither good nor bad, the elements which comprise human nature are but raw materials from which one is shaped. In another form, this was the basis of the philosophy of Plato who regarded virtue as a kind of "order".

THE THOUGHT OF BARON FRÉDI PIERRE DE COUBERTIN

Coubertin had an artistic and aesthetic nature. He based his concepts of the revival of the Olympic Games upon the Greek ideals learned from his classical education, upon the spirit and attitude observed in English sport and its wide application in the United States of America. He talked of freedom, equality of opportunity and social peace, "Il faut au sport la libertée; il faut le respect des individualities."[2] He wished to reach the masses and make the Games available to all. He was an educator non pareil, a visionary and a fighter for what he deemed to be right, most of all he was an example to be followed.

THE THOUGHT OF AVERY BRUNDAGE

For twenty years from 1952 this man, born in 1887, guided the destinies of the Olympic Movement. He kept proportion; although not articulate, some of his pronouncements are profound in their simplicity and purpose. He said what he thought and he meant what he said.

In his very first speech made in Lausanne when taking over the Olympic reins from Sigfrid Edstrom he stated:

> We must be careful and keep our proper balance remembering that we are concerned only with sport and not with politics business. At the same time, we must prevent others from exploiting or using our prestige for their own personal purpose. Our sole strength is our independence and our high ideals. We have no money and we have no army. To protect ourselves against those who wish to take advantage, we must keep our motives pure and honest, and clean and we will retain the respect of all.[3]

In his presentation made at the 48th Session of the I.O.C. on 17th April 1953 in Mexico he gave, clearly, the purpose of the Modern Olympic Movement:

> The Baron de Coubertin would be proud indeed if he could view what can be seen here in Mexico . . . almost every square metre of available space was found occupied, with thousands of boys and girls engaged in a dozen different kinds of sport . . . many think the Olympic Movement is concerned only with a few champions in each country. They forget that for one who makes an Olympic team, thousands, try, and in so doing not

only gain the physical benefits of participation but also learn the Olympic principles of fair play and good sportsmanship.[4]

At the 49th Session on 10th May 1954 in Athens he expressed his understanding of Olympism's philosophic origins:

> Of course, de Coubertin's idea was a most virile and dynamic one with its roots extending back two thousand five hundred years, to the days when the foundations of modern civilization were being laid in ancient Hellas . . . it is only because we have strayed widely from the wise teachings of the gifted Greek philosophers that we are in trouble today.[5]

In the same speech he talked of the Olympic Games saying:

> One must be amazed that such an idealistic enterprise has grown and prospered in the commercial atmosphere which prevails today. It is a testimonial to the innate good in man and to this desire for a world ruled by honesty, fairness and good sportsmanship, a world where all have an equal opportunity, a world where victory depends on ability and hard work, on personal skill and efficiency, and where the reward is based on merit.[6]

THE OLYMPIC CHARTER

In all versions of the Charter prior to 1991, there was no mention, or definition, of "Olympism", but in its fundamental principles it was abundantly clear what the aims of the Olympic Movement are, and it is these statements which give those who work for the good of the Olympic Movement a mandate authorizing aid to encourage and firmly establish ways in which they can influence the establishing of sound philosophic bases for youth and its understanding of, and implementation of, Olympism.

The aims of the Olympic Movement are:

- to promote the development of those physical and moral qualities which are the basis of sport;
- to educate young people though sport in a spirit of better understanding between each other and of friendship, thereby helping to build a better and more peaceful world;
- to spread the Olympic principles throughout the world thereby creating international goodwill;
- to bring together the athletes of the world in a great four-yearly festival of sport.

OLYMPIC SOLIDARITY

Many programs have been initiated to spread the Olympic ideals in a practical way in the five emblematic areas of the Olympic Rings. Reading *Olympic Review* gives a clear picture of much that is being done through Olympic Solidarity in the realms of sports, administration, by financial aid to enable delegates to attend sessions of the International Olympic Academy, technical assistance, sports medicine and in the conducting of sports courses, particularly in areas where expertise is not readily available. Olympic solidarity shows and helps many areas which could, and can be, of service.

WHAT CAN BE DONE?

It is only by example that youth can be influenced through sound, qualified help and demonstrated efficiency. These matters come about by belief—one has to believe in the concept of Olympism to be effective. If each of us does not have a personal philosophy of life, it is difficult to influence others to have a purpose and a realisable dream. Each in his or her own way can strive to be the best, but that is not the only way. Each can, however, influence another for his or her own good. There is such a tradition to draw upon. The whole concept of both Ancient and Modern Games is in our favour, but more than that, the continual effort of those, known and unknown, who have presented worthy ideals gives strength and courage to our efforts.

To build a personal philosophy, one has to have influence. Educators, specialists in medicine, administration, physical activity, participant or coach, parent or intelligent observer, have, by attitude, enthusiasm and encouragement the moulding and fashioning of the future. By abiding, and by seeing that others adhere through rules and regulations, a stability and a surety are formed. Faith, trust, reliability are the cornerstones upon which others will build when these qualities are identified. For it is you, the reader, who matter, you are destined to be leaders of society. You and your actions determine how people think, how they move and react. By your educational standards and the quality of your thought, you will be identified, sought out and followed.

WHERE DOES ONE REQUEST AID?

There are practical problems of nutrition, deprivation, injury, lack of opportunity and facilities, terrain, geographical location, certain religious and social factors of which all are aware in one's own and other countries which inhibit full opportunity for every child to take part in full, free, vigorous activity every day. But this is a worthy aim (not only an ideal), but, in many areas completely realisable and which should be a birthright for all.

To aid in this simple action, co-operation of, and at, the highest echelons of national influence is needed. National Olympic Committees must be the organisations through which help is sought. There are educational authorities, and their influence must be prosecuted so that others might benefit.

PHILOSOPHICAL CONSIDERATIONS

Philosophical enquiry provides understanding by considering the nature of the information already possessed, what it amounts to or what it means. In order to understand the character of philosophy one should realise that there is a difference between doing something and describing it. In order to be effective in creating situations and attitudes, our own philosophic approach must result in action.

Philosophy is an active endeavour rather than a body of knowledge which has to be acquired. One cannot learn to swim by listening to lectures about it. So one cannot learn to philosophise by hearing or simply reading what the great philosophers had and have to say. In each case it is necessary to have excellent guidance, but in neither case can one succeed without active participation.

Philosophy must be regarded as the development of critical, rigorous, independent thinking—this needs practice, which further enhances the point that to develop a personal philosophy in accordance with the humanistic principles of Olympism, one must have expert leadership and example. Furthermore, one has to be given the opportunity to think, and, through quality of thought, concepts are developed which enable one to act.

Where is there a better place for contemplation, discourse and action, than in the academic setting of the International Olympic Academy or in one's own National Olympic Academy?

Philosophy therefore must be deliberate and aid in clarification of the causes of social strife, ideas and ideals. Philosophy is not a special way to something which does not comprehend suffering, enjoyment, knowledge, beliefs or action; it is a criticism, a critical analysis of familiar things; yet philosophy attempts to carry things further, pursue them methodically, to introduce clarity and order. The chief role of philosophy is to make paths straight, unblock the roads of thought and open the avenues that lead to the future. Philosophy has still much work to do by turning its considered thought to why MAN is often alienated from MAN and how it will give intellectual direction to international society to make our world one; in fact, one of significance and worth.

THE DEVELOPMENT OF A PERSONAL PHILOSOPHY

The development of a personal philosophy is never by imposition. Attitudes and ways of behaving, so necessary to the continuous and progressive life of a society, cannot take place solely by direct conveyance of beliefs, emotions and knowledge, but only through the environment in which these factors can be expressed. Excellent teaching is essentially an expression of principles—yet one must know from what those principles come.

The whole attitude of a people is the outward and identifiable sign of a worthy pride and a way of dealing with all matters pertaining to living. A country is really the sum of its people. One tends to submit one's individuality to the State instead of acting with the belief that constitution, laws and administration can be the very means of furthering the ends of a society of free individuals. Through this it becomes our privilege and right to influence others, in the name of the non-political internationalism, which is Olympism.

Only if each one has a personal philosophy will it be realised that, inevitably, we are involved with the course of events. Philosophy is vision, reflection, imagination, considered thought and opinion yet these functions modify nothing and resolve nothing. Philosophy requires action and it is this action which must come from those bases of vision, reflection, imagination, considered thought and opinion. In this regard, because of its worthiness and because it has no signs, signals and symbols, it—through deeds, attitude and living of Olympism, in whichever circumstances one finds oneself, will shine through and may encourage others to follow. Because it has international prestige, the lead must come from the International Olympic Committee, through National Olympic Committees, International Federations, the International Olympic Academy and its siblings, National Olympic Academies.

This hierarchal way is progressive:

1. The I.O.C. can influence governments;
2. The N.O.C.s should apply the Olympic Movement's principles through education;
3. The International Federations will supply the techniques and training;
4. The International Academy is, and national Academies are, the institutes of learning, the places where principles are put into practice; of living the philosophy, by seeing, feeling, enjoying it—in action.

We need to create an Olympic world—consciousness, and for our individual philosophies to be devoted to the vibrant living struggle of our own Olympic age and time. Films, books, pamphlets, articles produced or published and/or games and contests conducted under the aegis of the International Olympic Committee and in the name of Olympism, must be the product of all. Were each of us to write one article (and have it published in paper or magazine), it would help firm our own philosophic position and further the humanistic aims of Olympism.

EDUCATION

Education is the key which unlocks doors. All education comes through an individual's social consciousness, the process begins at birth; initially it is almost unconscious yet it continually shapes abilities, eventually saturates consciousness, forms habits, arouses feelings and emotions, guides ideas, and fashions the way one will go. Education is the very process of living now—not for the future, it is a continuous process of personal belief and growth and, those who receive education, are those who give it. Leadership becomes education's privilege.

PRACTICAL MATTERS

1. Competition, at all levels for those incapacitated mentally and/or physically, as well as for those who are whole, should be an aim, should be fostered, encouraged and extended, particularly at the Olympic level.
2. History, both ancient and modern, concerning the mythological, actual and future aim and objectives of Olympic participation should be taught in schools. Olympism as an ethical concept should be included as should "fair play".

3. Olympic films, both historical and those giving specific techniques, should be introduced in school settings, FROM AN EARLY AGE.

4. Lectures given at the International Academy since 1961 should be widely used, reproduced and distributed by national Olympic Committees.

5. A film of the work of the International Olympic Committee ought to be made available and internationally distributed by the I.O.C. in various languages.

6. N.O.C.s should use national and international athletes, lecturers and teachers to spread the essence of Olympism at all levels of society.

7. Through the I.O.C. each N.O.C. should develop a package of films, slides, pamphlets, pictures, records, Olympic music, de Coubertin's and Dr. Carl Diem's works, to be available to each country for showing in schools, clubs and like organisations through the use of travelling I.O.C. vans.

8. Internationally an Olympic Day should be proclaimed in *every* country, thus the spirit of Olympism would then be experienced in a practical fashion by all nations simultaneously. This "Day" should also encompass on Olympic Run for all to enter or see.

9. Television and radio should be encouraged—and/or authorised—to show techniques of the various Olympic events, as well as the rules, regulations and conduct of international contests. In these ways, elements of competition would be learned early and in the best context. The whole Olympic Movement would benefit by media presenting Olympic principles, regularly.

10. The appointment of one young I.O.C. representative for each of the five continents to travel, talk and help at this official level with matters Olympic, to help N.O.C.s and represent them to I.O.C.

These are some of the ways in which a personal philosophy may be aided and firmed.

The greatest influence, however, will be example, the example of one who is known and admired, but preferably the example one sets oneself in all that one says, does and thinks in relation to Olympism to make this ideal of international amity a reality.

REFERENCES

1. *Aristotle, Ethics*, III, 14, 1119a. 11 (Weldon's translation).

2. Speech by Baron Pierre de Coubertin - Opening Meeting of the XVII Plenary Session of the I.O.C. Antwerp, Tuesday, 17th August, 1920 - published privately by the author, 1920.

3. *The Speeches of President Avery Brundage, 1952 to 1968,* published by the Comité Internationale Olympique, Lausanne, 1970, p. 7, p. 102.

4. *Ibid.* p. 9.

5. *Ibid.* p. 13.

6. *Ibid.* p. 14.

CHAPTER XI

Creating an Olympic World

TIME

Time is Man's enemy, Time's Man's friend,
    Time gives us time in which to mend
Or right the wrong wrought on a friend
    Long lost 'cause we took no time to bend.

Mentally stiff and staid are we
    For judgement is, so easily
Made by those of us in authority.

    We forget the kindness shown to us
Which gave us time to catch the bus
    That took us on our way to opportunity
It seems so long ago.

Time to reflect, for a given time.
    Then time takes us all
In its own good time.

J.T.P.

CHAPTER XI
Creating an Olympic World

Nothing in progression can rest on its original plan. We may as well think of rocking a grown man in the cradle.

Edmund Burke (1729–1797)

INTRODUCTION

This Chapter will be, probably, the most nebulous one of this book, not because it deals with the intangibles of belief, hope, wish and idealism, but because, in these troubled times for the whole Olympic Movement, it expresses the necessity to prosecute the Olympic Idea.

We are all sensitive to, and aware of, the forces, pro and con, concerning attendance at the Games which will herald the XXVIth Olympiad to be ushered in at Atlanta in 1996. Whilst each of us abhors oppression, dominance, deprivation of freedom, discrimination, invasion of privacy and the piratical acts of war and their aftermath, we also believe that MAN is not necessarily only the greatest killer but is, of all creatures, capable of showing the greatest love and compassion.

Aspects such as non-Olympian acts made in the name of Olympism have touched upon motivational roles necessary to be made by the International Olympic Committee and the national Olympic Committees, politics of the Movement itself, of reforms and recommendations.

OLYMPIC PRINCIPLES

Even from the time of ancient legend, there has been a willingness, even an eagerness to understand and associate with one, who in adversity has triumphed—within the rules. This is so today.

Those who are scientists through belief and training look with scepticism that Olympism—that strange word found in no dictionary—and the practice of the ideals it espouses, can be the new way to living adequately. There are those who believe, as fiercely, that olympism is worth saving, in fact that Olympism must be saved so that it may save the Olympic Movement.

I write about a nebulous "something"—how to create an Olympic life.

Perhaps the task is not as obscure, paradoxical, ambiguous, vague, or as unrealisable as it appears to be. Were it so, why are you reading? Perhaps you already believe that the Olympic Movement, its ideals and principles from which Olympism has risen, is worthwhile. Therefore, this theme will be listened to, although not necessarily agreed with.

Before conducting any study each of us has an hypothesis, a proposition assumed for the sake of argument, a theory to be proved of disproved by reference to facts and if one factor does not fit, then that aspect is rejected and another substituted; but if that part does not properly suit the whole, the hypothesis is changed.

My hypothesis is that the fundamental principles, as expressed in the aim of the Olympic Charter, are, if practised, adequate for each of us, individually or collectively, to build and to live an Olympic life:

The principles of the Olympic Movement are well known.

The threats to Olympism through the use of athletes as pawns on the chess board of the global game of international politics are also known, this has always been so. Not one celebration of the 21 observances of the Modern Summer Olympic Games has been unmarred by international incident—yet we are on the lip of hailing the advent of the XXVI Olympiad, that measure of time which wars and tribulation will not alter and which gives us the time to prepare educationally, morally and athletically for yet another festival of sport's expressions.

Because the International Olympic Committee can stand above government, does not have national delegates on its committees, is solely responsible for the Olympic flag, symbol, flame ceremony and motto, it can request members to conduct games and contests between individuals and not between countries. The International Olympic Committee is a body corporate by international law, has judicial and perpetual status. Its objectives are:

- to encourage the organisation and development of sport and sports competitions;
- to inspire and lead sport within the Olympic ideal, thereby promoting and strengthening friendship between the sportsmen and sportswomen of all countries;
- to ensure the regular celebration of the Olympic Games;
- to make the Olympic Games ever more worthy of their glorious history and the high ideals which inspired their revival by Baron Pierre de Coubertin and his associates.

Because youth and sports have become intertwined from the dim dawn of human history, Baron Frédi Pierre de Coubertin resolved that athletics and education should go hand in hand to encourage international amity and, because he was a visionary he saw that the human spirit could triumph over disaster, could forgive and forget provided there is an unseen world-force prepared to exert its influence, for good.

MAN, the destroyer, can also be the builder. There are millions of people who live the Olympic principles every day because they are soundly based upon acceptable concepts. Living an Olympic life only requires a willingness to do so, to abide by rules applied to others, as well as oneself.

If youth is believed in, and brought up to abide by, principles of fair play, honest endeavour and conscientious work then that is all one can do. For the future belongs to youth and youth is the hope of the world. Through its efforts it learns to manage, to take over, to apply, and this grows into a new culture.

The whole web which is Olympism as expressed by the Olympic Movement relies on the vigour of youth, its idealism and the example it has been set. The necessity to give the opportunity for expression of the subjective ideals, within the framework of Olympic endeavour, makes worthwhile the intangibles, the inexplicable within life, and allows principles to be put into practice. The Olympic Ideals are acceptable, but only if believed in, and can only become reality if each wishes them to be so. This must be accepted; it is known that there has been upset and political intrusion in every Olympic celebration.

A Few Examples:

1. The 5-day athletic celebration had become so crowded at the holding of the 77th Ancient Olympic Games that Kallias, the Athenian boxer protested that the chariot, two-horse race had so delayed the programme that the boxers were compelled to fight by moonlight.

2. For the *1st celebration of the Games* of the modern era, teams arrived too late because the Greeks were using the Julian Calendar rather than the Gregorian. Interestingly a French sprinter wore white kid gloves because he was running before Royalty, and the swimming events were held in the cold waters of the Bay of Zea, one mile from shore. Most the competitors had to be rescued because the waves were four metres high.

3. *In 1900* the U.S.A. team refused to compete on the Sabbath although many of the North Americans had qualified for finals on that day. Michel Theato, a French athlete, won the marathon but it was 12 years before he was informed he was a gold medal winner; the Paris Olympic results had been mislaid, no wonder, the programme dragged on from 20th May to 28th October and included such activities as leap frog, angling, cannon-shooting and three-legged races. Once again the Games were mixed up with a World's Fair.

4. *In 1904* the Russo-Japanese War was being fought. But (as an adjunct to the Louisiana Purchase Exposition) the Olympic Games were being held in St. Louis, Missouri and Alice Roosevelt presented the prizes. The British did not send a team, neither did the French, and athletes from Yale, Penn. and other Eastern universities boycotted the Games, yet they ran smoothly. The motor car had just been invented—its fumes badly affected the 31 Marathon runners and Fred Lorz of the United States of America was overcome by leg cramps and exhaust emissions after the first ten miles. However, he hitched a ride in a taxi and 15 minutes before Hicks (also of the U.S.A.) ran into the Stadium, Lorz did so, to finish "first". Hicks was later awarded the gold medallion.

5. *The Games of 1908* were originally scheduled for Rome but were transferred to London, where, of course, it rained for the whole two weeks of the festival. Insults and accusations also reigned. The U.S.A. and Swedish flags were forgotten. Irish athletes fumed when told to march behind the Union Jack. The Finns carried no banner because the Russians insisted that the Finns carry only the Russian flag. The protests over British officiating were incessant, resulting in the International Olympic Committee handing over to the International Sports Federations the detailed control and direction of actual Olympic competition. So the four-yearly celebration was growing up—and people were learning.

6. After the fiasco of the 1908 officiating, it was recommended that the Olympic Games be abandoned as they fostered international enmity rather than international amity, but the *1912 celebrations* in Stockholm proved the pessimists wrong. Twenty-five visiting teams attested to the fact that the Swedish people proved marvellous hosts. For the first time, electric timing was introduced as was photofinishing and sadly the first Olympic death occurred when Portugal's Francisco Lazaro collapsed and died of heat exhaustion in the Marathon race.

Swedish law at that time banned boxing, so none was held but after nine hours of wrestling in the light-heavyweight division neither contestant had a fall—the judges then declared the match a draw, giving neither a gold medal, but a silver one each instead, This too was the scene of the tragedy that would befall Jim Thorpe.

Soon World War I would take lives, rearrange geographic boundaries, alter mores, destroy friendships and would force the cancellation of a modern celebration of the Games.

7. The Games scheduled for Berlin in 1916 were held in *Antwerp in 1920,* proving to the world that the Olympic Spirit had come unscathed through the violence and stupidity of war. Belgium rallied behind the world's youth, and even though awarded the Games only in April of 1919, did a remarkable piece of organisation, presenting the start of the VII Olympiad with contests in 21 sports. However, the defeated nations, Soviet Union, Turkey, Germany, Hungary, Austria and Bulgaria were not invited to participate. It was here that the beautiful flag (now handed from mayor to mayor of the next Olympic city) was first unfurled. Baron Pierre de Coubertin had adapted the five rings (first seen on a Delphic altar) to symbolise the interlocking unity of the five continents of the world. In fact two days after it was presented, it was stolen, but after the arrest of the culprits it was again displayed.

Nurmi, Charlie Paddock, Hannes Kolehmanien became the idols of young people the world over, setting standards and ideals worthy of emulation. But, yet again a scandal arose—this time in Association Football (Soccer). Czechoslavakia and host national Belgium were the finalists. After 40 minutes the Czeck team walked off the field, down two goals, after one of its players was sent off—had Czechoslovakia been treated unfairly?

The proof of the Antwerp Games was that not even war could spoil international competition and that sisterhood and brotherhood would prevail.

8. *In 1924* the world celebrated the 30th anniversary of the renewal of the Games, and Pierre de Coubertin stated his wish to retire as President of the I.O.C. as he wished his own country to host *his* Games (again) whilst he was its undoubted leader. It was also here in Paris that a French schoolmaster, R .P. Didon, coined the Olympic motto: "*Citius, Altius, Fortius*". What a Games it was, the North American Robert Legendre, broke the world's record in the long jump at 25'6" in the Pentathlon—he was not even entered in the individual competition. Willie de Hart Hubbard of the U.S.A. was the first black contestant to win a gold medal and the Reverend Eric Liddell of Scotland abided by his parishioners' wish that he not compete (in the final of the 100 metres) on a Sunday but he entered the 400 metres on a weekday and won in a new Olympic record time.

It was in this year that the 1st Winter Olympic Games was celebrated. The Olympic family was growing, there was becoming something for everyone. The opportunities would grow, the ambitions would be more worthy, youth would have a sports purpose, changes would take place, but not in the concept.

9. *On 17th May 1928 in Amsterdam* the Modern Olympic flame burned for the first time—it was dedicated to the youth of the world and it was the time (because the Baron had previously opposed them) that more events for women were included. Then Germany was allowed to participate for the first time since 1912, Uruguay's team won the soccer title, Argentineans took two boxing first places, even Haiti had its athlete win a silver long jump medal and it was here that the inspiration of Paavo Nurmi made itself lastingly felt—at 32 years of age he won his 7th gold decoration. For the third successive Olympic celebration Johnny Weismuller swam to fame with three more absolute triumphs.

The 1928 celebration was quite the most successful, yet questions of "amateurism" raised their ugly heads and eligibility questions were imminent. Still more problems to solve. So it has always been; so with MAN, that irascible, unpredictable animal who has made his/her own environment and is never content to live within it.

10. The Depression had plunged the world into introspection, despair and caution, yet Los Angeles determined to see the work of a modern lifetime come to fruition, thus *the 1932 Games became a reality.* The world needed an inspiration. From 37 countries, 1,520 athletes provided it; for the first time in an Olympic village, and the "star" of the Games was a woman—the late "Babe" Didrikson. These Games of the Xth Olympiad showed the vibrancy and spirit which can rise above adversity. This is the essence of Olympism.

11. And so, *in 1936 to Berlin* to sense, feel and see the panoply of power of the then greatest blatant political show every staged, and yet a tiny miscalculation took

place. It was to the late black J. C. Owens, who brought back perspective and showed the world the light which cannot be dimmed, that friendship (with the late Lutz Long) and individual athletic excellence, surpass all the cultivated nationalistic biases of domination and transcend national ideologies. Furthermore world Jewry had been lastingly insulted by Hitlerian ideology of a blond Aryan race.

For the first time the Games were broadcast, televised and every jump, throw, vault, step, every splash and fall in every event was captured on film.

12. Once again was cancelled a celebration to be held in Tokyo in 1940 for in 1938 the Japanese found its war with China too demanding, and the I.O.C. re-assigned the Olympic Games to Helsinki. In 1939, the U.S.S.R. began its rape of Finland and the Olympic ideal was trampled under winter skis and marching feet until international hatred was so implacable and deep that it seemed impossible ever again to reunite the world's nations through friendly competition. The year 1944 came and went even though the Games had been assigned to London. In August 1945 the I.O.C. made it official—the Olympic Games were to be held just three years hence in bomb-scarred England. The Winter Games preceded them in February 1948 in St. Moritz where everything went wrong—the U.S.A. even sent two ice-hockey teams; the weather was ghastly. Someone tampered with the U.S. Bobsledders' runners but Gretchen Fraser and Dick Button won the first gold medals ever by U.S. citizens in a Winter Olympics.

The *austerity Games took place,* almost totally ignored by eight million Londoners. yet the British muddled along and at the *1948* Opening Ceremonies, Wembley Stadium was transformed with pomp and pageantry into a carnival of colour and the sun shone presaging an unprecedented heat wave, the first for 80 years. Later, of course, it rained.

From these Games was learned an important lesson that the Olympic spirit could survive even a lapse of 12 years. Athletes would compete no matter what the condition of the world and at the Closing Ceremony, Sigfrid Edstrom, the then President of the International Olympic Committee said:

> The Olympic Games are not able to force peace, a supreme gift to which all aspire, but in the youth of the entire world being brought together is the opportunity to find that all men of the earth are brothers.

Enough; we all know the problems of the day, the exodus of nations *from Montréal in 1976,* the *murders of 1972,* the student *massacre of Mexico in 1968,* the withdrawal of Indonesia and North Korea in *Tokyo 1964* and the banning of South Africa; and Rhodesia, although it had always sent a mixed team to the Olympics. The *1960 Games* forced the Republic of China to parade under the name Formosa and, as its team passed the reviewing stand, a placard was flashed "Under Protest"—never to appear again, and C.K.Yang received at this time his country's only medal. *1956 was the Australian* summer celebration on

New Year's Day, the first Olympics in the southern hemisphere and *in Helsinki 1952* saw athletes for the first time since 1912 from the U.S.S.R. competing.

We've experienced the disrespect to a nation's flag, seen a U.S. athlete proudly standing on the top dias, hand on heart but hat on head, observed militant defiance of black gloves and socks all because of mistake or intent, but before the world's largest audience, yet the celebrations go on. They survive, even thrive because they are worthy, and the efforts of millions through continuing periods of time are dedicated to an aim—even sacrifice of time, effort, energy, disappointment. This is life; were not the Olympic concept sound, the result could not be good, life is worth living. Those who strive towards a goal are already leading an Olympian life, with its mistakes as well as its joys.

ONE ASPECT OF POLITICS WITHIN THE INTERNATIONAL OLYMPIC COMMITTEE

The debate surrounding the venue for the 1980 Olympic Games created a dilemma for many of the world's sportswomen and sportsmen. Their anxieties brought both sympathy and understanding for South Africa's athletes who had, for too many years, been denied the opportunity of representing their country in company with the world's best. Of course, there are differences between Olympic participation and sporting links with a country which was still considered beyond the pale because it continued to practise Apartheid.

There is no suggestion that the athletes of the then Soviet Union should pay the price of their government's aggression, Their athletes were free to compete in the United Sates in the 1980 Winter Olympics and in whatever similar meeting which might take place before 17th July 1980—this is as it should be. The question is one which concerns the venue which, given the unparalleled prestige of hosting the Olympic Festival, has an importance all its own.

In the case of South Africa, it was the athletes themselves who were denied various forms of international competition by those who allege that policies of racial discrimination deny equal opportunity to black sportsmen and sportswomen, yet the government of South Africa recognised the autonomy of the controlling bodies in national sport, and mixed sport was commonplace. No-one argued that South Africa's case was good, there are so many, however, which are bad. But why the injustice of victimising South Africa for "political reasons" when "political reason" such as unprovoked aggression, genocide and the denial of the whole spectrum of human rights pass unnoticed?

Clause 24C of the Olympic Charter (1979) reads.

"N.O.C.'s must be autonomous and must resist all pressures of any kind whatsoever, whether of a political, religious or economic nature".

So by defending the Moscow venue, how did one ostracise South Africa's athletes? Even with internal discrimination, within the I.O.C.; the Olympic Games must go on but what must be asked is "are we boycotting freedom, individual freedom, and not the Games?" Do these considerations fall away now that the Republic of South Africa has been reinstated into the Olympic Movement and that the U.S.S.R. is no more?

THOUGHTS AND SUGGESTIONS

The eminent novelist and philosopher André Gide once said in a lecture, "All this has been said before, but since nobody listened, it must be said again". We often hear but we don't always listen. Admittedly not everything is worth listening to—but how do we know unless we listen? Someone who has an opinion listened to is happy and one may then talk freely—those who are unhappy will say the reverse. Are we listening to the voice of youth? It wants the Games—youth is the hope of the world and is its future leaders, thus these expressions of young people's opinions are worthy of official recognition. They come from IOA discussion groups—in 1993.

- Through educational programmes the whole history and idealogy of the Olympic Movement should be taught in all countries in all schools;
- The simplicity of the Olympic Principles should form the base of attitude to sports and games taught from an early age. These Principles set standards which are desirable as long as it is recognised that people cannot, and must not, be standardised. People can be influenced and persuaded to accept certain standards but will persist in thinking and acting in individual ways. Standards have a vital role to play in human affairs as criteria to live up to—standards of fair play, standards of excellence as epitomised in the Olympic Principles. Standards are more effective if they are agreed upon voluntarily and acknowledged as necessary. Unless we believe in the Olympic Movement through its Principles, it cannot survive.
- The I.O.C. should sponsor official films pertaining to:
  a)   training methods;

b)   techniques and coaching skills;

c)   drug abuse, the dangers and penalties involved;

d)   nutritional aids and adequate diet;

e)   content of educational programmes and materials to be used at all levels within school, college and university settings.

(These should be made by National Olympic Committees from I.O.C. grants as the N.O.C.s know the circumstances in each country.)

- The unofficial points scoring tables published in the world press, pitting country against country, gives the general public a biased view of Olympic participation and thus should be banned by the I.O.C.;
- Olympic solidarity should be vastly widened in scope as an educational medium;
- The example of Spain, Taiwan, Canada and the United Kingdom, and the 70 other National Academies in established National Olympic Committees should be emulated by *all* other countries;
- The I.O.C. should give serious consideration to the establishment of a permanent Olympic site, in Greece. Each member of the Olympic Movement should purchase a share, in land, thus allowing permanent facilities to be built. The facilities could be of such an international nature that they should reflect the various cultures and this centre could become the meeting place for Symposia, scientific meetings and all issues pertaining to Olympism. This should be planned for 2000, with television royalties being set aside for administrative purposes;
- The work of the International Olympic Academy should be advertised and this centre of intellectual endeavour be encouraged to be a free forum for viewpoints of every nature;
- By the elimination of the playing of the national anthem each time a victory is celebrated, much of false nationalism would be eliminated. Flags could continue to be raised.

It is tragic that sport and especially the Olympic Festivals are used for political and chauvinistic purposes, but such is human nature. We can only create an Olympic world by giving and living a life which we would advocate for others and by willingly abiding by applicable rules based upon principles by which we are prepared to abide. If the Olympic concept is worth saving, then it is only we who can save it.

Effort is given to less worthy causes; why not give more to ensure that sport can rise above its adversaries and that the Olympic flame will burn brightly, and light the way for future generations to see what their struggles will be and how they may overcome them?

As Pindar wrote in his XIth Olympian ode, "without toil there have triumphed a very few".

We must press on. The concept of Olympism is threatened. At the time of writing, the athletic world is in turmoil. If we believe, and work for the Olympic Movement and are flexible and prepared enough for change, the Olympic spirit will be seen again, felt again and be worthy of our intellect and our efforts once more.

CHAPTER XII

Olympism, Sport and World Society

OLYMPIC FRIENDSHIP

We really don't know each other—we hardly know ourselves.
Yet we're all here—a common bond compels.
We all believe in amity, in vigor, having fun,
The circled entwined rings, the colours, unity,
The one idea Olympic, the binding bond of wish,
The strengthening of new-found friendships—they are all
                                    upon our list.

We hope, we want, we need, yet even now we fear
Some politician's curse upon something we hold dear.
To be spoiled by twisted concepts polluting what we very
                                    badly need.
Yet each Games wins a battle, each Games plants a seed.
We need many an Olympiad to nurture it, and to stop our
                                  heedless greed.

We all know what we want, we all know what we need.
We know it takes some sacrifice, we fully know its creed.
For every little effort, for every handshake meant
For every smile we give, for every help that's spent,
We make our contribution as we reach to show its worth.
And love brings folk together to achieve real peace
                                  upon this earth.

J.T.P.

- 152 -

CHAPTER XII
Olympism, Sport and World Society

The historian . . . is apt to forget that sport in some form or other is the main object of most lives, that most men work in order to play, and that games which bulk so largely in the life of the individual cannot be neglected in studying the life of a nation.

Sir Arnold Lunn
(Inventor of the Slalom)

OLYMPISM

. . . Olympism is grounded on the spirit of "harmony" of man, not on the principle of exercises strictly for the body. Olympism is, in the words of Coubertin, the "essence" of a "distinct culture of the body".

Omma Grupe, from 'The Sport Culture
and the Sportisation of Culture'.
Published in *Sport—the Third Millenium*,
Les Presses de l'Universite Laval,
Sainte-foy, 1991, p. 135.

SPORT

How many interpretations, how many concepts are possible from that simple word? Sport is seen as physical activity, organized, long-term, individual or community expressed, demanding personal commitment and having intrinsic values; it has history and it has a future.

WORLD SOCIETY

This phrase encompasses nations, peoples, cultures, philosophy, social and physical anthropology, politics, economics, commerce, thought and opinion from individual to collective or national points of view. Thus World Society is political, economic, racial, religious, philosophical, strategic, climatic, communicative, and also possessing of a history and it has a future.

As one who has studied and participated for six decades in the areas loosely termed "sports" and physical activity", it is known that, as the physical and mental aspects of an individual are indivisible and that one reacts biologically and thus holistically to all situations, so growth and development of each individual proceeds throughout life in those co-indivisibles—the mental and the physical.

Generally speaking, *Sport* means "to play"; *Society* is a "body of individuals living as members of a community"; *World*—"the earth and its inhabitants" and *Olympism* epitomises the attitudes towards living adequately, friendly rivalry in absolute competition, exhibiting fair play within the rules. In the context of this Chapter, consideration is given to Olympic sport and its influences upon society and vice versa. In this sense then, *Society* is a definitive term suggesting common language, activities, social relationships, strata, organisations—all subject to the influence of politics, poverty, literacy, science, art, patriotism and internationalism.

Sport to one social group is not what it seems to be to another. One must not, can not, should never judge either sport, or another society from one's own limited personal knowledge or viewpoint.

AN ANCIENT CONCEPT

In Plato's theory of sport, the elements of strenuousness and self-discipline dominated all others. How lofty was Plato's concept of sport and how great was its value in his scheme of morals and politics? It was difficult, then, to adhere to his discipline of mind and body and judged by his standard, much of what is called "sport" today would be condemned as spurious.

Plato, in his last dialogue, *Book of Laws,* written about 340 B.C. addressed some remarks on the various forms of sport to young men:

> I hope no yearning, no passion for sea-fishing or angling will ever get hold of you, nor any pursuit of water animals nor the idle sport of setting day and night wheels. . . .
> Alone, and surpassing all, stands the pursuit of wild animals with horse and hound by the hunter in person. By racing, fighting, slinging and chasing, in personal encounter, those prevail who have at heart the ideal of manhood.

Plato's preference for the endurance—survival—encounter sports persisted throughout many ages. Vegetius in A.D. 400, wrote in the *Art of War,* "I hold that anglers and fowlers must not be allowed anywhere near a training camp but hunters of stags and wild boars will be welcome recruits".

In more modern times, King Edward III of England, during his wars in France, kept 60 couples of staghounds, and 60 pairs of harriers so that his officers and men could run, chase and maintain fitness for fighting. The Duke of Wellington kept a pack of foxhounds for the same reason.

Sallust, the Roman Historian, in his *Bellum Catilinae,* published in 43 B.C., echoes Plato, saying: I have no great admiration for mere athletic training or muscular prowess; but a man whose mind has sovereign control over his body neither weakened by self-indulgence nor debased by wealth or sloth and luxury may take his sport on the mountain, or on the sea, and I will admire his body rejoicing in hard work and his limbs growing under this toil".

Sallust—is correct—stressing that enjoyment is the essence of sport.

INFLUENCES UPON SPORT

The Greeks, masters of every form of art and literature were also masters of the essence of sport. The Greeks are entitled to the honour of having found the most attractive and genuine formula for sport—sport for the harmony of the human organism, for the smooth balance of body and mind, for the utter joy of feeling oneself intensely alive, well and functioning fully.

The ancient Olympic Games, for 1,276 years since 884 B.C. the greatest continuing festival of sport recorded, were developed and sustained through a philosophy linked with the worship of the Greek gods who were idealised athletes excelling in their godlike games and sports. The Greeks brought their gods down from the skies into the everyday life of sports and war, and other activities and the human athletes strove to excel, to achieve victory; the outstanding athletes becoming national heroes. The last phrase is pertinent today for outstanding athletes still become national heroes.

Throughout history, sport and religion, sport and worship, have intermingled in a very practical way. Just to give examples some have been taken from England. For centuries in pre-Reformation England, when the church had great influence over the amusements and leisure of the populace, the parish churchyard was the public playground on Sundays and Holy Days, and after Matins and Mass. The rest of the day was spent in games and revelries. Foot-the-ball, field hockey, singlestick and quarterstaff were the recognised winter games; in summer foot-racing, leaping, nine-pins, wrestling, long and cross-bow shooting and, always, hobby-horse and Morris dancing were associated with religious celebrations. Church ale was also made, and then sold, the profits were for "repairing the church and helping the poor".

By the *13th Century* it was necessary to ban from the church grounds wrestling "and all such sports, games and dances as engendered lasciviousness". In *1472,* Wrestling, Football and Handball were forbidden under penalty of "twopence forfeit". In *1542,* Bonner, the Bishop of London banned all sports from church precincts and in *1600* the puritan clergy were vehemently opposed to Sunday sporting activities. In fact, an inscription on a stone as part of a stile leading to the churchyard at Llanfihangel Discoed, in Monmouthshire reads:

> "Ye that come here on Sunday
> To practice playing ball
> Take care that before Monday
> The devil won't have you all."

Then in *1618* came the Declaration of Protestant King James I, permitting Sunday indulgence in lawful sports such as "Dauncing either of men or women, Archery for men, Leaping, Vaulting and other such blameless Recreation" and the "having of May-Games, Whitsun Ales, Morris-dances".

This was a remarkable piece of legislation *using sport to rebuke the Puritans* and to sway the masses from Catholicism to Protestantism. Charles I appended a further declaration in *1633* allowing freedom for ". . . all manlike and lawful exercises". In 1644 however Charles *Book of Sports* was banned by the Puritan Parliament which ordered all copies to be collected and burned.

It was only under Good Queen Bess that "Merrie England" became sports-free once more.

> "When Tom came home from Labour
> And Cis from milking rose, Merrily
> went the tabor
> And nimbly went their toes".

Sport in society has always been a potent force. Theodosius 1st in *392 A.D.* banned the Olympic Games, because of their deterioration through exploitation and professionalism. Richard II, *1389* banned soccer as it took too much practice-time from archery. Theodore Roosevelt was prepared by ban Rugby football in *1905* unless the rules of "the brutal game" were changed.

SPORT IS INTER-RELATED WITH MAN AND HIS SOCIETY

Frederick W. Hackwood wrote in his book "*Old English Sports*" published in 1907:

"The sports of the people afford an index to the character of the nation. They show how the people have met the stress the exigencies of life by varying their pursuits during those hours of leisure stolen from the more serious efforts of bread-winning; how they have taken advantage of their climatic and other physical environment for the purposes of recreation; what progress they have made along the paths of civilization towards culture and moral refinement; and, generally it may be accepted that the temperamental qualities of a people not infrequently manifest themselves in the outlets they seek for their super-abundant energies."

Sport has always been used to whip the imagination and firm the resolve: *Harrow's* "Forty Years On" cries out:

"God gives us bases to guard and beleaguer
Games to play out, whether earnest or fun;
Fights for the fearless and goals for the eager
Twenty and thirty and forty years on."

and *Henry Newboult's*:

"To set the cause above renown,
To love the game beyond the prize,
To honour, while you strike him down
The foe that comes with fearless eyes."

John Gaisworthy confirmed this with:

"Sport, which still keeps the flag of idealism flying is perhaps the most saving grace in the world at the moment with its spirit of rules kept, and regard for the adversary whether the fight is going for or against. When, if ever, the fair play spirit of sport reigns over international affairs, the cat force which rules there will slink away and human life emerge for the first time from the jungle."

In the present Olympic, social, political and economic climate this appears to be "the impossible dream".

MOTIVES BEHIND SPORT—A LITTLE HISTORY

When considering sport and world society, motives behind sports need analyzing. These are many, including the mechanism evolved for action-survival, latent adversary instincts, adventure, distinction, economic gain, leisure fulfilment, relaxation, distraction, play instincts, physical improvement, gregariousness, social pressure, release of tensions, physical preparedness, physical excellence and discipline.

Note the motives cited by these famous and articulate men in the way they expressed Sport.

F. L. Paxson, the North American historian, called it "the social safety valve that replaced the frontier", but *Thorstein Veblen* wrote—"sport is no more than an expression of the barbarian temperament". *Albert Parry,* in the Encyclopedia of the Social Sciences, terms sport: "an instrument with which the masses are to be kept in check, awed or distracted", and he continued. . . "The wide interest of Anglo-Saxon masses in horse racing, football, baseball, and similar sports tends to allay social unrest and lessens the possibility of political uprisings". At the International Olympic Academy, in his speech "Modern Training Theory", presented in July 1962, the late *Carl Diem* stated:

> "Sport is a physical exercise under mental control. By Sport we mean a game which we take seriously, enjoy, govern with strict rules, and in which we strive for top performance."

Sport is involved in Politics, and Politics manipulates Sport:

Zimbabwe (Rhodesia) competed in the 1964 Olympic Games, was not invited in 1968, ousted in 1972, despite her fully representative team, and was reinstated for the 1980 Games.

The late Avery Brundage stated his upset about the banishment of Rhodesia in Munich:

> "For the first time in 20 years the International Olympic Committee refused to accept my recommendations and succumbed to political pressures."

Fifteen nations of the 123 invited to compete in Munich threatened to "walk out" if Rhodesia competed—the I.O.C. vote was 36-31 to retain the team. The conditions set by the I.O.C. for Rhodesia's participation were:

1. Rhodesia must field black athletes,
2. Compete under its old name of Southern Rhodesia,
3. That it must carry and fly the Union Jack,
4. Sing "God Save the Queen" after any Rhodesian victory.

Yet Rule No. 1 of the Olympic Constitution then read:

> The Olympic Games are held every four years. They assemble amateurs of all nations in fair and equal competition. No discrimination is allowed against any country or person on grounds of race, religion or political affiliation.

In an article in the Toronto Globe and Mail of 9th March, 1976, it stated: "Africa and friends of Africa will boycott the Olympic Games if New Zealand competes while persisting in its "support for racist South Africa", according to Abraham Ordia, President of the Supreme Council for Sport in Africa". B.E.Talboys, Minister of Foreign Affairs for New Zealand answered on 16th March: ". . . We believe also that sportsmen and sporting organisations in New Zealand should be free to associate with those in other countries if they wish to do so, regardless of race, colour, creed or internal politics. Sportsmen have the same rights as other New Zealanders and this Government intends to uphold them. There will be no more political interference in sport . . .".

The Republic of South Africa withdrew itself in 1961 from the Commonwealth of Nations, was cast out of Olympic Competition in 1964 and officially in 1970 was unacceptable to other African nations for Pan-African competition and internationally banned from team competitions with other countries, yet, in 1970, 1976 and 1981 the Rugby Football series was played by South Africa with New Zealand; in December 1976 and 1980 the South African Track and Field athletics team brought back 17 gold medals from the Pierre de Coubertin Games and Argentine's University Soccer team played in South Africa. But the bans had their effects where delegations and ambassadors failed—*sport was the instrument* by which apartheid was challenged and being changed. The South African Games are still held annually, great sports festivals are held regularly, incentives are high, tours are encouraged internally for whomever will visit. The need for international competition was always fully understood—not for the participants solely, but as an extension of governmental policy. *Sport* then is important *as a tool*. By being debarred from the Olympics by the I.O.C. (a Sports body) South Africa's political and ethical attitudes were bared. *Sport* was used *as a weapon*. Now the weapon is sheathed. South African athletes competed for the first time since 1960 in the 1992 Barcelona Summer Olympic Games, twice being placed on the victory stand.

On New Year's Eve 1975, the presence of Titus Mamobola, the first South African to be invited to participate in the annual road race in Sao Paolo, Brazil, caused a political storm when the all black team representing Kenya was instructed to withdraw because of Mamobola's presence. Sport, again, was being used to focus a political light even though *all* athletes were dark.

The superb performance of the Kenyan men's field hockey team in the 1972 Olympics; Africa's first sub-4 minute miler Kipchoge Keino, Wilson Kirpugut Chuma, Saraphino Antro, Amos Biwott, Tembo, Koga and now a succession of other jumpers and runners all have put Kenya "on the map". Would the world have known as much of Kenya had it not been for the athletic successes of her sons? Is this not so also for Ethiopia through the efforts and image of long distance runners the late Abebe Bilaka, of Wolde, and Mirus Yifta? The 7' 1½" (2 m. 4.51 cms) high jump made by Minister of Sport, Idriss of Chad in 1964 focused attention on its country as did efforts of the Tunisian 10,000 metres runner Gammoudi, and on the happy, ebullient 400 metres hurdles champion, but poorly techniqued, Akii-Bua (one of 44 children by one father) of Uganda. Never has Cicero's statement held more truth, helping to bring back proportion in sport.

"Natural ability without training has oftener raised many to glory and virture than training without natural ability." *Pro Archia Poeta,* Chapter 7, Sec. 15.

Sport projects a *national image* too.

ATTITUDES TOWARDS SPORT

One of the saddest and most incomprehensible uses of political power was the Canadian Government's action, based upon its *United* Nations stance, for the exclusion of a multi-racial South African paraplegic team from the 1976 Para-Olympics scheduled in August, in Etobicoke, Ontario. The reality: forfeit $500,000 in federal funds plus $1-million contingent provincial grant if the South Africans compete. The losers were 1,700 disabled participants, including Canada's 88, and 22 South Africans. This denial of monies to those already denied much, to whom training (and re-learning) has become epitomised in "Sport", was positively cruel.

Look again at Canada—who, because she could not win any more in amateur international ice hockey, withdrew from the Winter Olympics of 1972 and 1976 until 1980 in that event. Another viewpoint, can anyone conceive of anything more ridiculous than to have the *"World"* Series of baseball, and the *"World Champions"* of American football? Especially when no one else is invited to compete. *This is sport by exclusion.*

How does one feel when a late Vice-President of the United States is reported in the *Congressional Record* as follows, on 12th September, 1962: "The Soviet Union uses competitive sports for many purposes, not the least of which is prestige—individual and national prestige", ". . . the United States must make an all-out effort to prepare for the Olympics if we expect to avoid being clobbered by the Soviets", and "Mr. President, in my view the United States must not lose a day in preparing to win the 1964 Olympics. "? But no nation *WINS* an Olympic Games. *This showed ignorance of the purpose of Sport.*

In 1948 *Soviet athletes* were unknown quantities; in 1956 and 1960 they burst upon the sports world in ice hockey, track and field athletics and gymnastics. In the '70's Olga Korbut became the darling of the United States through television. Then it was Nadia Comaneci of Romania. Soviet coaches were welcomed all over the globe except to China where now ex-East German coaches abound and the supreme U.S.S.R. triumph was the celebration of the Olympic Games in Moscow in 1980.

East Germany and its ideologies were thrust, by exquisitely trained athletes, sparklingly clad, in sports of all seasons, upon a reeling world, not quite ready for such excellence. *Hungary* has its whole educational system geared to participation by youth and its early, almost Spartan, selection for élite coaching. To quote Mihaly Kocsis—Director of the General Sports School, in a personal letter:

> The Sports School does not conceal its aim which is to raise efficient competitive sportsmen. It selects its pupils, it has a rational curriculum and it works with the most up-to-date methods adjusted to the requirements of the different age groups. The school raises an élite, and it follows two purposes: a direct and an indirect one. It develops the abilities of gifted pupils, and through this élite it wants to attract other young people and arouse their attention and interest for sport and physical education.
>
> The best encouragement, apart from facilities, is the success of others.

An evaluation of sport based solely upon accumulation of Olympic medals confirms his view.

Medal Winners in only Four Summer Olympic Games Over a 40-year Period

Country	1952	1956	1960	1992	Population
Indonesia	0	0	0	5	87,800,000
Egypt	3	0	4	0	29,000,000
Australia	11	35	22	27	10,050,000
Hungary	42	26	21	30	9,940,000
Finland	19	15	5	5	4,435,000

ANOTHER ATTITUDE

Baron Frédi Pierre de Coubertin believed the solution to moral decadence lay in the development of the individual as he wrote: "The foundation of real human morality lies in mutual respect—and to respect one another it is necessary to know one another".

The late Avery Brundage, the last human bastion of amateurism, stated, not long before he died—"The ancient Greeks used to stop fighting to stage the Games—now we stop the Games to stage our wars", and, "However, people of all nations will turn to the high ideals of amateurism and away from the tragedies of war". But Paul Gallico wrote ". . . Brundage suffers from the dangerous illusion that public competition on the athletic field engenders good sportsmanship, makes nations love one another and is good for peace". ". . . It is nothing of the kind. It's the finest stewpot for cooking up international hates between wars and keeping them alive, next to a round-table gathering of diplomats".

See an ice hockey match, watch the fights; observe the "no body contact" game basketball; lots of "character" is shown—often bad character. Games and sports bring out what is there. They do *not* "make" character. Competition can bring out the best in people, but it also brings out the worst. We happily remember a pleasant incident but unpleasant ones become too numerous to relate. The competitor is usually well-motivated, dedicated, self-demanding and self-sacrificing in terms of time and hard work. But the various systems which "use" the competitor are open to question—many questions. Also the systems within which an athlete competes and/or plays must inevitably influence the participants.

SPORT AND YOUTH

This was the theme for the 16th Session of the International Olympic Academy held just prior to the Montréal Games, and speakers explored what young people expect from sport. A survey of opinions disclosed many expectations, varying from "nothing" to "it's part of my life", and that it is a fact that many of North America's and Europe's youth expect gain, not merely participation or satisfaction from Olympic representation.

In the main, at the highest echelon, the professional makes sport into lucrative work, and the politician gets a lot of mileage out of athletes' efforts.

SPORT AS ENTERTAINMENT, PROFESSION, BUSINESS

That sport is all these is fact. Spectator sport is excellent entertainment, professional sport is usually financially rewarding, even more profitable is investment in sports franchises and promotions. There is nothing intrinsically wrong with any of this, other than the obvious anomalies, imbalances, and frequent apparent limitless financial settlements.

In the decades to come, the average sportsman or sportswoman will be no better, and no less rewarded, than the average performer in any of the performing arts—the "greats" will still achieve stardom but there are many potential greats pressing on their heels—and the athlete as performer is limited by one inexorable fact—age.

In the context of world society, identified professional sport (tennis, golf, football, basketball, baseball, to name a few) is no problem. The aspect that bears watching, and needs regulating, is the professionalism of so-called "amateur" teams and individuals, when in amateur competition with genuine amateurs, however few. Professional, full-time, life-long training of "amateurs" has been mentioned already in relation to sport in politics.

We know how games and sports start—why we indulge in them initially. Each of us knows why he or she played—or plays—games and sports. Without exception, we play, or played, because we like or liked to do so—there is, there was, no ulterior motive—it was fun. We had no *need* to play, except the biological *need* to move and we fashioned activity to suit the mood and urgency of our need. We invented games, copied activities, indulged in them because they and we were there. But what have games and sport become? That is a most interesting statement because it shows clearly education's failure in creating satisfying situations in sport in early life which would allow for "non-achievers". All children should be enabled to achieve to each individual's satisfaction and potential, at whatever level, whether physically or mentally disadvantaged or not. Because there is joy in being able to participate, however badly.

CONCLUSION

Time is running out. What of the changing attitude towards women's sport in India; Purdah in the Middle-East; of the exploitation of women through skin-tight sweaters and short skirts as sex adjuncts at the Galdiatorial contests in Western-world athletic arenas; of starvation and poverty in the so-called 4th world nations where no-one is able, or can afford the luxury of play; of statistics which may be shown to reflect whatever a particular programme wishes to be reflected; of sport as a substitute for war; of latent fear which motivates segments of populations to participate in sport; of the incalculable and vastly powerful effects of the media upon body and mind through sports-listening, reading and watching; of the differences in individual and national aspirations; of the manipulation of sportsmen and women; about the nation of China, its approach to Sport and Olympic sports participation; about the non-competitiveness of the Inuit?

One bright spot regularly shining on Sport's horizon is the International Olympic Academy. This calm vale in the Peloponnesus is the centre where opinions are expressed, ideas are thrown about, caught, talked about and where resolutions are made and firmed by young intellectual and vibrant people who have all the ability, capacity and the willingness to act for the good of Olympism. This university of academy intensity, tolerance, joy and happiness was created and built by belief and integrity for the meeting of each other. It is a rock of principle.

In this imperfect world, the International Olympic Academy stands as a force for good. Many marvellous things start and happen there because all are willing to try, willing to understand, to speak openly, freely and make friendships which transcend political frontiers, and the inadequacies of language.

Were the spirit of Olympism generated there to be maintained throughout the world of sport, there would be few worries because it would achieve the epitome of excellence it has every right to attain, untarnished and thus undimmed.

This cannot be without unrelenting toil. Each person who has attended the Academy has a vital part in the unseen plan which is always exposed in sports' excellence, fairly contested by able people in the name of Olympism.

Like every other instrument that man has invented, sport can be used for good or for evil purposes. Used well it can teach endurance and courage, a sense of fair play, and a respect for rules, co-ordinated effort and the subordination of personal interests to those of the group. Used badly, it can encourage personal insanity and group vanity, greedy desire for victory and hatred for rivals, an intolerant esprit de corps and contempt for people who are beyond a certain arbitrarily selected pale.

Aldous Huxley in *Ends and Means.*

A FINAL THOUGHT

Who is the absolute athlete—an Olympic champion? This can not be so because an Olympic champion's reign is limited to a given number of years. The ultimate athlete is one's own self who has within him or herself the ability to achieve the absolute, which he or she deems possible.

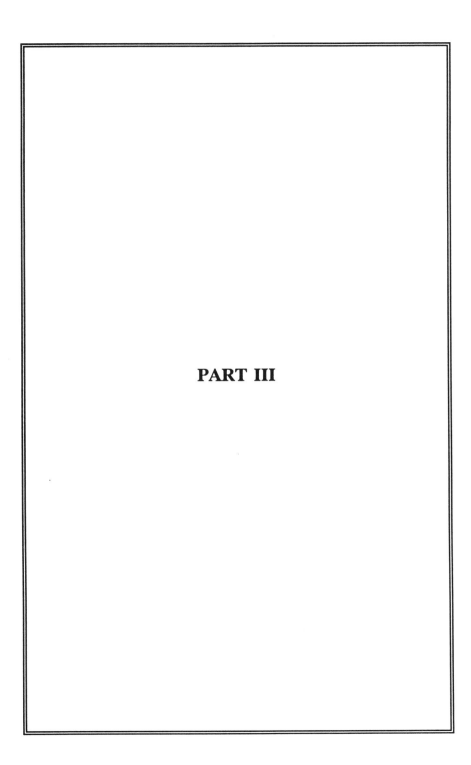

PART III

CHAPTER XIII

The Development of Olympic Athletes
Are Laboratory Methods Enough?

CHAPTER XIII
The Development of Olympic Athletes
Are Laboratory Methods Enough?

"Why investigate athletics, why not study the processes of industry or disease?" The answer is two-fold: 1) the processes of athletics are simple and measurable and carried out to a constant degree, namely to the utmost of a man's powers: those of industry are not: and 2) athletes themselves being in a state of health and dynamic equilibrium, can be experimented on without danger and can repeat their performances exactly, again and again.

A. V. Hill, *Muscular Movement in Man.*
McGraw, Hill Book Company, 1927, p. 3.

INTRODUCTION

Racial, genetic and nerve patterns are real and more permanent than laboratories, apparatus, sports facilities and coaching methods. However, even those patterns can, and do, change as a result of cultural demands, environmental pressures, inter-breeding and the different physical and emotional standards set for, and demanded by, sport.

Sport permeates many levels of society, it touches and deeply influences race relations, ethical values, status, language, political opinion, the concept of 'hero" and "heroine" and is an indicator of national outlook. Yet many peoples have neither the leisure nor the affluence to indulge in Olympic Games and Sports; poverty and malnutrition determine the minimum level of existence for others. However, climate and geographic location ensure that few nations will take part in the limited events of a Winter Olympic Games and elevated standards of performance are necessary to even allow of adequate representation in the growing number of activities within Summer Olympic Festivals.

THE ROLE OF EDUCATIONISTS

Physical educationists in particular are interested in the means by which youth is progressed towards Olympian excellence as well as enjoying the reflected glory of youth's successes. Furthermore, there should be an awareness of what constitutes sacrifice, compromise and expectations by government, the society, parents and young athlete and whether or not teachers and coaches are unwittingly encouraging exploitation of an individual by fostering the voracious appetite of "excellence" and its offspring, "waste". Educators have to be particularly careful that the cause is worthy.

Is it sufficient to win, whatever the price? "Winning is not the most important thing, it is the only thing."[1] or "An athletic field is no place for a gentleman."[2] Dr. Ward dismisses the concepts of fair play, the good loser, and sport for the fun of it, these are "myths" created by the press and public he says. "There are no illusions as to the existence of such things among successful athletes."[3] He continues, "Learning to be a good sport and a gracious loser is neither good nor desirable. Among athletes good sports and gracious losers are nonexistent."[4] George Allen, a U.S.A. football coach was heard to say, "Losing is a little like dying." Are these statements true, do they reveal what élite competition is really like; are we deluding ourselves in thinking it otherwise? Or is the real winning expressed in Vince Lombardi's "The will to excel and the will to win endure, they are more important than any events that occasion them."?

CHEATING

Under the pressure of instant acclaim through victory, ideals are often lost. Cheating, attempts at cheating, the setting of rules to prevent cheating or to punish cheats, are, unfortunately, part of sports. It has always been so. The ancient Greeks had to prove they were true Greek to take part in Olympic, Pythian, Nemean and Isthmian Games. The 23rd Chapter of the *Iliad* records the cheating perpetrated by gods, goddesses and heroes in the Funeral Games. The Zanes, to be passed by Hellenodicae and athletes prior to entering the Olympic Stadium, proved and warned against cheating, and ancient Spartan youth, in training, were expected to steal food. Thus cheating was taught, and, if found out, discipline was enforced and order maintained. However, punitive measures never have, and never will, ensure fair play.

As ancient Olympic competitions became more intense so privileges and prizes proliferated. Eventually the Games themselves were disgraced and banned.

Does cheating have a part in our sport? If not, why does the International Committee for Fair Play exist? What an indictment on our society that such an organisation should have to function to reward good sports behaviour that which ought to be normal. If so, what is being done about it?

On the eve of the 1972 Olympic Games, the International Olympic Committee published its first Medical Commission's booklet on all aspects of doping. On page 4 is this statement:

Investigations of this type can take place only in an environment marked by understanding, frank co-operation and mutual assistance. Only under these conditions will we be able to prevent incidents incompatible with the Olympic Ideal and the dignity of our athletes.

Yet it is some of these very athletes who take unfair advantage, risk health, censure and reputation to win, at all costs, by cheating and abuse. It seems that for the very few any means is legitimate, provided it results in victory. Governments are known to "bend" immigration rules to allow a noted athlete to compete for his/her new country. Victory, and the hope of victory at any price, is seemingly understood and acceptable. Has nothing really changed, is it only a matter of degree?

LABORATORY TESTING

In the desperate search for observed and acknowledged athletic "firstness" the only, present, untouched area known is human selective breeding; even this was attempted by Hitler with his concept of "ein Volk", the blue-eyed, blond(e), pure Aryan. As a people, we have our own natural selection methods which, however pleasant, are rather "hit or miss".

The age of champions in Olympic contests is lower than four Olympiads ago. The International Olympic Committee acknowledges this and ". . . will encourage the International Federations to set up, from a medical point of view, a lower age limit, where reasonable or justified, should it have not been established already".[5] How then are these young athletes chosen? It is often too early to identify by natural ability, but there are signs which are translated into prediction, which are then tested, proved or disproved in laboratories. it is known that structure can determine what sport people contest but that function can change structure, if started early enough; that the onset of puberty can be delayed, that blood doping can and does increase oxygen carry in the system, that the ingestion of anabolic steroids will create muscle mass through hard work, that androgenic steroids and the use of progesterone oral contraceptives may be utilised to regulate the onset of the regular menstrual cycle.

What is tested? Everything possible. Anthropomorphic measures through X-ray are made concerning structure, predicted height and body density at a given age, biomechanical assessments concerning the attachment of muscles, their distance from joints and consequent mechanical efficiency, intelligence tests, motivational, stress and skill tests are performed as well as the whole realm of organic and motor fitness performance measures. Then the "successful" child is catered for; an environment of absolute specialisation and devotion to detail is created and the potential champion, devoid of social life is made not a representative of, but an exception of society . . . what for? The hope of achieving a gold medal; what of the young person then? Adulation, fame, fortune, travel, "friends", publicity, and if anything goes wrong—anonymity. Educators, beware. Sometimes, to keep a prospect "at the top" and in the public's "eye", unethical practices are resorted to.

FACTORS FOR SUCCESS—HEIGHT IN PARTICULAR

What then are the factors involved in athletic success? Sport is an extremely diverse field and abilities and attributes which contribute to success in one sport are not advantageous in another. Consider just one aspect, height: it is obvious that a tall player has physical advantage in basketball, shotputting and high jumping. But this may be a disadvantage in gymnastics, wrestling and weight-lifting because the ratio, strength to mass, is greater for the small competitor thus beneficial when managing one's body weight.

What contributes to success in a given event? Aerobic capacity, the ability to use anaerobic reserve, balance, mobility, agility, speed, power (realising that there is not one second-class lever in the body's make-up), endurance of the repetitive kind, endurance of the sustained type, skill, perfected technique, tactics, high intelligence, hand-eye co-ordination, acute hearing, excellent eyesight, peripheral vision, reaction time, experience, perceptual ability (anticipation), large hands, motivation, concentration, dedication; adequate rest, food, sleep, preparation; economic security, excellent schooling, coaching, facilities; emotional stability, emotional support from family and friends, specific physical preparation? These, and the countless other psychological reinforcements and physiological factors to cohere, aid achievement. Naturally all athletes do not possess all these characteristics nor do they have all these features at their disposal.

By virtue of being a sprinter, the structure and temperament, when compared to a 5,000-metre runner are different. The sprinter of quality is invariably mightily muscled in shoulders and arms and volatile in nature suiting the violence of reaction and the necessary force applied. The 5,000-metre runner is more slenderly muscled and often more introverted; but to revert to the factor, height, this single measure alone separates the 100 metre sprinters almost completely from the 5,000 metres competitors.

The longer-distance runner derives an advantage from slight muscles, not mechanically but physiologically, because long-distance running demands the maintenance of the maximum rate of oxidation within the muscles, avoiding the creation of an oxygen debt and the production of lactic acid. There is no reason why the efficiency of oxygen utilisation is related to physique but efficiency of blood supply and cardiac output must be beautifully balanced, and delicate muscles may have an advantage over massive ones in this regard. Height is, usually, not affected by training; therefore, size is natural. The size of a 100 metres Olympic finalist is not that of the 5,000 metre finalist. Just as if one is short, one will not reach the highest echelon of high hurdlers or the final of the 400 metres dash; body shape, in the sense of skeletal proportions is inherited and when growth is over, unaffected by training. No amount of training will alter the proportions of trunk and thigh, or breadth of shoulders and hips. This is not so with musculature when training becomes a vital influence. But do sprinters have big muscles because sprinters sprint, or are people sprinters because of inheritance and favourable environment in which they grow? Probably the latter.

Many women and men are born with the possibility of developing the necessary physical requirements but only the few have the compelling wish to excel. More and more children are being given opportunities, fewer and fewer achieve Olympian excellence. Struggle, conquest, suffering, skill and freedom are the rewards for exceptional talent. At each Olympic Games celebration, performances are more spectacular and new records are set in both endurance and skill. Improvements in equipment, lighting, surfaces, methods, availability of coaching plus increasingly efficient psychological, physiological and mechanical research, better medical supervision and control over infection all contribute to the achieving of excellence.

The improvement lies within the athletes themselves. However, are they more gifted than previously or is it that training methods, more fierce competition and natural endowment account for better and better performance? In what way, or ways, is the modern athlete better? By the time the final is reached, even physiques seem to become matched—the only factor left is the will to win because athletes are born *and* made.

THE HUMAN FACTOR

If even one small detail is not tested, one feature ignored, or not identified, the whole is incomplete and that minute element becomes of greatest importance. I know, for I have been Olympic Coach, international competitor and work physiology researcher. That which is immeasurable is the human spirit. It is when a practical error is made, a mental lapse occurs, a physical disability has to be coped with (such as a cold or an ingrown toenail) that the courage, the essence of an athlete comes to the fore. This is that which makes the champion, when one gets up to continue, to summoning of an incredible driving force, the will to succeed, the inability to surrender to adversity; these are the qualities of invincibility so necessary in a true Olympian victor. But is it wise to allow such an athlete to persist? To not do so would destroy, because every contingency has been covered, every factor has been prepared for—except for the unexpected—to cope with this and triumph within the roles, is indeed, success.

Scientific methods are used to coax every centimetre, every fraction of a second, every ounce of energy out of an athlete who is considered to be almost a machine, then coaching through constant honing and polishing wears down all the knobs and excrescences and makes what often seemed like ordinary abilities into a co-ordinated, smoothly functioning organism. All this is possible, but only because the athlete wishes it. Thus many athletes are unwittingly used to serve ideologies and systems' purposes.

Ask a topflight Olympic winner "was it worth it?". And the answer is usually "Yes". The pain, agony, upset, deprivation, discipline, the beating of self, the hours, days, months and years of effort are soon forgotten. At the moment it is sufficient but it has taken everything, the total involvement of body, brain, senses plus the knowledge that physiological and psychological limits are nowhere in sight, that records are made to be broken and that the intricacy of the web which binds performer and environment has created the circumstances that enable the achieving of excellence. These the athlete knows through experience. The limits of language constrict ability to express adequately all that is meant by devotion to achieving a goal, of what sacrifice really means, of what it is really like to experience the height and sensitivity of participation at the élite level. The truth lies beyond the ability of language to express it. The performer knows but is never able to adequately articulate the essence of experience. One can never recount an aesthetic moment.

What of tomorrow, the future, of being beaten, of being forgotten? If, and only if, the athlete has been progressed through an educational process in which nothing can be dissociated from the achievement of an aim, that values are an integral part of life, that decency and concern for others are paramount, can the champion's will come through unscathed.

CONCLUSION

The solution to the problem of unethical behaviour lies in education. Belief in the elixir will always live as have other myths since time began. Education in Olympism, the Olympic ideal, the concept of the Olympic Movement are essential if athletes, however young, are to be guided to make choice. The educational process against unethical practice is not only the domain of those involved in sport. It belongs deep in society, the home, the church, school, in peer behaviour. If aspects of unfair advantage are to be countered, knowledge and communication as well as co-operation between physicians, educators, parents, athletics governing bodies, investigators of scientific data, the media and athletes are essential. The goal is distant but worthy of pursuit.

True educators understand that the nub of Olympism is a set of inner principles expressed in deeds of accountable human activity and from concern for supreme and honourable effort—it is a way of life. It is the educator's responsibility to keep this at the core of preparation for Olympic representation and to achieve it, it is necessary to introduce the concept of Olympism into schools at the earliest opportunity and to have it as an ethic for all programmes of physical activity.

If young people have a worthy example to live up to, they respond and attempt to emulate observed behaviour. Youth needs example, leadership, and to see courageous decision. It is an educator's privilege to give each of these.

REFERENCES

1. Jim Tatum, Head Football Coach at Marlyand University quoted in *Sport - Mirror of American Life* by R. H. Boyle, p. 63.
2. Dr. Stephen D. Ward, "Some Observations on Athletes, Psychiatric Communications, University of Pittsburgh, January, 1959, p. 6.
3. *Ibid.*
4. *Ibid.*
5. Resolution at the Baden Baden Conference. 11th Olympic Congress Bulletin (8th edition). Published by the National Olympic Committee for Germany, 1981, p. 39.

CHAPTER XIV

Sport
- Aggression and Violence -

ANTICIPATION

The eastern sky will turn a golden-red before
    The sun, like a human lip, kisses the horizon's rim,
To become a faultless, orange orb pulled
    As though by magic strings.

Mounted, it will speed into a dappled mix
    Of orange, red and blue to shine
And keep on shining above our
    Troubled, waking world.

But before we see Helios's promise
    Of a sun-blessed day
We will be silent, and still, in order to believe,
As a cool soft breeze, which does not even stir the leaves
    Stirs us, and we will feel—but what?
As we anticipate this unique phenomenon.

J.T.P.

CHAPTER XIV
Sport
- Aggression and Violence -

The swaying and the struggles of history will continue, but little by little knowledge will replace dangerous ignorance; mutual understanding will soften unthinking hatreds.

Baron Pierre de Coubertin,
From a speech at the close of the 1936
Olympic Games, published by the speaker.

INTRODUCTION

There is a danger in writing about aggression and violence because there is the tendency to be forceful in presenting such a controversial topic. One must be most careful not to be bitter or to be fierce, not to be vehement and not to unintentionally upset, for were one to be misunderstood, words could lead to hatred which is a seed which soon grows into violence. To be better understood, what I consider to be the meaning of certain words used in this text follow:

Aggression—

Self-assertiveness is seen as either a good characteristic, revealing energy and initiative, or as a sign of emotional instability, it is offensive rather than defensive, and is the first act of hostility or injury, the initiation of a dispute, quarrel, an intrusion or even an unprovoked attack.

Violence—

The exercise of physical force in order to inflict injury on, or to cause damage to a person, persons or property; an action to force someone from, or to a place or to do something, or to stop someone doing something. It is undue restraint applied to some natural process or habit or forcibly interfering with personal freedom. It is shown in vehemence, impetuosity, force, outrage, profanity, injustice, fury, infringement, fierceness and oppression.

Competition—

The action of endeavouring to gain what another wishes or others are trying to gain at the same time. The striving of two or more for the same objective. It is rivalry.

Partisanship—

Where one either takes part, or takes sides with another. A blind, prejudiced, unreasoning or fanatical adherence to, or supporter of, a person, a team, a nation or a cause.

Hatred—is active dislike.

Enmity—is illwill.

Fanatic—

Frantic, furious, frenzied, it is the characteristic of a "possessed" person leading to excessive enthusiasm, wild and extravagant ideas and actions.

To Fan—to act with the object of widening, expanding or making a display.

Fan—an instrument for agitating the air. It is also an abbreviation of the word "fanatic".

Sport—An entertainment or a pastime, a diversion or a recreation. To play.

AGGRESSION

Biologically, aggression is a normal feature of the human make-up. Aggression is behaviour intrinsic to Man's being and to his or her ability to interact with the environment.

Man's very nature is aggressive, the process of creation, the sperm's efforts to be first, the demand to be born, the child's fight for breath, the demand to be fed. All life is conscious or unconscious competition, struggle to know, to be first, to be heard, to be seen, to be recognised.

One use of aggression common in Man is as a means of communication. Much of the aggressiveness shown by children is a means of obtaining attention. "Watch me, Mum.", "My father's bigger than your father.", "I'll beat you.", "I'll race you . . .".

Within aggression there is no need to be destructive, vicious or ferocious, the only necessary condition is that aggression be directed towards a focal point. Man's learning ability makes possible the use of aggression to achieve objectives rather than the harming of an opponent.

Individual and/or corporate social actions are integral of the hominid way of life. Had aggression no advantage to the human it would not have replicated itself through natural selection, through the interaction of genes and environment giving rise to a predictable pattern in human response. This however neglects the influence of Man's rapid cultural evolution which has placed Homo sapiens in circumstances quite different from those in which natural selection originally operated. Characteristics selected by early man for survival may be maladaptive now.

Is aggression beneficial to the species because it ensures that "fitter" individuals gain priority? Is "fitter" equated with "more aggressive" implying that the more aggressive ones are those needed by society and that their perpetuation is beneficial to society? Here it should be noted that the occurrence of aggressive behaviour in itself provides no evidence for the nature of its cause.

In his book *On Aggression* Konrad Lorenz makes clear the genetically innate (nature) and culturally determined (nurture) theories about aggression[1] whereas Ashley Montagu in his work *Man and Aggression* states that "Man is man because he has not instincts, because everything he is and has become, he has learned, acquired from his culture."[2] Erich Fromm[3] and Rollo May[4] have expressed yet another point of view attempting to proportion the genetic, social and environmental determinants making Man what he is.

What then is aggression? What creates it? Is it only overt acts perpetrated to gain attention; an athlete's action of driving the pole tip into the vaulting box in an attempt to clear 6 metres in the pole vault; the mob's vocal threat to a football referee; the violation to one's own integrity and one's physical self by the subversive act of taking drugs or the slow mental and physical torture of a political prisoner? All these are not acts intent on destruction, they are acts to construct, to protect or to destroy, they have no common cause. All acts of aggression are not "bad" as Ardrey stated[5] in *Social Control,* we must properly ". . . distinguish between aggression and violence", otherwise ". . . the constructive debate becomes a wasteland of words".

SPORT:

Sport probably originated from highly ritualised hostile fighting, through the introduction of strict culturally developed rules, and the aggressive instinct which is competition being usually directed towards others of the same species. Aggression is a major component of competition, it is a competitiveness not a combat. Even when there is no body contact e.g. gymnastics, diving, skiing, speed and individual ice skating there is contest. One competes against oneself, one does as well as possible in the circumstances. The competitor has also other antagonists—not the environment, not oneself, but time, or the judge who subjectively assesses the performance.

Sport is aggression and that aggression is the self-motivation to perform. The aim of aggression is self-identity, status, security, it is integral of the process of survival.

In 1908, Adler in a paper "On the Origin of the Striving for Superiority and of Social Interest"[6] considered aggression an instinct and that an individual's fulfilment is dependent on each one's power over others as well as over environmental circumstances. What more is sport?

Adler wrote of "striving for perfection" and "striving for superiority" and:

Whatever name we give it, we shall always find in human beings this great line of activity—the struggle to rise from an inferior position to a superior position, from defeat to victory, from below to above. It begins in our earliest childhood; it continues to the end of our lives.

So, aggression is shown by action, the assertion of one's individuality over self, over others and/or the environment. "Ago ergo sum"—I am because I act.

VIOLENCE:

Violence is a perversion of man's drive to live, express and be recognised, it is destructive hostility.

Violence erupts when someone cannot resolve his or her needs for power, in normal ways. It is the expression of impotence, the inability to do something about a situation in normal ways. Violent actions give a sense of strength, identity, and significance and, although socially disruptive, harmful to the perpetrator and destructive to the victim; the means seem to justify the ends.

Violent action is the expression of acute feelings of psychological and physiological inadequacy and vulnerability; it is energy denied, frustrated or blocked. Man becomes violent only because of inadequacy. Inflicting pain, causing destruction, killing, are all cancerous malformations of Man's inner need to compete.

SPORT, VIOLENCE AND SPECTATORS:

The relationship between violence and sport is of vital concern because violent actions which would not be condoned outside of sport are legitimate within certain sports, e.g. ice hockey, North American Football, boxing, albeit within the bounds of rules and regulations. Increased violence by professional athletes in game situations[7] as well as spectator violence are in need of constant attention.

Within the last twenty years "soccer hooliganism" has erupted in clashes and confrontations between rival groups of "fans" (fanatics) as well as between the police and these same "fans", at professional association football games—particularly in England. But these destructive, vindictive acts extend far beyond the football arena. Members of minority groups, public and private property, trains, buses are the focus for the pent-up expressions of these mobs composed mainly of frustrated, working-class but often unemployed young people (mostly men) who dress in distinctive clothing, who are fiercely loyal to a chosen team and who have symbols, songs and chants, such as:

We'll take the Tottenham in half a minute
We'll take the Arsenal and all that's in it
With hatchets and hammers
Carving knives and spanners
We'll show the Tottenham bastards how to fight.

Blood and Guts—Violence in Sports[8]
Paddington—New York, 1979, p. 309.

- 185 -

With unemployment and the economy as it is there is little hope of untrained and unqualified British youth achieving satisfaction or advancement so, what has arisen is a cultural and status stress between young people and society generally. Both television and the Press have some responsibility for this situation because the Press exaggerates and makes sensational the character of the problem, and the television cameras tend to isolate the violent aspects.

In *Football Hooliganism*[9] Hall is quoted:

> Newspapers thrive, not simply by printing the most newsworthy stories by highlighting the most newsworthy *ASPECT* of a story. So there is a progressive tendency to rework and process stories so as to isolate and identify for your readers the most dramatic angle.
>
> It follows of course, that you can increase the news value of a not very dramatic story by *ADDING* a sensational touch or by selecting an unusual angle on a perfectly usual story. This *VALUE-ADDED* effect is especially strong in the fiercely competitive circumstances in which newspapers presently operate.

Again, in Ingham, et. al.,[10] Marsh on page 75 in interviews with "fans", found it quite normal for them to try to appear on television. In an interview he quoted:

> ". . . where you find television cameras you'll find trouble because people say, you know, "oh, I'm gonna get myself on telly." When there is no television coverage ". . . no-one runs on the pitch".

So it appears that to stop violent behaviour one must stop it first by the contestants on the field of play, because this stimulates spectator response.

Sporting events are exhibitions which show power, strength, co-ordination, co-operation, skill, aesthetic features, grace and other human attributes. They are also dramatically contrived, goal orientated, and in many instances violence is seen or is just under the surface. The underlying themes of competition are akin to war and the language used is surprisingly similar e.g. attack, defence, "the bomb", shoot. Newspapers, books, films, magazine articles, advertising posters, the theatre, even music testify to our fascination with violence. The more powerful the production the more violent the reaction.

Where are the violent *crowd* reactions in synchronised swimming, rhythmic gymnastics, golf, tennis, track and field athletics? Fan violence occurs because of betting, ingestion of drugs and/or alcohol, partisanship and through watching rough players in the rough sports which have violence in their make-up.

There is yet another type of violence caused by boredom. It is violence for pleasure, it is an end in itself done for the physical experience, for the search for superiority, for living vicariously through the players or performers.

Many people have either not played games or sports or, when they did play them were considered not good enough for representation in school, club or other teams. These are often the people who considered themselves excellent but who were turned down by a coach and through frustration and jealousy became violent, feeling unjustly treated and that they could still perform better than those on view. Violence thus follows disrespect.

VIOLENCE AND OLYMPIC FESTIVALS:

Why is it that there are so very few violent acts in the celebrations of Olympic Festivals?

Of course there was the unforgivable violence of murder in the 1972 Munich Olympic Games celebration, but this was a fearful political manoeuvre to attract world-wide attention to a cause. Admittedly Olympic participants were involved, but it was the concentration and focus of all the media which were used by the terrorists for their own ends. There was also the pre-Olympic massacre of militant students seeking reforms in Mexico City in October 1968; but neither of these dreadful occurrences was pertaining to the Games themselves.

There are incidents, there is rivalry, fierce unrelenting opposition, aggression, pride, nationalism, hate, objection, spite, cheating and a play of all heightened emotions throughout the various contests; yet there is no violence in the stands amongst the spectators. There is partisanship, there are shows of patriotism, overt bias and preference exhibited by clusters of watchers. There are accusations against judges and referees and there are occasional displays of petty stupidities. There are exclusions of teams and boycotts—but no violence.

EDUCATION:

The opening and closing ceremonies, although officially very short have now been surrounded by remarkable shows, ingenious, innovative and colourfully rich in ethnic contribution, full of delightful music of composition, voice and instrument, through sight, sound and colour when all the senses are whetted. Everyone is absorbed and involved.

The opening of the Olympic Festival involves representatives from all the participating nations and all the games and sports to be contested. Through justifiable pride the peoples of the athletic world are drawn together in an harmonious atmosphere of goodwill.

The closing ceremony is full of symbolism; it becomes the quieting note on which to go away, to reflect, to contemplate in awe what one has been a part of and what one has witnessed. The informal mixing of all athletes, vanquished or victor, in a huge burst of international amity helps to create a better understanding of each other—violence is furthest from one's thoughts.

Furthermore, the arts and cultural programmes with representatives of every discipline from all over the world enrich the Olympic environment.

Sport and cultural activity play fundamental roles in society by contributing to an individual's physical and mental well-being and by strengthening group cohesiveness. So with conjoint participatory ceremonies the Games are opened and closed like the opening and fading of a beautiful flower but with the hope it will bloom as well, again.

The purpose of the Games is known. Once, every 2 years the watching world throws its attention to either the Winter or Summer festivals of physical activity which are the manifestations of a universal value system of fair play, the embodiment of Olympism, when peoples of all nations are reminded of the equality of Man. The Olympic arena is as much a testing ground for man's ideals as it is for athletic excellence.

The aims of the Olympic Games are 4-fold: to promote the development of those physical and moral qualities which are the basis of sport; to educate young people through sport in a spirit of better understanding: to spread the Olympic principles throughout the world thereby creating international goodwill and to bring together the athletes of the world in a great festival of sport. Gradually, through education these principles are being understood and applied.

In the Olympic Games it is not as though there are just two individuals, or two teams battling for supremacy. The whole atmosphere caused by the mixing of cultures, of language, political persuasion, different religious, physical, mental, moral and emotional groupings softens, rather than hardens absolute feelings. Tolerance is demanded, violence and thoughts of violence recede. Each country and every individual representative is attempting to present the best, through flag, colour in uniforms, sound in national anthem and particularly through dedicated performance. Every aspect is heightened and accentuated—violence would spoil the Olympic atmosphere.

Spectators have their allegiances. Many have sacrificed much to watch a contest, to be part of the pageantry. Naturally one has hopes that someone, some specific someone, or team will win. What happens if that person or team does not pass to the next round. The spectator stays, passes allegiance to another, to an "underdog" or to a previous affinity. Many people have moved from one culture to another, have past loyalties, past memories, friendships, have emigrated or created new ties. So viewers have not only the one single purpose when watching an Olympic event as there would be in, say World Cup Football elimination play, the focus is diffused; people at the Games wish to be seen on the television screen but not as "trouble makers". People do not wish to draw attention to themselves for the wrong reasons and they do not wish to spoil the spectacle for others. Because of the costs involved, and the time needed to attend Olympic Games, the spectator is usually more affluent and, perhaps better educated and thus less given to express him/herself violently.

In watching Olympic participation one is always conditioned by, not only the consistent brilliance of exceptional performance but by the understanding of what each individual athlete has had to overcome in the pursuit of excellence.

Athletes seldom resort to violence for this would defeat the purpose of representation. Athletes would always rather win an Olympic Gold medal than become just a world-record holder.

Athletes and spectators alike know that where thousands compete greater numbers watch; and television, the Press, and radio, show, reveal and tell to an eagerly waiting world every conceivable action unfolding or about to take place. All wish to be seen in the best light, and as the object of athletic competition is to win one must do so within the rules to achieve the highest acclaim.

CONCLUSION

The final period in any sequence of development—biologically speaking—is marked by what is grotesque and extreme; that is the picture of violence. An example is the reason for banning of the Ancient Olympic Games. Today, the glorification of winning, at whatever cost, has reached a peak. Things are already out of proportion even though we cherish the beauty in many games and sports. Only through education will the unplumbed potential of energies needed to keep the Games viable be released.

The more one experiences the more one realises the wisdom held within the Delphic inscriptions, on an arch within the inner sanctum of Apollo's Temple, "Know Thyself", and "Nothing in Excess". Herein lie the built-in warnings to the eruptions of violence in self and society and of misdirected aggression to others which, acting together, could quickly engulf and destroy the Modern Olympic Games. To guard against this we must avoid extremes, excesses and complacency.

REFERENCES

1. Lorenz, K., *On Aggression*, Bantam Books, New York, 1970.
2. Montagu, A, *Man and Aggression*, Oxford University Press, New York, 1973, p. 73.
3. Fromm, E., *The Anatomy of Human Destructiveness*, Holt, Rinehart and Winston, New York, 1970.
4. May, R., *Power and Innocence*, W.W. Norton Co. Inc., New York, 1972.
5. Ardrey, R., *The Social Control*, Athenium, New York, 1970, p. 242.
6. Adler, "On the Origin of the Striving for Superiority and of Social Interest", quoted in Ardrey (1970:105) of Adler's article 1967:104.
7. Gilbert, B., and Lisa Twyman, "Violence: Out of Hand in the Stands". Sports Illustrated, Vol. 58:4 (31 January, 1983: pp. 62–74.
8. Atyeo, D., *Blood and Guts - Violence in Sports*, Paddington, New York, 1979, p. 309.
9. Ingham, R., S. Hall, J. Clarke, P. Marsh and J. Donovan, *Football Hooliganism*, London, Inter Action Imprint, 1978, p. 24.
10. *Ibid*, p. 75.

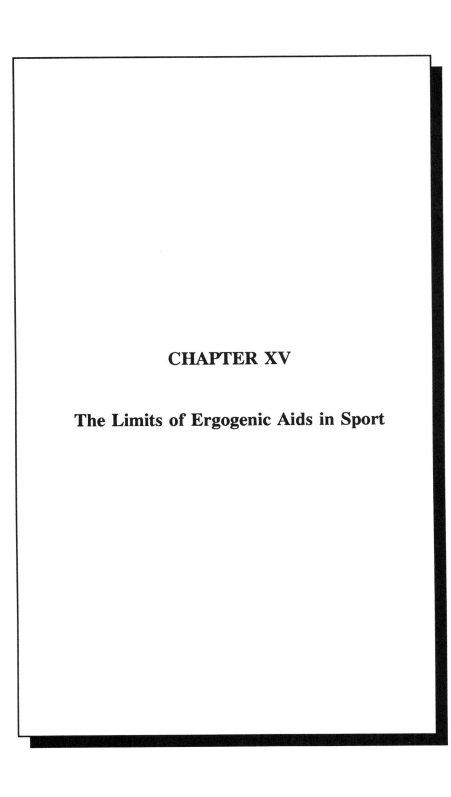

CHAPTER XV

The Limits of Ergogenic Aids in Sport

THANKS FOR THE MEMORY

We forget—we forget even the names, the records set.
    We're fickle—we fail to think; what of the athletes
Hours, days, months, years of discipline, sacrifice, training,
                            sweat.
    We chose to forget.

A champion, once brilliant in our eyes,
    Is now not even in our mind.
You see, we need the thrill, the spill, the upset,
    'Cause we cannot do it any more, and perhaps we never could
And now we're not even kind.

We live vicariously through others' efforts, joy and work
    How strange to have this particular quirk,
And we clap and shout and stamp and when our hero
    (already yesterday's) gets cramp
And comes second, it's not good enough for us,
    Why the fuss?

It's now "ex-champ" whom we quietly cheer;
    For God's sake let's have another beer.
All of past glory, glitter, slap, touch, smile, flowers
    And autograph are gone—to another.
But will we remember? Oh, brother!
    We paid our money, we licked the honey of his or her success.
So sweet that moment, will there be another?
    Oh yes, I guess—then, we can forget.

                                   J.T.P.

CHAPTER XV
The Limits of Ergogenic Aids in Sport

*One never knows what is enough until one knows what is
more than enough.*

William Blake

INTRODUCTION

It is reasonably safe to say that the majority of people take some sort of pill or have an injection. The reason is clear, the treatment taken or given, is in order to *make one better.*

Many take drugs of some sort or another which have been medically prescribed. Others treat themselves, purchasing over-the-counter concoctions or by using home-made remedies.

Just because a medical practitioner prescribes the ingestion of some substance is it ethical to do so? Where does a medical practitioner get his or her moral values?

We tend to use the words *"ethics"* and *"morals:* interchangeably. Actually morality concerns behaviour whilst ethics comes from reflection.

It is time that we should get together to work out a code of conduct in *ALL* sporting matters with an elucidation of the philosophy on which it is grounded. Otherwise the major world sports festivals will give way to the "Bionic Games" and sportswomen and sportsmen will become products of "high tech" processes, instead of being people. Sport will become, no more, a service to society but a blight upon society.

Being concerned, being appalled saying how disgusting it is, "tut tutting" will not solve the moral problems which arise from the use of drugs in sport. The genetic, surgical, medical improvements possible in athletes or the use of pharmaceutical substances slipped to opponents are out of hand.

One might say that the advancement in training methods, of running surfaces, landing mats, fibre-glass vaulting poles, overflowing swimming pools, running shoes, the legitimate training at altitude for future running at sea level, the taking of special diets are all recognised so what's so bad about taking some sort of ergo-genic aid or a few pints of blood—especially if it's your own *to make you better?*

Some hard thinking has been done. More is required. We need the aid of philosophers, medical specialists and scientists but most of all we need a consistent, concerted public sport consciousness about the use of ergogenic aids in sport.

Where do you stand on the issues of behaviour modification, genetic engineering and the use of drugs in sport? The way we think and act in one area influences the way we think and act in other areas. Sport (there is truly little left) is faced with the prospect of being subordinated to commerce and to technology—not served by commercial interests and technological advances. Think of the interference of a young girl's puberty, just because she demonstrates a talent for gymnastics, what an abuse of science. Advance this interference into schools, clubs and amongst the lotions, potions and pills there'll be other substances such as "greenies" and "bennies", to change, by their use, weight, stamina and speed.

Some years ago it was thought possible to transplant brains. Take out Jack's brain, split it, give half to Bill, wake them up, ask them who they are. Both will say they are Jack. Send them away, bring them back, re-unite the brain in Jack's head, he'll claim to have been in two places at the same time. Many men are said to be wanting babies, that fertilised ova will be placed in men's stomachs and after 9 months of massive hormone therapy caesarian sections will reveal a child. We tend to believe, fatalistically, that whatever is scientifically possible will, one day, be scientifically actualised.

It is not only a matter of drug use by sportswomen and sportsmen or of nerve-ending transplants, its conceivable that sporting types can be bred to order. What a waste of those seven-foot giants in professional basketball—why not encourage stud-farms? You'll like a weight-lifter, sir? Blue or brown-eyed? A swimmer, madam, male or female, short or long-distance specialist?

The sperm and ova of world-class athletes have a price on them, today. Where does society stand in these matters? We rely on medical ability and scientific integrity for guidance but as George Eliot wrote in these matters we need ". . . good sense, not common sense". Until now we have been guided by an understanding of human nature and a Judeo-Christian code of conduct and tradition explained, primarily, with the aid of Greek thought. That tradition is suffering from neglect and considered inconvenient by many.

SPORT AND ITS INFLUENCE:

Sport has always had its problems. Today's problems are greater. The coverage by the mass media, the intrusion and acceptance of commercialism at every level has led to an acceptance of "gamesmanship" and disgusting examples of violence which ought to have no place in human activity. Sport has such an immediate as well as a lasting effect on youth, on spectators and followers. Add these effects to the physical, emotional, mental and societal effects of drugs and science and the scene is set for the future.

What are the limits of these influences?

A SHORT HISTORY OF DRUGS:

Drugs, in one form or another, have been with mankind since antiquity but only in the last 100 years has the pharmacological industry undergone tremendous growth.

Vaccines, antibiotics and tranquillizers characterised the three major drug revolutions.

We are now in the fourth revolution which is two-fold:-

1. The increased emphasis on the use of drugs for pleasure.
2. The use of aids to enhance physical performance.

Toffler in his book "Future Shock" predicted the development of an entire industry to pleasure through drugs, and that it would be common for many to start the day with orange juice laded with amphetamines. And we all know the devastating effects of the use of anabolic steroids to enable the building of muscle mass and excitable behaviour.

HISTORY OF ERGOGENIC AIDS:

The first recorded incidence of doping was when Adam and Eve believed the apple would give them God-like powers.

Man has always sought for the elixir or life, the magic potion, the secret ingredient, the aphrodisiac to make one bigger, stronger, faster.

The writings of Philostratus and Galen tell of the athletes of the Ancient Olympic Games, at the end of the 3rd Century B.C. who ate sesame seeds and used strychnine hoping to improve performance. There are 13 black marble slabs on the left of the entrance to the Crypt as one enters the archway to the stadium in Ancient Olympia. On each of these blocks was a statue of Zeus. Engraved underneath each was the name of a man who had cheated in an Olympic festival. The name of the village or city from which the athlete came was also chiselled. The city or village was never again allowed to enter an athlete in the 4-yearly festival—the athlete was banished. Today, the Athletes' Commission of the International Olympic Committee has recommended the life-time ban of athletes caught cheating by using performance enhancing drugs.

Verified cases of unquestionable doping have been identified since 1865 when Pini reported doping proof amongst Canal swimmers in Amsterdam.

It is known that the Berserkers in Norwegian mythology used bufotein, Andean Indians still chew coca leaves, Australian aborigines chew the pituri plant for stimulation and anti-fatigue effects.

In 1879 the famous 6-day Cycle race was held for the first time. French racers used caffeine, Belgians sugar-soaked bread in ether and others were known to use nitroglycerine for the final sprint. Heroin and cocaine were used by the trainers of those days but in 1886 Linton the English cyclist, in the 600-kilometre race Bordeaux to Paris, died having taken massive doses of a strychnine-based drug given him by his manager and bicycle firm, Belgian owner. Later English and Belgian soccer teams made attempts to better performances through use of oxygen. This was in 1908. Boxers in that year were found to be using strychnine pills and mixtures of brandy and cocaine.

The first case of "drugging to lose" came in 1910 when James Jeffrie—having been knocked out by Jack Johnson—asserted his tea had been doped. This method of manipulation, nowadays called anti-doping or para-doping, has become the favourite excuse of doping offenders who have been discovered as we well know from the 1988 Seoul Olympics Summer Games and from the 1993 February episode.

In 1889 the word "doping" first appeared in an English dictionary which referred only to a mixture of narcotics and opium administered to horses. Today's word comes from the Bantu tribe of Xhosas in Transkei, South Africa. The work is "Dop"; later absorbed into the Afrikaans language. Initially the Blacks used this hard liquor as a stimulant at worship, later it became the pace-setter for doping in today's sports. As early as 1910 and 1911 the first scientific proof of doping was established in Austria.

The Austrians brought to Vienna the Russian chemist Bukovski whose methods revealed alkaloids in saliva. Later Dr. Sigmund Frankel—Professor of Chemistry at the University of Vienna—conducted 218 saliva tests and appropriate sanctions were taken.

In 1919 in England, Dr. Emden conducted extensive tests on the ameliorating effects of phosphorus compounds and later the pharmacological effects of benzedrine.

In 1934 the first clinical observations of the effects of benzedrine on physical performance were made.

In the second world war, in Germany, Hauschild developed the drug pervitin, and, in England, methadrine was concocted. Each was used to keep pilots awake during night flights; for long marches and in Commando raids which required feats of concentration and endurance.

By 1933 the word "doping" was in general use and the first definitions were written. Also advanced were expressions of moral—ethical points of view, yet athletes and their coaches (called Trainers then) as well as medical practitioners who had an interest in doping, created confusion, concerning the administering of drugs by simulation of ignorance of regulations.

From 1950, doping cases noticeably increased and in the Winter Olympics of 1952, in Oslo, broken ampules and syringes were found in the speed-skaters' changing rooms.

In the 1955 Tour de France 25 urine tests were conducted—5 proved positive.

In my own published study on the theoretical use of energisers and tranquillizers in 1965 I was concerned to whom one was talking when that person was on drugs and who really was competing in athletic competition, a person or a drug?

Also in 1956 Lothar Alpler in the amateur (a word used no more) world cycling road race in Zurich, Fritz Gallati and many others were discovered taking amphetamines; some racers were found to have up to 18 amphetamine tablets in their jerseys, yet others who used drugs, such as the Dutch cyclist Scheepers were treated as martyrs and heroes and the medical doctors who conducted the tests were maligned in the Press.

In the Helsinki Olympics of 1952 the random sampling of Marathon runners' food proved inconclusive and it was only after many fatalities that public opinion was roused. Danish cyclist Knut Enemark Jensen collapsed in the Rome (1960) Olympic Games after his trainer has given him a compound of nicotinic acid and amphetamines.

Dick Howard (USA), third in the 400 metres final at the 1960 died of an overdose of heroin. The dramatic increase in drug use in sport was in 1960.

In 1961 the Italian Football Association's study showed that 17% of all players took psychotics and 94% of the "A" league professional club players used some sort of drug, even for training.

In boxing, Welterweight Billy Bello died of heroin poisoning in 1963.

Even tennis has not remained untainted, Andreas Simeno (Playing in the 1961 David Cup against Billy Knight of Great Britain) received a large injection of testosterone.

This is enough to establish that doping in sports is not a sudden problem only just identified, except to record the tragic death of 26 year old Birgit Dressel the German heptathlete on 10th April, 1987.

In the course of her career she received, at least, 400 injections from her specialist.

In 1962 the International Olympic Committee at its meeting in Moscow passed a resolution against doping. In January of 1963 the Council of Europe made a significant contribution by making a clear definition of doping.

Doping is defined as the administering or use of substances in any form alien to the body or of physiological substances in abnormal amounts and with abnormal methods by healthy persons with the exclusive aim of attaining an artificial or unfair increase of performance in competition. Furthermore various psychological measures to increase performance in sports must be regarded as doping.

In the same year the definition was confirmed by the 1st European Doping Colloquim in Uriage and by the Sports Doctors Congress in Barcelona. Most significant in sport was the re-establishment in 1967 of the I.O.C. Medical Commission chaired by Prince Alexandre de Morode who is still Chairman of this Commission.

The first dope-controls were initiated at the 1968 Winter Games in Grenoble continuing in the 1968 Summer Olympic Games of the XIXth Olympiad in Mexico.

Rightly, the I.O.C. took its lead, and still maintains it, in supporting continuous scientific research and control of drug use in sporting activities.

The I.O.C. Medical Commission now includes four sub-commissions all dealing with different aspect of sport and medicine:

1. Doping and bio-chemistry of sport
2. Sports medicine and orthopaedics
3. Biomechanics and Sports Psychology
4. Co-ordination between International Federations and National Olympic Committees

The projects of the I.O.C. Medical Commission for the future are many and complex. Already, the I.O.C. has established sports medicine courses in each of the 5 continents and 20 accredited Dope Control Laboratories.

Gradually it is being accepted that, from a biological and a medical point of view, the use of ergogenic aids in sport is an unnatural and highly dangerous way for winning. In fact a victory gained, at too great a cost.

FAIR PLAY:

The medical aspects of doping rank second to the ethical considerations of sporting fairness. Drug-taking to enhance performance is always unfair and contrary to all sporting morality. I see it as unethical in the extreme, morally wrong, physically dangerous, socially degenerate, legally indefensible and an expression of an inferiority complex and that it has become a social disaster. It is considered to be a refusal to live within one's natural limits and usually represents a refusal to be individually responsible for one's own success or failure.

Yet, many athletes take drugs. I took a survey of 80 top-class women and men track and field athletes in 1986. My question was this:

"Were I to give you a substance which would ensure your winning of an Olympic Gold medal in 1988, but you would die within three years of winning—would you take the substance?". In each case the answer was "Yes".

THE PARADOX OF DRUG TAKING

The paradox arises from the fact that many authorities have concluded that no pharmacological preparation can enhance human athletic performance.

It has been shown that the performance of top athletes was significantly improved after taking entirely inert substances provided that the athletes believed them to be effective drugs.

Also, the administration of a potent compound gave no effects when the athletes thought they were only placebos.

The power of suggestion is strong. Many coaches and their "pep" talks have some effects.

The BBC television programme QED, titled the *Steroid Myth* presented evidence, when aired on 3rd January, 1990, that, from Great Britain, Italy and USA "The idea that steroids enhance performance may be another damaging myth". The thrust of the programme was that the mental impact of taking steroids is as effective as taking anabolic steroids.

Athletes have rationalised the taking of an "aid" as:

a. a direct influence- advantageously of the *physiological* capacity of one or more of the body's systems which will contribute to performance *or*

b. the "aid" will remove *psychological* restraint thus enabling the physiological capacity to be extended.

It is this search to find *the* substance which will exert both psychological and physiological effects that drives athletes to find the "magic potion".

What then are the limits? Are there any? Should there be no controls? Should athletes, and others, be freely able to use whatever ergogenic aids they so wish and take whatever consequences result?

Have we searched enough for the cause? Is winning everything?

Nationalism, profit, fame, recognition, money. The more liberally these reasons have been used, the less their intent has gone beyond verbal confrontation. If one could eradicate its causes doping would become pointless.

The evolution of our society has turned top-class athletes into workers, just like anyone else.

Athletics is a demanding job needing intensive preparation, it is a profession.

In the individual sports there is an undue number of competitions. The workload, the travel-demands tax, often unbearably, normal limits of endurance and ability. Hormonal shortfalls in athletes need to be brought back, officially into balance. Athletes suffer from overwork and are often treated like patients in order to justify practices incompatible with usual medical ethics.

Athletes have a short "life". There is no security, no guarantee in case of accident, no degree, no higher educational opportunity, no profession except sporting performance. Dealing in dope, taking dope to keep one "on top" for just a little longer is tempting. What is the top athlete's position in society? Athletes are so easily forgotten both as heroes and as workers. We have come to doubt genuine drug-free performance; have we developed an attitude that sport is "tainted" at any level? If so, this attitude will ultimately destroy a respect for, and the perceived value of, sports activity at EVERY level. Sport is too important, too valuable a component of the world's cultures to allow it to be diminished in this way. Sport and its inherent integrity, as a positive societal force, must not be compromised further by the activities of those who cheat by indulging in doping practices. How will we look at the participation, and the results of, the Commonwealth Games in Victoria, 1994? Will we expect, will we accept diminished performances, lower heights, less distances done, slower times or are we only interested in the expected monetary "clash" of two, three or four sprinting "giants"? Has all been forgotten, has all been forgiven?

LIMITS

There are strong indications of intrusive effects of doping throughout society in general and some nations indicate the remarkable measures being taken to curb, identify and control this scourge. The taking of ergogenic aids in sports is not an isolated phenomenon; it is closely linked to a host of society's ills, concerns and problems, it is only one aspect of pollution, for example. If society is not possible without a moral base, sport is not possible without rules. Our wish and intent should be not to control the use of ergogenic aids in sport, but to eliminate them.

EDUCATION

Such a great deal has been written and said about the illegal use of anabolic steroids, about banishment for athletic life, the need for a national policy of drug abuse, the expected International results of the Dubin hearings so far ignored, the casting of responsibility on to medical practitioners, physiotherapists, masseurs, trainers, coaches, administrators, the I.O.C. and the I.A.A.F., random testing, restricted lists of substances, banned substances, rights of athletes, sanctions, penalties, legislative and financial matters, efforts to prevent the spread of doping to regions of the world where the problem is non-existent, that we seem to have forgotten the powerful influence upon youth; in fact the whole of the educational aspects concerned with drug abuse. Education, communication, discussion at all levels are essential to a better understanding of the use of dope in sports.

CONCLUSION

What is meant by "limit"; a value, a position, or something which may not be passed? It is not likely that chemical limits have been reached, but have human limits of performance been reached without dope? Records are made to be broken. Records challenge, records are incentives. What are the limits of human endeavour? Were we to know life would not be worth living; struggle, striving, practice are worthy, but can be spoiled by false objectives to be achieved by false standards and false practices. Our limits and our integrity will be challenged if we are intent on making sport worthy again. We will determine by our efforts whether ergogenic aids will win or whether by our concentrated effort their influences will be limited.

CHAPTER XVI

- Sport-Teaching -
Art or Science?

CHAPTER XVI
Sport-Teaching - Art or Science?

"The educator's part in the enterprise of education is to furnish the environment which stimulates responses and directs the learner's course."

John Dewey
Democracy and Education

INTRODUCTION

This subject is a challenging one, not controversial but complex and one worthy of considered opinion as is expressed by Plato in *Republic, VIII* 352d ". . . our discussion is on no trifling matter, but on the right way to conduct our lives."

All those who teach have individual idiosyncrasies, ways of presenting the subject taught in order to give the greatest impact and to stimulate learning. The whole object of teaching is to encourage thinking and subsequent intelligent action.

DEFINITIONS

It is important to differentiate between teaching and coaching.

Teaching comes first, is concerned with the introduction of ideas and principles to as many as possible, whereas *coaching* is essentially involved with the few (the exceptions of society) and with the applications of techniques at the élite level. Teaching introduces and creates the initial shape, coaching knocks off all the knobs and excrescences to produce "the finished product". It is also assumed that *Sport* means "to play" and that, for this Chapter sports, games, dance and exercise are synonymous as they are all concerned with movement. Furthermore "Art" should be considered as practical skill, guided by rules, and methods of doing certain actions, and *"Science"* as systematised knowledge, ascertained truth and that which refers to abstract principles.

EDUCATION FOR SPORT TEACHING

There are two premises on which this point of view rests:

1. An holistic approach to human movement based upon the biological sciences because the essence of biology (Bios) is life, and life is identified by movement.
2. The purpose of sport-teaching is to make optimal movement possible for others—the practice of which principle is the essence of the discipline.

It is necessary to digress in order to recognise the fundamental factors which are necessary for an adequate education particularly at the school level where emphases should be upon experimentation, concept and width. Only at college and university levels do concentration on specific aspects of individual subjects of choice take precedence.

Education can be likened to a circle. it being as strong as its weakest link. For humans the product of an education makes him/her only as strong as his/her weakest thought and weakest ability.

All the methodology of *how* to teach, the knowledge of biochemistry, functional human anatomy, human nutrition, human genetics, work physiology, psychobiology, sociobiology and axiology will not make a teacher. A teacher is *not created* even though put through the machinations of technique and technology and given the tools—a teacher is one who has emotions (which can not be systematically employed or appraised) as well as human values. The *act* of teaching is not like inducing a chemical reaction, (although a true teacher must be a catalyst, staying the same but enabling things to happen) it is much more like painting a picture, individual and not always by formula, even though some so-called "paintings" are created by filling in numbered areas in given colours. The *act* of teaching is comparable to the act of high jumping; one must throw one's heart over the bar as well as one's body, otherwise one's work, one's students and one's self are spoiled, by being unfulfilled. Because teachers are human they may substitute dogmas for hypotheses, popularity for hard work, novelty for depth of thought and propaganda for fact. The very aspects which need enquiry, discussion and opinion and which ought to excite intellectual interest in young people are often poorly prepared and inferiorly presented by teachers of sport. Far too much time in sport-teaching is given to inessentials. Whilst rules, dimensions and regulations are necessary to be understood, these can be learned from readily available books. Sport in *all* its forms needs simultaneous physical, emotional and mental expression. Its essence is expressive movement, not constraint, being participated in, up to the ability level of those enjoying the activity. Sound sport-teaching is based necessarily upon knowledge of the organism, principles of force and work plus the cultural and psychological needs of the individual. There can be no rejection of any aspect of learning by the potential teacher, for excellent teaching can only flow when the teaching becomes reality.

The preparation of those devoted to becoming efficient teachers must be scientifically based; the biological sciences forming the core. But no one aspect of concentration is sufficient. There must be an historic progression with constant opportunity for expression *at every level.* One of the worst aspects of the education of those wishing to teach any sphere of physical expression is the "in house" method where all subjects are taught within one discipline. The essence of true education is in its liberalising effect. We who study the art and science of human movement must be educated enough, *and brave enough* to encourage involvement with other disciplines, at all levels and heartily reject "special" courses conceived by others for students who wish to specialise in the teaching of Sport and other aspects of physical activity.

We are often encapsulated by our own mediocrity, by our acceptance of narrow aspects of other subjects to the exclusion of the broader aspects of them. Limitations worry, freedom excites. the only way to freedom of leaning is to release the reins of constraint so that *choice* is encouraged. Therefore there must be many options, *after a firm base from which to choose has been laid,* and that base lies firmly in the sciences which establish analytical thinking, logical progression and knowledge about the *human as a unit,* so that considered judgments can be made. Whilst it is essential that various streams, avenues and opportunities cater for the different personalties and ambitions of those who make up the sports-teaching profession, it is wise to have *a common base of knowledge,* then, and only then, should choice be made. Education gives the right to choose—without it considered decision is impossible. To teach adequately within the world of overt physical expression whether to the mentally disabled, physically "illiterate", physically and mentally handicapped or to those blessed with seemingly normal reaction and to those of the élite minority, preparation must be adequate; interest and devotion intense. The only thanks a teacher of physical activity will receive will be noted in the smile, the shout of exultation, the indirect joy of another's achievement, the observed mastering of a skill, an achievement in another's mind yet not revealed to us, *in a victory, not assessed as one, by us* and sometimes through a lifetime friendship.

The complexities and range of the human mind, even our own, are still mainly beautiful mysteries. The physiological capacities of the human organism, the psychological ramifications of encouragement, praise, help and/or censure, the social implication, the inner needs and justification, are not known. None of us is capable of knowing the limits of anyone—even ourselves.

Each teacher has sought "truth". Whether searched for through the mental beliefs of a religion, the thrill and inspiration of an art, or the exact prediction of the purity of science does not matter—it relies upon the absoluteness, the intensity, the belief and conviction that "this is a way". And that is enough, for the teacher is dedicated to bring out the statue from the stone, just as Michelangelo took a rejected, marred piece of marble and created the statue "David". A small boy had stood, daily watching Michelangelo chip away at the cracked slab of rock and eventually the expressive and beautiful statue appeared—the young observer said, quite simply, "How did you know he was there?". The teacher of human movement must have that hope, that vision, belief, ability as well as knowledge to be as that sculptor, to bring out that which is there. That is the inspiration, motivation and essence of a teacher—belief and hope—that somehow, sometime, someone will be touched by a thought, an idea, a feeling that there is a need to know, to learn more, to express, to feel more deeply, to have a purpose, because one's life is unique and one can make a contribution, through the privilege to influence aright, just someone else.

Man is so magnificently irascible, so unpredictable, so impossible to characterise, stamp, label, "pigeon-hole" that the study of Man, holistically, is the only way to understand how and why Man moves and acts as he does. Not that human behaviour will ever be solved, for every thought, concept, idea, feeling, reason, can never be assessed at any given moment; thus Man frees himself so soon as he is "captured" and reason is never exact, adequate or "right". It is difficult to say what and when something is "right" or "wrong", "good" or "bad", adequate or inadequate. There are so many factors to be identified, adjusted to, encouraged, stressed, eliminated, that expression (through physical movement) bares all the limitations, inhibitions, reliefs, emotions, strengths, weaknesses, hates, loves, which through excellent sport-teaching may become canalised into expression—adequate or inadequate in the eyes of—whom do you think—the teacher.

Teaching is hard work—not inspiration alone. For the successful teacher, of that which has been grouped together under the term "sport", such aspects as balance, speed, mobility, force, memory, ingenuity, concentration, strength, work and endurance can be either assessed or measured scientifically and the findings used to aid more fulfilling performance by others, simply because the teacher of human movement *does* direct human behaviour. No-one can behave without a neurological mechanism. breathe without respiration, be maintained without nutrition or a circulatory system. It is thus assumed that Man acts and reacts as a biological entity and, unless illness is present, will do so with efficiency and integrity. Yet Man's behaviour is more than just the body's response to stimuli, there is the environmental effect to consider, mental decision, individual belief and relationship to others. The teacher of expression through physical activity becomes a conjoining force which fashions a world of expression, equalising and balancing many pulls and pushes in each individual into a cohesive recognisable whole. This is only done by losing oneself; in other words, by stopping being conscious of self by being conscious of others.

Teachers of human movement must have spontaneous self-expression, ingenuity, problem-solving ability and creativity *but* to be creative in teaching demands knowledge and understanding. Any "education" ignoring these points is not making a realistic effort to promote creativity in teaching. Originality is also a necessity, but techniques of teaching do not ensure that the creative teacher of diving will also be a creative scientist, even though he/she may be a splendid science student. Does this then suggest that some potential teachers of sport fall foul of the "educational theory/educational practice" dichotomy? Often, in the educational context, theory and practice are dramatically opposed. "I'm a practical teacher, I've no time for all this theory." is sometimes said, or, "It may be fine in theory but it won't work in practice.", the implications being that theory is one thing and practice another. This is the way many who wish to teach sport-activity view science, as against art.

There are different kinds of "theory" or different senses in which the word "theory" is used but it will be readily agreed that the theories of biological (natural) science have enabled us to get somewhere. Controlled experiments form an integral part of the natural scientists' procedures and the possibility of these forms of research, achieving technological application, is always present. So far as the biological sciences are concerned, the dramatic advances of the last thirty years give a reminder of the successful and happy marriage between theory and practice. Thus, with a successful science of nature so there is now a successful science of Man and it is here that the practical teaching of Man, in movement, can thrive; for theory will modify practice just as practice will modify theory.

Philosophical theorising alone cannot provide teachers of sport with a set of techniques which will ensure a successful lesson or practice session, neither can theory provide someone who has personality defects with the absolute means of controlling or stimulating action. Neither do theories provide *certainties.* Aristotle wrote in the Nicomachean Ethics I, (iii), 4:

> . . . for the man of education will seek exactness so far, in each subject, as the nature of the thing admits; it being plainly much the same absurdity to put up with a mathematician who tries to persuade instead of proving, and to demand strict demonstrative reasoning of a public speaker.

Naturally, there will be differences of opinion on educational issues but teachers of sporting activity must be prepared to exercise reason, powers of critical thinking, use the proven facts of physical laws, the results of work physiologists' experimentation, the social sciences' conclusions, *and* one's own ideas, opinions and theories concerning training methods built upon experience. The delight of, and the privilege of being in teaching is the inevitability of disagreement but with the opportunity to express oneself. There is no such thing as an absolute answer or even a similar class to teach—neither would be desirable. There are *no* definite answers—there *is* constant searching, there is *no* perfect teacher, there is *always* room for the considered idea; thus teaching will *always* be a challenge, ever new but based upon given "knowns" which must be applied; for excellent teaching lies in the ability of *putting principles into practice.*

Teaching may also be compared to selling something but no one can sell unless someone buys, yet there are teachers who believe they have done a full day's teaching irrespective of whether the students have learned anything or not. The only way to stimulate learning is to augment the quantity and quality of learning opportunity, because the learning is that which the student must do for him or herself; the initiative lies with the learner, as was so well put by the then headmaster of Rugby School in England, Thomas Arnold (1797–1842) who, in an address to the school said: ". . . the boy must build himself, his own manhood, with the material supplied by environment. Nobody else can do it for him."

The teacher is a guide, the leader. The way to direct the energy that propels the teacher lies in the belief of what and how something is taught and from the eagerness of those who are leaning. The more a teacher is aware of the intellect of those being taught, of *their* hopes, ambitions, objectives, aim, interest and past experience, the better the teacher will understand the forces at work, how they can be harnessed, directed and utilised for intelligent thought and action *in* those who are leaning. If there are faults, these lie with the teacher, not the student; some teachers are quick to establish blame, for not comprehending, upon the student, when the teacher (him or herself) has not clearly communicated what is expected of the student. This applies in all teaching, but the *opportunities for communication* are heightened in the realms of sport. Here the teacher has freedom unknown within the restrictive classroom setting; but the control, direction of the functioning, vital, moving and energetic body bring added responsibilities which can only be met by adequate preparation.

A competent teacher of sports activity must be prepared, and suitably dressed to demonstrate what is needed, or to see that an adequate demonstration is given by another. To meet the changing needs of those who learn, the different climatic, cultural, ethnic and social impositions demand all of a sensitive and understanding teacher—*herein lies the art of teaching*—the ability and willingness to change and adjust to each situation as the circumstances determine. The relationship of teacher to student is a societal one; the teacher must be aware and alert to the social expectations demanded of teachers equally as well as understanding the import and value of the subject matter taught.

DISCIPLINE

For successful sport-teaching, personal discipline is essential and is learned through the willingness to be patient and to acquire this feature through the scientists' duty to observe, for it is discipline which will be the guide. There is also the need to accept the challenge of difficulty and intensity which breed selectivity. This should be done without compulsion in choosing courses of study, not "easy" ones but those which one identifies to be essential, however, arduous, challenging or difficult. Without effort there is no reward. This was stressed by Pindar in his XIth Olympian Ode, when he wrote: "Without toil there have triumphed a very few".

Stephen Leacock hit it well when he asked what courses a student was taking. The answer was "Greek, Music and Architecture". Leacock asked did the student intend to become a choirmaster in a Greek Orthodox Church? "No", said the student. . . "those courses come at 9, 10 and 11, Monday, Wednesday and Friday.".

EDUCATIONAL INTENT

What has this to do with Olympism? Everything! For unless the principles of the Olympic idea are incorporated into the daily teaching of every child in every school, the Olympic Movement is doomed.

The whole concept of Olympism lies in its universality, its commonality, in its inherent fairness. Based on simply expressed principles, it is adequate for each culture, each stratum of educational level and for each individual. In classroom, in pool, on field and track, Olympic principles of fair play and international friendships can be explained, observed and practised—unless this is maintained, the whole Olympic ideal will be lost. The Olympic Games, as the ultimate expression of Olympic thought, precept and action must go on, they must transcend every adverse influence imposed by Man upon them.

The spotlight is on, the spotlight illumines this human arena where every facet of human behaviour is based, intensified, magnified, judged—but by whom? It is we who judge ourselves. Educationalists should ensure that adequate teaching will prepare youth for the opposition, the challenge which will continue to come to destroy the freedom Olympism brings. The Olympic torch lit and carried should be the light to enlighten world educational authorities to a movement which is an inspiration, an incentive and a worthy ambition for millions of young people. It is one of the few world-forces for good left in this complex universe we have made. Educationally it relies solidly upon our influence, leadership and belief, not to exhibit once every two years but every year, all year, every day that, in and through sport, through and for youth, at all levels of art and science—*Olympism is a living communication.* It is the Esperanto of nations, the language of mental and physical expression in the open air, in art galleries, in and through poetry, in music, writing, drama, gymnasia, upon tracks and on fields instead of just talk. Decision through talk in stuffy conference rooms in isolated countries concerned with narrow matters of national prestige can all be changed, by happy youth competing in equitable rivalry in a world festival, in amity and with jubilation, free from oppression and restraint.

CONCLUSION

Teaching is an art—not a science, yet the application of scientific principles is essential to successful teaching. It is not possible to teach well without adopting the physical, chemical and statistical laws, thus adequately allowing full expression of human movement. To understand sport, one must also be thoroughly versed in morphology, genetics, physical and social anthropology, logical aspects of the development of Homo sapiens—but *not* in separate compartments. That is one of the fundamental errors made by those of us who study the complex animal—the human being—that we attempt to segment when study must be inter-, cross-, multi-disciplinary and holistic. Man cannot be separated from his environment for Man constantly creates it. Thus one must be highly qualified by being thoughtfully *prepared,* for sports teaching and any other aspect of the human movement spectrum.

The general public has a vociferous disrespect for those who teach aspects of physical activity for it is thought to be either easy or needing little qualification. You have noted how "everyone" tells the teacher of sport what is good for his/her child, how anyone can "teach" someone how to swim, play basketball or softball and run the 800 metres. But it takes knowledge and the *knowledge is scientific* but the way the *teaching is done is the art.* One can not survive without the other, each is complementary to the other. The science and art of teaching of physical activity are like functional arms and legs guided by a thoughtful mind. Michel de Montaigne in *Essays,* written in 1580 gave the essence to this thought:

> It is not a mind, it is not a body, that we are training up; it is a man, and we ought not to divide him into two parts; and as Plato says, we are not to fashion one without the other, but make them draw together like two horses harnessed to a coach.

There are far too many people involved in curricula who are limiting the options of those who wish to teach by excluding essentials in the study of Man, just as there are teaching Colleges and Universities which accept those neither fitted for, nor truly interested in, the sport-teaching professions. These are underlying problems which, until eradicated will, solely by being problems, drive the wedge between the necessary components of a liberal education through science and art.

Curriculum decisions, as educational decisions, rest upon individuals' systems of value and often upon cultural, linguistic or nationalistic aims. These (varying with time and place) will bring about variations in curricula practices based upon them. The real questions are "which major lines of enquiry ought to be pursued?" and "whether human intellect and society at their present level of evolution can survive the next truths?"

Sport-teaching can neither be satisfying nor satisfactory if it is not a true blend of fact and spontaneity. The *science* of *teaching sport* lies in the naturalness of adequate understanding of function and structure, their limitations and potential. The *art* of *teaching sport* is in the identification of intent and the ability to draw out hidden resources, of purpose, adequacy and fun. For when teaching becomes fun, it is free from restraint and individually has meaning: *BUT* only knowledge frees the body and mind.

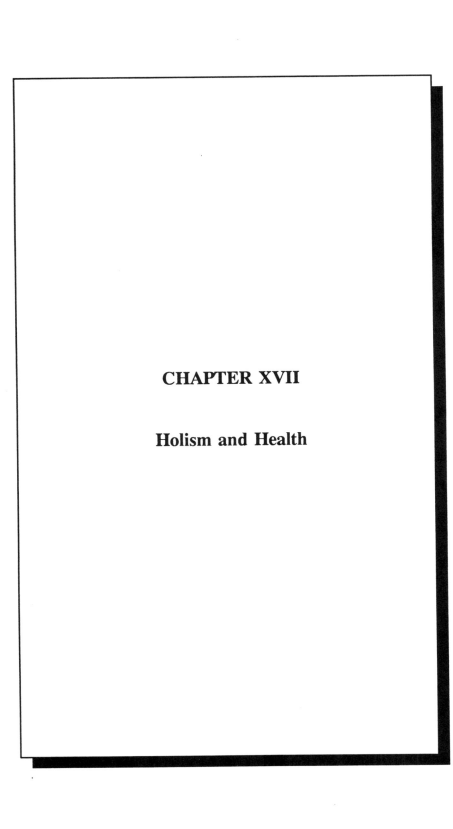

CHAPTER XVII

Holism and Health

TIME AND TIDE

Roar, thou mighty ocean roll,
    And leave firm strands for us to walk upon.
Where wind and tide combine their force in lashing spray,
    As we implant our tell-tale marks,
Though soon they will be gone,
    On drying corrugated wrinkles as we stroll
Impatient for bronzed skin, to attest a holiday.

Scudding clouds, the wind's whip-lash 'round our knees
    The ever-present humming of the wild erratic breeze
Which presses lungs to fill with full
    Clean, clear, yet salty air.
And the sugar sand whips eyes and straightens out our hair.

The rocks seem insignificant from a viewpoint upon high
    But now, close by they're massive and the sea surges to get
                                         by,
I could watch the sea for ever with its wondrous changing hue
    Determined by the clouds and weak sunshine peeking through.

The inexorable tide smashes 'cross the rocks
    And the changing weather patterns our hope
And forever mocks, as wind and tide
    Combine their strength in glorious intertwining play
As though to know we wish that on the morrow
    It will be, at least a sunny day.

                                                J.T.P.

CHAPTER XVII
Holism and Health

Look to your health; and if you have it, praise God, and value it next to a good conscience; for health is the second blessing that we mortals are capable of: a blessing that money cannot buy.

Izaak Walton: *The Compleat Angler*
(Chapter 21, 1653)

INTRODUCTION

For the purpose of this Chapter, I have defined PHYSICAL ACTIVITY—FITNESS—HEALTH.

Physical Activity: Voluntary movement which requires any of the features of walking, running, applied strength, mobility, speed, muscular power, balance, agility, dexterity, endurance. It may be enjoyed alone or in a group and includes sports, games, exercises and dance.

Fitness: The ability to do a job of work well, without tiredness and to be able to repeat that work as efficiently as previously and still be mentally and physically alert. Physical fitness is only one aspect of total fitness.

Health: Personal fitness for full, rewarding and enjoyable living. Health is positive and not simply an absence of disease, and may be depicted as a unit of three inter-related features, each influencing the other: physical fitness, mental health and spiritual conviction.

Thus, a healthy person with optimum fitness is able to carry out usual and everyday tasks without undue fatigue, having reserve energy enough to enjoy leisure-time activity and capable of meeting emergency situations.

WHAT THEN IS HOLISM?

The term was coined by the late Field Marshall, the Honourable J. C. Smuts—one-time Prime Minister of South Africa. The terms comes from the Greek (ὅλοΣ) meaning whole. Smuts defined it in his book *Holism and Evolution,* published by McMillan Company in 1926. It is the theory that the fundamental principle of the universe is the creation of wholes, that is, complete and self-contained systems from the atom and the cell by evolution, to the most complex forms of mind and life. Holism is fundamental in nature.

I was introduced to the book in the 1930's and it had a great influence upon me and the formation of my concept of human kinetics which took me over 30 years to formulate and confirm into fact as an holistic scientific study of the genus *MAN* moving. Rightly considered a biologic science. The human kinetics concept had its origin in Guelph, Canada in 1965. Because holism is everywhere and in everything, I believe it to be the key to the interpretation of health.

WHOLE AND HEALTH

It is most interesting that the words "whole" and "health" stem from the Old English word "hale" which is defined as "the condition of wholesomeness". The expression to be "hale and hearty" is well known. The word "whole" is defined as "something made up of parts in combination of mutual connection". It is an assemblage of things united so as to constitute one greater thing—a complex unity. What more is health? To be made whole is to be healthy, thus health is a condition of wholesomeness.

There is a trend in Canada (although started in the United States of America some 30 years ago) to use the term "wellness" rather than "health". Wellness is not health. Health is positive and tangible shown in its expression through human satisfaction and efficiency, whereas "wellness" is a feeling, a phase; health is a state with respect to soundness, a particular manner of being, of the unity of mind, body and spirit. The whole is not something additional to its parts; it *is* the parts in a definite structural arrangement and with mutual activities that constitute the whole. The essence of the whole is that whilst it is formed of its parts it, in turn, influences those parts and affects relations and functions.

A thing does not come to a stop at its boundaries, it overflows because of its action. It passes beyond its bounds and its adjoining fields—it has an effect on other things. Health is action which overflows. Health is both cause and effect which interlock, embrace, influence each other through inter-penetration of their own influences. Everything has its field and it is the intermingling of these fields that allows things to happen through creativity or causality in nature as well as in life. Nothing ever happens in space alone or in time alone but always in both, together. The ideas of space and time interweave with each other and are dependent on each other. The inmost nature of the universe is active energy or simply action which involves the interplay of tremendous positive forces. That is why I consider health to be positive and not simply an absence of disease. because health is a mixture of many things and forces. What are these things and forces which enable us to have health, if health is optimal personal fitness for fine living?

The word "fitness" is far from being the narrow, one entity aspect of physical fitness. Fitness is for living and being ready for all the exigencies of the day, for the unexpected, being able to react to it, and cope with it, effectively.

FINE LIVING

What does "fine living" encompass?

1. *Work*—this is related to contribution and ability within the environment in which ones finds oneself, or has created.
2. *Play*—the outlets we need to stimulate ourselves.
3. *Civic and Societal Contributions*—which each of us must make.
4. *Love*—affection of all forms.
5. *Worship and Personal Faith*—these forces and things conjoined typify health, that positive state of being, enabling one to live to the fullest—and being thankful for it.

I see **HEALTH** as a circuit—a circle without a broken link—no weaknesses, all parts of that continuum being of equal strength, purpose and value, no factor counting for more than another.

But I said **OPTIMAL** personal fitness for fine living. We are not equal, we do not all have the same genetic background, the same structure, the same opportunities, the same nutrition, the same working or living environment, but does that mean to say that we cannot be healthy with one leg, one breast, or one eye? Certainly not. We can be optimally healthy (as healthy as we can possibly be) with that loss.

HEALTH AND DISEASE

As we talk of HEALTH, perhaps we should talk of DISEASE. The word derives from the Latin—dis-aese, dis meaning "part", and from the French—aese, meaning "comfort or content". Disease is a morbid condition, a deviation from health, a disturbance of structure and/or function of any part of the person, or the person as a whole. And this applies both physically and mentally—and these are caused by deprivation of some sort or other—disease is caused by the lack of essentials. Throughout all cultures, health is identified as Harmony—Balance—Order, and disease as Disharmony—Imbalance—Disorder. It is appropriate, however, to realize that one doesn't treat a disease but sick people.

It is salutary to reflect on famine, poverty, hunger, starvation and to focus our attention that in many societies, there is no play, no expenditure of unnecessary energy, no laughter, no singing, no hope, but there is mass disease interpreted on the basis of *ALL* factors; the host, the agent of disease and the environment.

Claude Bernard stated that the healthy being is ". . . a piece of constancy living and moving in a world of variables." With disease there is no constancy. The genesis of infectious disease and of epidemics is more than a single reaction between *MAN* and his parasites; disease affects everything. To maintain homeostasis, i.e. the constancy of the internal milieu, *MAN* must have access to the balancing factors involved in the process. Unless *MAN* can obtain what is required to convert or eliminate what is in excess, *MAN* can not maintain homeostasis—or health. This lays bare another source of pathology, that of deprivation, and this is disease as a result of lack of essentials.

IS EXERCISE AN ESSENTIAL?

What do you feel about the old man who was asked how he was? His reply was "I'm remarkably well considering I've been remarkably well for so many years.". I wonder will it ever be that the terms Life Span and Health Span become synonymous? *Life span* is the theoretic length of time one is able to live. *Health span* is the theoretic length of time that one is able to keep active and healthy.

Is there any relationship between longevity (life span—life expectancy and average length of life) and exercise? To what extent is longevity determined by Heredity, Behaviour, Environment, realizing that the environment has a silent assimilative transformative influence of a most profound and enduring character on all organic life? What about these factors; do they affect longevity?—"Age", occupation, geographic location, standard of living, nutrition, education, medical care, "fate". How do we explain the fact that *both* sedentary living and life expectancy have increased in Canada since 1850? But is it longevity in which we are interested—categorically—NO! We are most interested in what we can pack into the years given us—rather than on how long we live. Already your experience has shown you long and useful lives as well as long and useless ones. Our nursing homes, hospitals, old-age homes are *full* of people just "ticking over", maintained in air-conditioned situations or thermostatically-controlled environments protected by drugs, maintained by full-blooded young people. This in no way disparages the wonderful work done by the nursing profession, the care, rehabilitation, exercise programmes freely given. *There is no need to do anything to live.* It is difficult to realize that one can still die of old age, but here we must ask ourselves, "how old is old?" If we go on like this will people live to be 200, 300, 500 years of age? But will they be healthy? Is there any joy in simply existing? My uncle Edmund lived until he was 89 and he lived an active, useful life. My father said he'd have lived longer had he not killed himself. "Killed himself?" I asked. "Yes," said Dad, "since he bought that car two years ago he never got any exercise—I could see him slipping from then on".

DISEASES OF UNDERACTIVITY

Are there hypokinetic diseases? Since the wheel was invented, *MAN* has attempted to substitute machines for the work our bodies were created to do. Today, many daily activities common to our parents and particularly theirs, are performed with minimal effort by us through machines—physical exertion has become unnecessary. Analyze your own life—your aches and pains and operations. Do you not feel like the woman who told her doctor that she'd always wanted to have a nervous breakdown but every time she was about to get down to it, someone in her family needed a meal cooked. *You* are active, you have a purpose in life, you fulfil your societal obligations—you haven't time to be ill; you're *healthier* because you just don't have time to entertain aches and pains. The older ones of us are still more accustomed to physical activity, in an average day, but those in the younger generations have to take special care and make specific effort to join exercise programmes. Exercise has become the modern substitute for the work our bodies were created to do.

Also, because of "double jobs" when both partners work, many people lack habitual exercise which has a partial overlapping with detrimental emotional factors leading to suppressed emotional responses; general disuse of mind and muscle; overstress; tension syndrome; lower back ache; internal diseases, e.g. cardio-vascular conditions; emotional and psychiatric problems, and ALL of them are inter-related. Exercise is not a specific cure for disease. Disease requires prompt and efficient medical attention; the value of exercise is in its preventative factors. The general principle is that progressive physical activity has the effect of adapting the body to cope with the necessary stress of modern life.

Psychosomatic diseases are so prevalent these days—we all need work to occupy our minds and bodies. You have interesting purposeful lives—many, many others don't! By our society's acceptance of mechanization we can see how the active function of mind and muscles has been eroded and gradually taken over by "labour-saving devices". We don't walk, but ride; we don't climb stairs, but use elevators; we don't lift weights; we don't mow lawns but have a machine to do it; we have vacuum cleaners; some of us have dishwashers; push button heating, and so on, but still we feel stressed.

WHAT IS STRESS?

Stress is essentially the rate of *all* wear and tear caused by life. Throughout life we try to preserve homeostasis, to maintain the constancy of the internal milieu despite the surrounding.

The Apollonian advice to "know thyself" and "nothing in excess" are as applicable as when carved on Apollo's temple arch at Delphi in 510 B.C.

Stress, however, is good; we all need stress to enable us to cope. Stress is biologic, but the effects of stress may often be bad. Many common diseases are largely because of errors in our adaptive response to stress rather than to direct damage by germs, poisons or other agents. Emotional disturbances, high blood pressure, gastric and duodenal ulcers, cardio-vascular, allergic and renal diseases all appear to be essentially *diseases of adaptation.*

The great, late Dr. Hans Seyle, the man who devoted his life to defining stress, explaining it and treating it, stated that it is through the G.A.S. (general adaptation syndrome) that our various internal organs—especially the endocrine glands and the central nervous system—help to adjust us to the constant changes which occur in and around us.

Life is largely a process of adaptation to the circumstances in which we exist. There is a constant give-and-take going on between living matter and its inanimate surroundings, between one living being and another, ever since the dawn of life.

The essence of health and happiness lies in a successful adjustment to the ever-changing conditions in this world. The penalties for failure in this great process of adaptation are disease and unhappiness.

Seyle suggested that everything we do goes in three stages:

1. **Alarm Reaction**—infections—mental problems—any exertion—a new job—reaction to a new boss—
2. **Stage of Resistance**—defence
3. **Stage of Exhaustion**, and death.

We all go through stages 1 and 2 many times, e.g. running produces a stress situation to the system through reluctance, through the weather, to the muscles and the cardio-vascular and respiratory systems. So, before we run we warm-up to prepared to be efficient. There appears to be a close relationship between the G.A.S. and aging. There are diseases of adaptation; they are consequences of the body's and/or the mind's inability to meet either external or internal agents by an adequate adaptive reaction. It is well to realize that there is no pure heart disease (in which all other organs remain perfectly undisturbed) just as there is no pure liver disease, or pure nervous disease. *EVERYTHING IS INTER-RELATED.*

When considering our own health we would be well advised to note *all* the influences upon us rather than just the symptoms shown. Just as when we receive medical care, we should hope that our ailments are considered in relation to all other factors that may be influencing us.

HEALTH THEN:—

Let us now go back for another moment of reflection to *Hippokrates* and *Asklepios:*

Twenty-six centuries ago, Hippokrates, the accepted "father of medicine", told his disciples in Greece on the island of Kos that disease is not only suffering (pathos) but also toil (ponos), that is the fight of the body to restore itself to normal. He wrote that there is a healing force of nature which ensues from within. Not every deviation from the normal condition of the body is disease. There is a power of restitution in case of damage of mutilation. The newt forms a new leg, the plant supplies the place of a severed branch with another, the broken whole in organic nature restores itself or is restored by the undamaged paths, but the more highly differentiated and specialized the organism, the smaller is the power of the remaining cells to restore the whole. He wrote that just because someone has lost an arm does not make that person ill for the rest of his or her life. The person may be physically crippled yet be in excellent health—in other words, to be optimally well. Because there is no Ponos (toil)—the fight was lost years ago—there is peace in that scarred body. Illness presupposes a clash between forces of aggression and our own defences.

It was Hippokrates who wrote the treatise on *Soils, Airs, Waters,* choosing Kos, the most sheltered of the Dodecanese islands with its mineral springs, green and smiling valleys rich with fruit and flowers, to erect Aesculapia. These were the first houses of medicine, or anatoria, where, on arrival, after bathing, a patient lay in the incupatio, drugged by herbs to sleep and the diagnosis of the disease being given dependant upon the dreams produced.

The essay of Hippokrates "On the Sacred Illness" (epilepsy) has become famous. He wrote:—

> It is not, in my opinion, any more divine or more sacred than other diseases, but has a natural cause, and its supposed divine origin is due to men's inexperience, and to their wonder at its peculiar character. The fact is that the cause of this affliction, as of the more serious diseases generally, is the brain.
>
> It is a question here, not only of epilepsy, but of other afflictions, which suddenly affect the patient with terrible force such as heart—asthma and brain—disease.

He noted the difference between acute and chronic illnesses; developed the skill of questioning, understanding causation, and diagnosed through close observation of a patient. He differentiated between 7 forms of gallbladder infection, 4 forms of jaundice and 12 different bladder complaints and defined "epidemic" and "endemic".

The Greek name of physicians, Asklepiadai, appeared about 600 B.C. Later they were called Hippokratics and today almost all the world's physicians take, or refer to, the Hippokratic Oath (4th century B.C.). Throughout the world physicians wear the symbols of Asklepios—the staff and the snake.

The cult of Asklepios came from Thessaly in the 5th century to Epidauros which, even today, the local population calls "the holy place". The springs of Asklepios are still considered to be especially healthy. For over 1000 years, with Epidauros as its centre, the cult of Asklepios developed on an international scale in the ancient world. In the Iliad (iv. 194), Homer speaks of Asklepios as an "irreproachable physician".

The principal symbol of Asklepios as a healer was his snake. With its periodic shedding of its skin, it was a symbol of rebirth, of beauty as well as a symbol of eternal youth and immortality. The shedding expressed the body's regeneration after illness thus becoming the symbol of medical cure. The snake was considered a healer, a wise creature and a leading expert on the identification of therapeutic herbs. The staff around which the snake enwrapped itself can be considered as a walking stick, since Asklepios and his trainees were always walking, which he considered to be the curative exercise.

It was Asklepios who developed psychotherapeutic treatments, the use of "medicinal springs" and hydrotherapy. Thank offerings were made to him and the difference between rich and poor was apparent only in the value of these offerings—he preferred poultry. When Socrates had emptied his hemlock-poisoned cup (399 B.C.) he asked his disciples to sacrifice the proverbial rooster to Asklepios.

We must ask ourselves, did these ancients treat their clients holistically?

HEALTH TODAY

We have all observed the growing fascination with alternative approaches to health care. More and more people are searching for alternative health therapies to replace traditional medical care. For some it is simply a dietary method, for others a way of life.

Holism has become a philosophy; it has changed it original meaning. It seems as though "holistic medicine" is conceived as being not whole at all but, in many instances, a devotion to one aspect in the treatment of, or the attainment of, health. One is advised to beware of charlatans and cults.

There are a numbers of holistic approaches to health:

Ayurvidic medicine
Biofeedback
Charkas
Chi
Coulourtherapy

Homeotherapy
Hydrotherapy
Magnetic healing
Reflexology—to name a few

Each has a declared aim, to treat each client as a whole.

HEALTH TOMORROW

Here is a strategy for improving the health of the nation over the coming decade.

The needs are:

1. Prevention of major chronic illnesses
2. Prevention of injuries
3. Prevention of infectious diseases and, *through the achievement of three main goals:*
   a. increased healthy life-span

b.   increased access to preventative health services

c.   reduced health disparities amongst peoples.

Objectives: these should include:

i.   reduced infant mortality

ii.   reduced tobacco, drugs and alcohol use

iii.   increased use of mammography amongst women

iv.   increased physical activity to include muscular strength, endurance training, development of flexibility. Two vital aspects are to increase participation in daily, light physical activity to at least a quarter of the population and, to reduce sedentary lifestyles. These objectives, if achieved, should result in overall *HEALTH* for all rather than overall physical fitness.

There are special populations of our society who are at particular risk, e.g. minorities, those who are disabled; those at low income levels, single parents, and it is in these groups that the above average incidence of disability, disease and death take place.

To effect this strategy everyone must be involved. Each person has a special concern, a special reason, a special interest. Foster your own intellect, enthusiasm and contribution for the sake of a healthier nation.

CONCLUSION

We have come full circle considering many aspects in the matrix of health. How one lives is much more important than how long one lives. The only way to ensure long, efficient, active life is to choose one's parents very carefully.

As for me, I agree with Jack London when he wrote:—

I would rather be ashes than dust!
I would rather that my spark should burn
Out in a brilliant blaze than it
Should be stifled by dry rot.
I would rather be a superb meteor,
Every atom of me in magnificent glow
Than a sleepy and permanent planet.
The proper function of MAN is to
Live, not to exist.
I shall not waste my days
In trying to prolong them.

CHAPTER XVIII

Aesthetics, Art and Movement

CONTEST

The stop-watch, then the churning water,
The sprinter's flicking feet, the discus turned
In flight, the vaulter's leap from gravity
The boxer's punch which turns to fright.
The triple Axel smoothed with grace is
reflected on the athlete's face, by thankfulness
—alone—not a job well done, until it's over.
The phycho/physiological release (it's never peace)
That pent-up emotion of breaking out becomes
A silent shout of joy forcing the
Bars of one's self-imposed prison—and inadequacy.
We are never as good as we hope we are
And the crowd's so fickle sometimes
Like an almost empty jar of rattled pennies.

Thanks for the memories.
If you've not been there you do not know
—so long to practise, oh, so slow
and yet in a trice it's over—gone,
never to be repeated; different crowd,
feeling, words, food, time of day, yes, it's gone.
The aesthetic moment was yours
and yours alone, it never can
be shared or shown.
It was the essence of the
internal inside song that sang
to you—because it *was* you,
you alone and only you.
The world thought it saw it
but yet it never did, that moment
it was *YOU.*

Not yours, but the
real you, the one you had
always wished to be.
The flowers, chants, the cheery words,
the judges' judgements in bold stark
numbers, the podium, the kiss, the
medal hung around your neck was
what we saw with television eyes.
But *you* know—at last it was you, you
had yourself revealed to you and
tonight you'll have your first fright-free
sleep, the first one you've ever had
since the days of trusting youth.

J.T.P.

- 228 -

CHAPTER XVIII
Aesthetics, Art and Movement

The spectator will always understand more than the artist intended and the artist will always have intended more than any single spectator understands.

David Best
(*Expression in Movement and the Arts*, 1974, p. 152.)

Aesthetics has had a history long before its name was conceived.

Aesthetics lay dormant within Man's potential where it gradually developed and was changed by Man's use of time. Through the acquisition of leisure and the opportunity for contemplation, the creation and fashioning of objects, as well as the different patterns for man's movement, were devised. It no longer became necessary for objects to be only utilitarian nor for Man's actions to be exclusively used for protection, gathering or hunting.

Because Man is the one recalcitrant creature who strives to force forward from the tangible to the intangible. from the known to the unknown realms in search of knowledge and truth through reason, he or she, is not content just to eat, to be warm, to sleep—*Man* moves. Just as civilization is not composed solely of work, play, shelter, clothing, food, companionship and comfort—but of the striving of human spirit. It is through the combination of movement and the intellect that aesthetics was conceived.

AESTHETICS

What is meant by aesthetics? Is it the sustained and self-critical enquiry into the meaning and value of our experiences of what we identify to be beautiful, both created and observed?

But why should "aistheticos"—perceptible by the senses—have had its origins in Greece?

The Greeks originated philosophy; the thinkers gave great philosophical speculation to the nature of reality. high premium to physical beauty and all forms of games and activities, to the advanced understanding of geometric form and the origin of mathematics, the creating of art-forms in temples, and to statuary, painting, oratory, lyric and epic poetry. They eulogized the moving body and made their gods in the likeness of men, and their goddesses in the form of women. As we know, the light of Greece is so clear, it floods the rather stark countryside revealing everything as it is—this gave yet another dimension to the clarity of observation of the early Greek thinkers. But, what kind of knowledge can be obtained by watching people and other animals move? What knowledge may be gained by regarding the forms of art; what is the function of art in all its varieties? These are the types of questions which turned philosophers into rigorous thinkers and lively antagonists in an attempt to find the truth and, in attempting to answer, they developed aesthetics.

In its original form a sharp distinction was made between thought and feeling; that is, things material (pertaining to things perceptible through he senses) as opposed to things thinkable or immaterial.

The source of aesthetic theory is contained in certain dialogues of the greatest of Philosophers—Plato, for whom the essence of the beautiful lies in appropriateness and symmetry resulting from the relation of the concept to the plurality of phenomena.

BEAUTY

It is not known whether Socrates lived; nothing of this philosopher is recorded except that of which Plato and others have given account.

General Xenophon, an admirer of Socrates, in his *Memorabilia* wrote that Socrates taught that there is no such thing as absolute beauty. As goodness, so beauty is to be defined with reference to the end a thing serves and the purpose it fulfils. He wrote that something is properly called beautiful and good, ugly or bad to the extent to which it performs or fails to perform the function for which it was designed. He gave the example of a dung basket saying it should be called beautiful if it is well adapted to be useful. He wrote that a golden shield is ugly if poorly designed to serve its purpose. Xenophon tells us that Socrates was convinced that, fundamentally the beautiful is the useful. However Plato's account of Socrates' opinions about beauty, present quite a different picture. Perhaps the more intellectual interpretation of Plato is responsible for the contrast from the soldier Xenophon's understanding?

In the *Hippias Major* of Plato the searching manner of Socrates is revealed, in the *Symposium* whilst the central issue is love, the dialogue concludes with Socrates' presentation of a soothsayer's views on the relation between love and beauty with beauty being either transcendental or rational. In another platonic dialogue—*Republic,* Socrates returns to the problem of defining beauty. Here he considers the aesthetic environment which will nurture good men, essential components of this environment are, he wrote, music, literature, visual arts and physical activity.

Aesthetics, as a critical enquiry (delving into beauty and all forms of art) was born in Greece and nurtured in Germany as it was Alexander Baumgarten (1714–1762) who coined the word "aesthetic", giving the new name to an old subject in his book *Meditationes* in 1735. Baumgarten believed in the primacy of reason; through this, clear and distinct ideas could be attained and rigorous logical deductions made. He said that to make beauty intelligible, what was needed was a science of the things we perceive, to go along with, and supplement the science of, things we know. Thus aesthetics became his science of perception as well as his science of logic. Aesthetics to him was "perfection of sensuous knowledge as such" and where there is a defect in sensuous knowledge, when it is imperfect, the result is ugliness; but what is ugly for one is not ugly for another.

Baumgarten had a "major problem", he was passionately fond of poetry (as was Plato). He considered poetry a "perfectly sensuous language" yet his science demanded he be perfectly factual, and whilst poetry expresses clear ideas it does so without being distinct. He eventually presented his conclusions in 1750 in his book *Aesthetica* resolving his concern. He wished aesthetics to be not only a science useful to explain the nature of artistic discovery but to be a science concerned with the means by which artistic values are presented and communicated. Thus, through Baumgarten aestheticism came to stand for a way of looking at life, a way of viewing art, literature and forms of movement.

EXPERIENCE

All learning for Man is experience. Because we are conscious and sentient, responsive and vital, moving and expressive, we experience. Experience is the general condition of our daily living. We are all different and we look at people, things and situations in different ways. There are those amongst us who are mystic, others scientist; some rationalist, others are sensualist, introspectionist; businessman or businesswoman; the scholar, the worshipper, the artist, the teacher, the sportswoman or sportsman; each devoting him or herself to different spheres within this broad spectrum of experience through the characteristic activities we pursue. But the word "aesthetics" will, for many, conjure up a vague rather insubstantial world bearing no obvious relation to experience. What is the relationship between aesthetics and movement?

Human movement is Man's most characteristic attribute, life is identified through movement; human movement is unique and, to give but one example, our hands enable us to do what our brain suggests we should do. The purpose movement serves will affect the observer and/or the performer's judgement of it. Movement which serves functional objectives is essential for every human; the more movement serves our function the better it is for us. Perhaps one then agrees with Xenophon's interpretation of Socrates' opinion that something is aesthetic if useful? When needs are met with skill this is especially satisfying.

Anyone who moves, (and feels that a certain movement, or sequence of movements satisfies the purpose for which it was created), enjoys an exhilaration. Looking at others move with pose, grace, assurance, range and co-ordination gives positive associative feelings to the observer. Some sports, games and related activities exist primarily as contest, yet even when points or goals scored are not to one's liking, or efficiency of the players' actions, the flow of movement gives pleasure. In some other activities, such as synchronized swimming, the various forms of Rhythmic or Olympic gymnastics, skiing, speed skating, pair skating, surf-boarding, wind-surfing, and diving, it is not only the competitive result of the act which is important but "the way it is done", the "spirit" of the performance, the quality and the factors injected through interpretation and one's own style which count.

Concepts of acceptable and unacceptable patters of human movement come from social, racial and even national bases, through customs, physical structure, individual and group expectations.

Some enjoy slow, smooth, ballistic, wide sweeping movements. Others enjoy moving fixations, accented, noisy, violent, jabbing, striking, jerky ones, some like to glide across a floor, others to stretch and reach high. Some need personal space, others like communal movement, some to touch, others to be free or to expand in breadth through open, striking statuesque movement. Attitudes vary to movement because each of us has preference as well as limitations of experience, ability, opportunity or of concept.

The extent to which our movement-habits and our preference for certain movement themes vary is related to our personality, and to our values which, unlike facts are usually private, sometimes unusual, often imaginary.

Every movement we do, every movement we observe has many meanings and differs in different situations and with different people. The same movement may mean different things to different people at different times of the day, month or year. Movements, so thoughtlessly or thoughtfully performed, or seen, have very many different connotations—these are characteristics of the genus, *Man*. Symbolism, (the identification and significance of signs and the relating of them to our experience) has its part in making each of us what we are.

AESTHETICS OF MOVEMENT

Aesthetics of Movement is concerned with the investigation and study of human response to environmental, visual, aural, tactive, oral and olfactory phenomena or stimuli. This statement does not imply limit of response to only those stimuli which cause feelings of 'beauty' and which heighten experience and transcend the norm of 'pleasure'. It is equally concerned with what some consider to be "ugly", plus the whole range or stimuli between the extremes "beautiful" and "ugly". In fact the aesthetics of movement deals with the complete spectrum of biological response.

BEAUTY AND ART

Beauty and art are not synonymous. The purpose of art is not necessarily the portrayal of beauty. There are so many experiences and things to which we apply the word "beautiful" which have nothing to do with art, as such. Is physical activity beautiful? Are sports, games, dance and exercise art forms? Is it "beautiful" to take part in activity, or is it only pleasurable, or not even that, especially when one is inadequate for the activity? Is it beautiful to watch an athletic spectacle . . . in the rain, without a coat, from a wet seat, however fine the athletic action?

SEEING AND DOING

Is this evanescent "something" called "aesthetic" possessed by something, or is it a quality conferred upon someone or an object by a perceiver? In aesthetics nothing works on principle; there are no rules. The crux of the aesthetic field is transactional experience which involves a perceiver and an object, it is not the event but the product of one's own effort to know, to understand, and to appreciate that matters. Beauty does not exist intrinsically in an object; it exists in the mind because of the stimuli which the object emits. The object remains the same but even the perception of it will change because the reference of experience changes, grows or diminishes. A statue is beautiful because of reference within oneself. A viewer brings certain stable features into a situation through biological, social and psychological similarities to other humans, yet each person introduces a wide degree of variability to situations which may happen at a particular time and in a specific situation. Also, differences in performers introduce further factors into the aesthetic field; these different variables account for differences in aesthetic response and judgement.

Is a performer an artist? If so, is she, or he, imitating things which have happened previously, or creating an original work. The imitative arts, according to Plato, give copies of copies and the practitioner of these art forms does not know the difference between knowledge and ignorance; otherwise, says Plato, the artist would seek to make actual things rather than fabricate copies.

"Imitation is only a kind of play or sport . . ."

(*Republic,* Book X, p. 602).

PERFORMERS AND SPECTATORS

In attempting to evaluate human movement from either the performer's or the spectator's view the concept of aesthetic perception must be central. Only when the immediate "world" before us is seen in terms of the particular performer and his or her interest and ability, can we succeed in reaching an understanding of the performance. This is difficult to do; for example, to dance, to release emotions and express oneself may well be an aesthetic "experience" not only for the dancer enjoying the movement for it is own sake, but also for the onlooker. The sheer beauty of physical movement is aesthetically appreciated in many athletic endeavours, but is it art?

A work of art is the presentation of, or the embodiment of, something formed from diverse but compatible elements as an entity. It is created by a "composer" with the intent to communicate an idea and to achieve a reaction. In dance this expressed emotion is fashioned into a unit portraying these ideas; but, however magnificently interpreted, the dancer cannot "feel" what the dance reflects. Only the individual in the audience receives the interpretation built through the dance's elements, each in themselves carefully selected, choreographed and executed. The dance is an abstraction from actual happenings or feelings which suggest meanings, and these are significant.

What is portrayed conveys the form of the whole, and it is this form which is aesthetically evaluated by the viewer who does not see every element but gains an impression through this integration. The whole becomes greater than the sum of its parts and the unifying process, by which form is attained, is composition. So, is all aesthetic response a response to form, and if so, is that a fundamental emotion of Homo sapiens and is this the way in which we watch all forms of physical expression; are we always looking at form, how something has been achieved as in springboard diving, in a quarterback's throw, a goal-keeper's save, a volleyball player's "spike"? The essential feature of aesthetics is "significant form", so, unless one makes a judgement that something has, or lacks significant form it is not an aesthetic judgement at all.

DOING

In engineering and in architecture "aesthetic factors" have become the province of the industrial designer who aims to create a pleasant and functional environment in which people can work and/or live. In human medicine one of the topics of psychology lies in the assessment of satisfaction gained through the "how" something is done. For the human-movement practitioner gratification is gained through making it possible for people to do things to their optimal level.

In prosthetics much has been achieved to design limbs to be as attractive as possible to the user, but, will a copy every be satisfactory aesthetically? Would not efficiency allow for greater well-being? Man only invented machines which flew when he stopped attempting to imitate birds' flight.

SEEING

How does one see ice dancing—innovative, creative, beautiful? If so, what is it that makes it so? Is it the great expanse of cold white or blue ice, blended costumes, blended movements, happy young faces, glorious bodies, the colours, the music, the synchronization of movement patterns, the flow and melding of co-ordinated actions all in rhythm, or, in fact, is the performance a piece of art? Transient, yes, reproducible on film or video, possibly, yet next time there is a performance there could be human error, the spectators may be different, the site, ice surface, the judges, the time of day—in fact, to some degree, everything will be different because there is no possibility of performers producing the "now". But what was seen, and to some extent recalled, is the overall form.

How does one watch dance, in the same way as one watches football, or will it be even the same people who will watch both these physical expressions? Will judgements differ?

Is football only structured play because there are rules that must be known to those who control the game and those who participate in it? Does this structure inhibit creativity; if so, can there be any aesthetic experience gained through taking part, or is the emotion only pleasure and that solely for the winning coach and partisan spectators?

Is any play self-rewarding, does one play for the sake of playing rather than for an extrinsic reward? Whilst there are aspects of play in every game, sport and activity, is true play only possible when it is dissociated from survival, and are football, and/or other games, activities of survival?

AESTHETIC EXPERIENCE

What is an aesthetic experience? Is it hedonistic, satisfying; does it require conscious reasoning; is it intuitive, is it a state of awareness, an integration and a being "one" with the experience that "does something" to us?

Is it possible to dissect, to agree on some essentials? Can it be similar for all people regardless of time, place or space and are aesthetic concepts of people in cities those of the Bushmen of the Kalahari desert? Were ancient Greece's values different to our own? Concepts of the aesthetic change, according to time, place and all the things *Man* has done and all the things that have happened to *Man*. But, are there values which continue for ever, are there immutable standards?

Biological change, technological discovery, social change, changes in values, prejudices, a change in the traditional acceptance of what is excellence are all being reflected in the whole range of "artistic" interpretations. Often the performer, the spectator and the artist have, seemingly, forsaken traditional patterns. As people and times change so do tastes and standards; however, to sift aesthetic criteria appears to be impossible for it is the whole person who reacts, bringing to any experience habitual responses, past influences, biases and inter-related values.

Each of us has perceptions and values for judging these perceptions, yet there appear to be very few identifiable and unchanging things about which all of us agree to be common to the aesthetic experience. What each of us considers to be "aesthetic" is affected by emotional state, imagination, physical condition, freedom, one's own idea of beauty, what is meant by "deformed", truth, pleasure, perceptual acuity, breadth or depth of appreciation, as well as one's own idea of reality, and experience.

Aesthetics offers no objective formulae, no proofs because it deals with the value part within perception. Aesthetics thus assesses values and these depend upon intangible standards. An aesthetic experience cannot be replicated; it cannot be relived; it is unique. Even the anticipation of hearing a passage in a well-loved piece of music, the sitting back, the waiting, knowing how pleasurable the experience has been and the expectancy of the joy it will give on hearing it again, cannot be classed as aesthetic because, always the circumstances have changed, but it is the same music. An aesthetic experience belongs to oneself exclusively. The majority of people have never had an aesthetic experience. Most people have fond memories, have enjoyed fleeting moments of exquisite joy, have been pleased, have shared delightful episodes, exulted in victory for oneself or for others and even when one's experiences have been recorded in sound and on film have re-lived, in part, those times. But the aesthetic experience has passed and can never even be described. Our levels of appreciation, because of our human circumstances of satisfaction and expectancy, are all different in degree through physique, injury, deformation, deprivation, level of nutrition, apprehension, genuine or imagined fears, repressions, opportunity or encouragement, in fact, through experience. But the anticipation of receiving an aesthetic "message" can become of the greatest importance for a particular individual who, through intellect can be more sensitive to the aesthetic potential within oneself.

CONCLUSION

The aesthetic field is a perceptual one invoking the full range of sensory responses of which the human organism is capable. Each human is the result of a unique combination of genes, acting together they form a whole personality. It is this whole personality, the whole person, which reacts mentally/physically to stimuli.

When we encounter physical response through our own movement or observe it in others, or encounter art in any of its interpretations, we do so biologically.

A. E. Houseman put this succinctly in his book *The Name and Nature of Poetry:*

Poetry indeed seems to me more physical than intellectual . . . I could no more define poetry than a terrier can define a rat . . . we both recognize the object by the symptoms which it provokes in us.

However, the delight which the beautiful gives directly is not sensible pleasure, the senses are conveyors only, being allowed to be so through the action of the intellect. The senses do not perceive beauty or experience the aesthetic. The essence of beauty involves order, proportion, symmetry and harmony which are, essentially relations which sense is unable to identify.

It is the intellect, not sense which apprehends the beautiful, and it is intellect which experiences the aesthetic.

The joy the aesthetic gives is Olympic in magnitude.

BIBLIOGRAPHY

Best, David, "Aesthetic in Sport" in British Journal of Aesthetics, Vol. 14, (Summer 1974) pp. 197–213.

Best, David, *Expression in Movement and the Arts*, Lepus Books,(London 1974).

Dickie, George and R. J. Sclafani (Eds), *Aesthetics a Critical Anthology*. St. Martin's Press (New York, 1977).

Ellfeldt, Lois, *Dance from Magic to Art*, Wm. C. Brown Company, Publishers (Dubuque, Iowa, 1976), pp. 122–130.

Fleming, William, *Art Music and Ideas*, Holt, Rinehart and Winston, Inc. (Toronto, 1970).

Gaunt, William, *The Aesthetic Adventure*, Johathan Cape (London, 1975).

Kraus, Richard, *History of the Dance*, Prentice-Hall, Inc. (Englewood Cliffs, New Jersey, 1969).

Lowe, Benjamin, *The Beauty of Sport*, Prentice-Hall, Inc. (Englewood Cliffs, New Jersey, 1977).

Moore, Henry, "Notes on Sculpture", in *The Creative Process*, (Ed.) Brewster Chiselin, Mantor Books (London, 1973).

Phenix, Philip H. *Realms of Meaning*, McGraw-Hill Book Company (Toronto, 1964).

Plato, "What is Beauty?" in "The Greater Hippias", Trans: Benjamin Jowett, in *The Dialogues of Plato*, The Clarendon Press (Oxford, 1953), pp. 11–13.

Reid, Louis Arnaud, "Sport, the Aesthetic and Art", in British Journal of Educational studies, Vol. 18, No. 3, (October 1970), pp. 245–258.

Smith, Hope M., "Human Movement and the Realm of Aesthetics", in *The Academy Papers: Realms of Meaning*, Human Kinetics Publishers (Illinois, 1975), pp. 47–53.